Headquarters Economy

Headquarters Economy

Managers, Mobility, and Migration

J. Myles Shaver

OXFORD
UNIVERSITY PRESS

OXFORD

UNIVERSITY PRESS

Great Clarendon Street, Oxford, OX2 6DP,
United Kingdom

Oxford University Press is a department of the University of Oxford.
It furthers the University's objective of excellence in research, scholarship,
and education by publishing worldwide. Oxford is a registered trade mark of
Oxford University Press in the UK and in certain other countries

First Edition published in 2018
Impression: 1

Published in the United States of America by Oxford University Press
198 Madison Avenue, New York, NY 10016, United States of America

British Library Cataloguing in Publication Data
Data available

Library of Congress Control Number: 2018945145

ISBN 978–0–19–882891–4

Printed and bound by
CPI Group (UK) Ltd, Croydon, CR0 4YY

To Jay and Russell

Preface

It is not by accident that I live in the Minneapolis-St. Paul metropolitan area—the "Twin Cities" for those of us who live here. Family considerations were a key element to relocating from New York City to the Twin Cities after I was informed of a potential job opportunity in the region. With my wife being born and raised in the Twin Cities and me being born and raised in Alberta, we wished to be closer to our families when we raised a family. However, it was also important that we both be happy in our careers.

For my wife's career, that required that we live in a region with corporate headquarters or large professional service firms. Being familiar with the Twin Cities area, we knew it was home to a number of large corporate headquarters; and this facilitated our initial investigation into moving to the region. However, in the process of deciding to move, preparing to move, and relocating, I was taken aback by the depth and breadth of headquarters activity in Minnesota.

This began as my wife explored employment options. The list of headquartered companies in the region was much larger than I had thought and in a wider range of industries than I had expected. What also struck me was that during her job search, my wife was often directed to talk with companies that were not headquartered in the Twin Cities yet had significant operations in the area. It quickly became apparent that a large number of companies had headquarters-like operations in the region (often divisional or business unit headquarters), although their formal corporate headquarters were in other locations.

As I settled into the region, I continued to encounter more companies with headquarters operations. In the classroom, my MBA students represented the breadth of businesses in the area. In addition, students in my executive education classes further highlighted the extent of business activity in the region.

As I interacted with academic colleagues from around the world, many would ask if I enjoyed living in Minnesota. I explained the personal motivations for living here and I noted how it was professionally engaging because the Twin Cities housed a dynamic business community. Moreover, the "local" companies consisted of headquarters of some of the largest companies in the United States. Although they had been aware of specific companies, my colleagues had not been aware of the depth and breadth of corporate activity in the region.

Describing the region and its economy only piqued their interested. They would ask me why—what lead to this? Although I live in the region and study location choices that companies strategically make when expanding—I did not have an answer.

And that was the genesis of this book. As I began to investigate this question, I noticed that understanding the prevalence and scope of headquarters activity was as foreign to Minnesotans as it was to my academic colleagues who lived outside of Minnesota. Despite driving past a few Fortune 500 headquarters and having a general appreciation of the businesses climate in the region, relatively few Minnesotans have an appreciation of the extent to which the Twin Cities is a corporate epicenter. Moreover, to the extent that people recognize and think of the concentration of headquarters in the region, their explanations for its existence center on "folk theories" about the weather or the Scandinavian heritage of many settlers to the region. Although these representations have semblance in fact, no one had really attempted to distinguish the empirical reality from the folklore.

As I dug into this question, it became apparent that any insights would have to go beyond historically recounting what happened on the banks of the upper Mississippi River. Likewise, I would have to go beyond describing the experiences of a set of entrepreneurs and business leaders who founded, built, and guided the companies that define the Twin Cities' corporate landscape. Rather, insights would lie in better understanding the underlying forces that created and sustained headquarters in the region.

As I describe in Chapter 1, the book follows the chronological progression of this multi-year research project. As I began to gain insight into this question, I expanded the work to look for ways to empirically verify my insights with data that I had not used to help shape my initial understanding. What also become clear, as I discussed the project with my professional friends and at universities around the world, was the interest in the insights I was generating. They were curious about the experience of Minneapolis-St. Paul, but quickly responded with how I could offer insights about a little-discussed path towards regional vitality and corporate competitiveness. Studying the head-quarters economy of Minneapolis-St. Paul allowed me to isolate factors that can shape regional vitality and corporate competitiveness in many regions.

Acknowledgments

I would like to thank many individuals and institutions for their support, assistance, insights, comments, and guidance over the multiple years of this research project. I could not have accomplished this research in isolation.

In terms of financial support that made this research possible, I am grateful to the University of Minnesota and the Carlson School of Management. Sabbatical support was instrumental in allowing me to initiate this project. In addition, the Pond Family Chair in the Teaching and Advancement of Free Enterprise Principles supported my summer research. I also acknowledge the support that I received from the 2015–16 Fesler-Lampert Chair in Urban and Regional Affairs through the Center for Urban and Regional Affairs at the Humphrey School. This too, enabled me to dedicate time to this project. Finally, Dean's Research Grants from the Carlson School aided my data collection.

Many institutions in the Minneapolis-St. Paul business community helped me advance this work. In particular, I am grateful to my interactions with the Minnesota Business Partnership and the Human Resources Executive Council.

I would also like to thank the following individuals for insights, assistance, and encouragement: Marilyn Carlson Nelson, Charlie Weaver, Doug Baker, Jim Campbell, Bert Colianni, Bonnie Holub, Rick Clevette, Peter Frosch, Richard Davis, Michael Langley, Lee Schaefer, Robert Price, Lynn Casey, Susan Brower, Bruce Beckman, Peter Horwich, Alyssa Callister, Brent Carlson-Lee, Greg Page, Jim Lawrence, David Mortenson, Deb Cundy, Dave Kvamme, John Campbell, Phil Miller, John Stavig, Vanessa Laird, Gary Cohen, Steve Kelley, Rand Park, Art Rolnick, John Adams, and Dave Beal.

I would also like to thank the following undergraduate students at the University of Minnesota for their research assistance on this project: Kelsey Robinson, Jacob Kleiner, Katherine Su, Haley Dahl, Marcus Lorimer, Jay Shin, Alison Oosterhuis, Catherine Weese, James Updike, and Madison Laird. Some of the data that I present in the book is a direct result of their careful efforts. They also collected additional data, which I do not present in the book but helped shape my understanding over the course of this project. Moreover, I am thankful to the Carlson School Undergraduate Honors Research Assistant Program for funding their research assistance.

Acknowledgments

I benefitted from comments during many research seminars where I presented earlier versions of this research. The individuals who engaged with the research and provided helpful comments are too numerous to mention. Nevertheless, I wish to acknowledge the institutions that hosted these research seminars. This includes the Copenhagen Business School, Duke University, George Washington University, Harvard Business School, London Business School, Purdue University, University of California Berkeley, University of Colorado, University of Minnesota (Carlson School and Humphrey School), University of Pennsylvania, University of South Carolina, University of Utah, Washington University, Israel Strategy Conference, London Business School Ghoshal Conference, and the Industry Studies Association Annual meeting in Minneapolis.

I have also benefited from presenting this research in many non-academic settings. In particular I would like to thank students in a number of my MBA classes where I shared these ideas—especially when this was still a work in progress. I also benefitted from being able to present parts of this research to meetings of the Minnesota Business Partnership, Human Resources Executive Council, St. Paul Chamber of Commerce, Carlson School First Tuesday, Rotary Clubs of Minneapolis and St. Paul, Minnesota Women's Economic Roundtable, Civic Caucus, Regional Council of Mayors, and the Minnesota Mayors Association. I would be remiss if I did not thank many of my former students and many managers for engaging discussions about this research.

All of my departmental faculty colleagues have engaged in discussions about this research and I thank them for their comments. They include Stuart Albert, Sunasir Dutta, Dan Forbes, Russ Funk, Martin Ganco, Aseem Kaul, Jiao Luo, Ian Maitland, Alfie Marcus, Evan Rawley, Harry Sapienza, Gurneeta Singh, PK Toh, Andy Van de Ven, Richard Wang, Alex Wilson, Aks Zaheer, Sri Zaheer, and Shaker Zahra. And I would especially like thank my departmental colleagues Mary Benner, Paul Vaaler, and Joel Waldfogel who have been generous with their thoughts and time—and especially patient in that they have spent hours listening to me discuss this project.

I would also like to thank many of my colleagues in the Work and Organizations Department at the Carlson School for taking the time to engage with my project. In particular, I would like to thank Collen Manchester, Alan Benson, Aaron Sojourner, Connie Wanberg, John Budd, and Theresa Glomb. I also appreciate the insights from my PhD students—especially Exequiel Hernandez, David Souder, Adam Fremeth, Cameron Miller, Min Jung Kim, Miguel Ramos, and Gary Dushnitsky. I thank Russ Coff for thoughts on the state of the strategic human capital literature.

Tarun Khanna, Mauro Guillen, Rob Salomon, Todd Zenger, Anne-Marie Knott, Andy Van de Ven, and Mari Sako provided helpful advice on undertaking a book project and finding a publisher for my book. I am especially grateful to Adam Swallow at Oxford University Press for his guidance and encouragement.

Finally, I would like to thank my family for their support and insights. We have spent a lot of time at home and in the car talking about the Minneapolis-St. Paul economy. Their knowledge of the region and its economy rivals anyone's. I extend a special thanks to my wife Susan—who wrote the survey that I use in Chapter 5; and to my sons, Jay and Russell, the reason—in expectation—for which we moved to Minnesota and to whom I dedicate this book.

Contents

List of Figures

List of Tables

1

Headquarters as a Managerial and Administrative Talent Pool

When people think of corporate headquarters two images generally come to mind. They picture engines of economic power and impressive infrastructure such as skyscrapers or glass-clad corporate campuses. Having immersed myself in the study of corporate headquarters, I see them as engines of corporate success and contributors to regional economic and social vitality. However, I no longer picture the physical infrastructure when I think about corporate headquarters.

When I look at corporate headquarters, my focus extends beyond the buildings, the offices, and the employee amenities. I am drawn to the essence of a corporate headquarters—the talent that utilizes this physical infrastructure. In particular, my focus turns to a company's skilled, professional managerial and administrative workforce. When I view headquarters in this manner, I better comprehend how headquarters influence the companies that they guide and impact the regions in which they reside.

Take, for example, the senior management of a company headquartered in the region where I live—the Minneapolis-St. Paul metropolitan area. This group of men and women possess an impressive set of credentials. They are business professionals. They have all made investments in their human capital—many with graduate degrees from prestigious universities. Their prior work experience spans a diverse set of vibrant industries including pharmaceuticals, consumer packaged goods, medical devices, chemicals, publishing, industrial controls, animal nutrition, and agribusiness. And it is clear that they have been effective in guiding and managing their company. A look at the company's performance shows that it doubled sales and tripled profits between 2006 and 2016. This is especially impressive in light of the economic climate over that time period.

What company is this? It is not a start-up or a mid-sized company. Many would not consider it to be "high-tech" or in an "industry of tomorrow"—although I am sure many within the company would rightly disagree. It is not even a publicly traded company. In fact, it is a cooperative.

The company is Land O'Lakes and I believe that it nicely depicts the talent that resides in corporate headquarters. To the extent many people have heard of Land O'Lakes, most know it as a mid-western business that sells milk and butter. It would not be a company that many people think about when highlighting the talent that can guide multi-billion dollar operations on multiple continents or foster regional vitality. But it should be.

Land O'Lakes is a Fortune 500 company with over US$13 billion in sales. A multi-billion dollar company—by its size alone—is a complex organization to manage effectively. But the complexity does not end there. The company operates in multiple lines of business. In addition to dairy foods, its other major business units are animal nutrition and crop inputs. And although Land O'Lakes' operations are primarily in the Unites States, it does business in over sixty countries around the world. Whether at home or abroad, its success must be realized within a competitive landscape that includes prominent multinational enterprises, such as Kraft Foods, Monsanto, and Syngenta.

To run this company requires many types of managerial and professional expertise. This includes general management skills—the ability to set a strategic course of action, communicate the company's direction to its employees, and execute those strategies. In addition to general management, there are other—more specialized—professional management skills that are vital to Land-O-Lake's success and reside within its headquarters. These include capabilities to manage the financial, accounting, legal, human resource, information technology, marketing, and logistics needs of the company. It also includes the expertise required to innovate and launch new products and services.

Sixteen miles southwest of Land O'Lakes' headquarters are the headquarters of Holiday. Holiday operates a network of over 500 gas station convenience stores in Minnesota, Wisconsin, Michigan, North Dakota, South Dakota, Montana, Wyoming, Idaho, Washington, and Alaska. Most of these stores are owned by Holiday, although the network also includes franchised operations. Nationally or internationally not many people will have heard of Holiday because of the regional footprint of its operations or because it is a privately held company.[1]

You might question whether the talent required to run a gas station convenience store has anything to do with the talent that would be required to guide multi-billion dollar operations or to foster regional vitality. This would be a fair question if we were to focus on the operations of any one store. However, if we consider the talent required to manage this network of stores, a very different picture emerges. With over 500 stores, Holiday generates approximately US$4 billion in sales. Forbes identifies it as one of the largest privately held companies in the United States. If it were publicly held and considered by the Fortune rankings, it would be placed within the Fortune

1000. Moreover, it must operate within a competitive landscape that includes a variety of firms—including large sophisticated companies. It competes with independent gas station owners who operate under the brands of major oil companies. It also competes in the "convenience visit" space with companies such as Walgreens, McDonalds, and even Target and Walmart as they enter this arena.

Once again, any business of this magnitude and in such a competitive arena requires expertise and professional management in order to flourish. And although it is in a very different sector of the economy, it draws upon many of the same professional skills that Land O'Lakes draws upon to run its business. In order to be successful, Holiday requires talent with general management, marketing, finance, legal, human resource, information technology, and logistics expertise. And that is the type of talent that it employs in its headquarters. Men and women who have invested in their human capital development. Managers and professionals who have work experience in an array of professional settings.

A little over 8 miles southeast of Land O'Lakes' headquarters lies downtown St. Paul. Here we find Ecolab's corporate headquarters. Although approximately the same size in terms of sales, Ecolab is in a very different set of businesses than Land O'Lakes. Ecolab provides cleaning, sanitation, and clean-water services to the industrial, healthcare, and hospitality sectors. It might not be a household name because most of its clients are other businesses and not individual consumers. Ecolab has a large international footprint and generates almost half of its revenue from outside of the United States—operating in about 170 countries. Its competitors are diverse and include many multinational companies. As with Land O'Lakes and Holiday, the managerial task of effectively running an operation with such size and scope requires a talented managerial workforce. A scan of the company's top management team confirms this. In addition, accolades such as being on the Ethisphere Institute's list of the World's Most Ethical Companies reinforces other dimensions in which the management of this company is accomplished.

Of course, this is not to say that managerial talent is the only talent that these companies employ. For example, Ecolab is also known for its technological focus as Forbes includes it on their list of the World's most Innovative Companies. Company-wide Ecolab spends over US$180 million per year on research and development (R&D) and has over 1,600 R&D employees—many of whom are in the Minneapolis-St. Paul region. Likewise, Land O'Lakes' different business units all rely on technological innovations in order to be competitive in the marketplace. For example, the Dairy Foods Research and Development and Test Kitchens are located on the corporate headquarters campus. Whether at Land O'Lakes or Ecolab, these talented non-managerial employees have an impact on their companies and the region. Nevertheless,

3

accounts of corporate success and regional vitality that overly focus on the underlying technologies upon which companies draw are myopic.

As I describe in greater detail over the course of the book, the attributes associated with the managerial and administrative talent that put these technologies to work in the marketplace differ from the scientific and engineering talent that generates them. In particular, all large successful companies are professionally managed. It does not matter whether a company is a "new economy" firm, an "old economy" firm, a regional player, a multinational, publicly traded, or privately held. When one considers the professional management within these companies, we see more similarities than differences. All successful companies need to set strategic directions, administer their businesses, and oversee their operations.

Consider, for example, the professional finance employees at Land O'Lakes, Holiday, or Ecolab. These professionals possess similar types of skills and their companies employ these skills in a similar manner—even though these companies differ greatly in the industries in which they compete and the technologies upon which they draw. This is not to say that the financial issues facing these companies are identical or that the finance professionals lack industry-specific experience and skills. It is to highlight that the expertise and professional experiences of the managerial and administrative professionals in all of these companies share commonality and are potentially transferable. It would not be uncommon for the finance professionals in any of these three companies to have previous work experience in one of the other two—or in many other industries.

Contrast this with other professionals within these companies such as engineers or research scientists. The research scientists in Land O'Lakes' animal nutrition business share fewer similarities with their research scientist counterparts in Ecolab's water reuse businesses. They draw on different knowledge bases and technologies. Although they might be engineers or scientists, it is unlikely that their skills are as interchangeable between companies as the finance professionals.

Viewing Headquarters as a Collection of Managerial and Administrative Talent

Viewing headquarters as a collection of managerial and administrative talent—whose skills are applicable across a wide range of companies and industries—allows me to identify four aspects of corporate headquarters that warrant greater attention. First, a regional concentration of such talent can give rise to a special type of economy that has received little attention—a headquarters economy. This is an economy that has a concentration of headquarters from diverse industries.[2] Second, it provides an explanation how regions with high concentrations of corporate headquarters create and sustain economic and social vitality. Third, it helps define what is, and what is not, a headquarters. Although "headquarters" is a commonly used term that is well-understood, defining what constitutes a headquarters in today's economy is not always obvious. Focusing on the managerial talent pool that guides a company provides a basis for defining headquarters. In addition, it is consistent with the observation that large companies have multiple headquarters. Fourth, focusing on the managerial talent pool of a company helps us understand where headquarters should locate, what would keep them there, and why they might move. I expand on these points in the following sections and further develop them throughout the book.

Managerial Talent and a Headquarters Economy

Viewing headquarters as a managerial talent pool whose skills can be applied across a range of different businesses identifies a unique type of economy that has not garnered much attention—a headquarters economy. A headquarters economy emerges when there is the collection of diverse corporate headquarters within a metropolitan area. One reason why a headquarters economy has not attracted much discussion is that we lack an explanation of what exactly it is, why it would emerge, what would sustain it, and how it can aid companies' competitiveness. However, viewing headquarters as a pool of managerial talent provides an avenue to address these deficiencies.

A headquarters economy is notable for several reasons. A pool of managerial talent, which possesses a range of experiences, guides businesses and drives the performance of companies within the region. As I demonstrate, the effect does not end there. A vibrant headquarters economy is home to innovative companies, evolving companies, entrepreneurial activity, and a high quality of life. Together, these elements create a reinforcing system—a virtuous cycle—that generates and sustains regional economic vitality.

Understanding what creates, sustains, or diminishes a headquarters economy stems from knowledge about the mobility and migration of its managerial talent base. To what extent does this talent migrate to a region? And why? To what extent does this talent stay in the region? And why? To what extent does this talent move from company to company within the region? And how does that impact the companies that it guides? I develop why these questions are important and argue how differences in patterns of talent movement among firms and between regions affect the formation and preservation of a headquarters economy.

Managerial Talent, Corporate Success, and Regional Vitality

Viewing headquarters as a highly skilled talent pool explains why corporate headquarters activities have a profound impact on regional economic and social vitality. When I talk with regional development professionals, the professional headquarters talent that I describe is exactly the type of talent that they wish to attract, develop, and retain in their region. The logic is that an educated, experienced, successful workforce is a powerful engine for regional prosperity.[3]

A talented workforce aids economic outcomes as it propels companies in the region. It guides existing businesses, reinvents companies as they face challenges, launches and nurtures new companies when opportunities arise. This workforce creates many positive spillovers to the community that go beyond the economic prosperity of their employers. A talented, professional workforce demands amenities such as good schools, cultural offerings, recreation, and a healthy environment.

But it not only demands these amenities, it fosters a region's ability to invest in these amenities. By managing successful companies, it fosters a region's ability to make investments in public goods through a deeper tax base. Successful companies also invest resources that build the community through actions like philanthropy and other forms of corporate engagement. Equally important, a well-compensated workforce facilitates individuals' investments in their community's quality of life amenities.[4]

In parallel, when I talk to corporate executives, they share the same goals with respect to attracting and retaining talent within their region. Although primarily concerned about attracting and retaining talent for their companies, these executives share the broader goal of attracting and retaining talent that is not directly tied to their company. Because they live in the region, they personally benefit from the amenities that this talent pool facilitates. However, there is also a business case for their interest in deepening the regional talent base. In general, businesses are always on the search for additional talent—and this is especially pronounced for successful, growing companies. Having a local talent base facilitates talent acquisition and can provide a source of competitiveness—especially vis-à-vis companies with more limited access to such resources.

In addition, the professional employees in their companies will often demand the same type of amenities that similarly skilled individuals in other organizations demand. When there is a critical mass demanding the same type of amenities within a region, it is more likely that these amenities can be offered and supported. As a result, greater pools of talent within the region and outside of their company can have tangible effects on their company.

Managerial Talent as the Definition of a Headquarters

Identifying corporate headquarters is no longer as simple as identifying a company's location of incorporation or searching for its address in an annual report. With geographically dispersed corporations and the ability of information technology to bridge where people work and where they live, the managerial and administrative talent of a company is often geographically dispersed. Moreover, with the geographic separation of incorporation from operations—made even more pronounced with corporate inversions—the geographic legal status of a company and the geographic footprint of its talent are not necessarily the same.

However, thinking of headquarters as a talent base rather than a legal address resolves many of these complications. For example, if a company has a legal headquarters in one region but the mass of its managerial talent resides in another (sometimes referred to as its operational headquarters), then the latter will be of much more interest if we wish to evaluate how the company contributes to a headquarters economy and to regional vitality. In addition, corporate decisions of where to locate and how to build its managerial talent base often have more pronounced long-term effects compared to decisions of where to incorporate the legal entity.

Likewise, many companies are decentralized with important business units headquartered geographically separate from the corporate headquarters. These divisional and regional headquarters can be multi-billion dollar operations, and house the requisite managerial and administrative talent to effectively operate a business of that size. For example, Thomson Reuters' corporate headquarters are in New York City. Nevertheless, the company's Legal Solutions Business is headquartered in the Minneapolis-St. Paul metropolitan area. This business division recorded sales of US$3.4 billion and employed approximately 7,000 in its suburban corporate campus in 2013. The size of its operations and the nature of the workforce that it employs make this divisional headquarters an important contributor to the region.

Because these divisional, regional, or operational headquarters are easily overlooked, I refer to these as "hidden headquarters." Hidden headquarters, due to their resident talent, are important elements of a headquarters economy. They can play as large—or an even larger—role in a region's economic and social vitality compared to many corporate headquarters. In addition, business units and regional headquarters can have greater or different managerial talent demands than their corporate headquarters. For this reason, analyses of headquarters economies require that we pay attention to these hidden headquarters, although they go unnoticed in many discussions. It also highlights that companies must make important strategic choices with respect to where divisional and regional headquarters reside and how they tap into local managerial talent bases.

Managerial Talent and the Location of a Headquarters

A requisite pool of managerial talent is necessary for a headquarters to exist. Although history anchors a company's headquarters location, it by no means makes its location permanent over time. So while key geographic features like proximity to ports, raw materials, or companies from which they were spun-out affect where a company is initially headquartered; the influence of these forces tend to wane over time. Companies expand, acquire, divest, merge, and change their business portfolios. As these events occur, the initial historical drivers of its headquarters location can become less relevant.

For example, in 2013 Archer Daniels Midland moved its corporate head-quarters to Chicago from Decatur, Illinois. Although the company wanted to stay close to its agricultural base, it chose to leave Decatur because Chicago "provides an environment where we can attract and retain employees with diverse skills, and where their family members can find ample career opportunities," said chief executive officer (CEO) and chair Patricia Woertz on the announcement of the move.[5] It is clear that if the company's preference is to keep its headquarters close to its agricultural base, then there are many locations within the United States that would fulfill that requirement. It then becomes other factors that tipped the balance towards one location versus another. In the case of Archer Daniels Midland, a key factor was accommodating the needs of its headquarters employees.

Likewise, when two companies combine through acquisition or merger they generally consolidate corporate headquarters. For example, Northwest Airlines was headquartered in the Minneapolis-St. Paul region until Delta Airlines acquired it in 2008. After the acquisition, Delta consolidated the companies' headquarters in Atlanta, which was Delta's headquarters.

These examples reinforce that headquarters are mobile. Because a region is currently home to a corporate headquarters is no guarantee that the head-quarters will remain for any period of time. Although headquarters can relocate—as in the case of Archer Daniels Midland, most headquarter changes of large corporations do not occur in this manner. Rather, they occur through changes in corporate control or corporate scope—as in the case of Northwest Airlines. In either situation, when it comes to thinking about what attracts and retains headquarters activities, it becomes important to understand what draws and retains managerial talent in a region. It also becomes evident that the access, attraction, and retention of managerial talent should play a central role in determining the post-acquisition geography of managerial actives when companies combine.

Although companies change structure and can move their headquarters, the focus on talent also highlights that individuals are mobile too. Because some-one resides in a region is no guarantee that they will remain there for any period of time. Regions that grow and maintain a managerial and administrative talent base are more likely to retain headquarters compared to regions that lose this talent base. Companies will continue to flourish in regions where they have access to this talent base but will likely wane if they remain in regions where this talent base atrophies. Therefore, access to talent becomes an important locational anchor for headquarters. Furthermore, this anchor becomes especially important when there are no other geographic anchors for the underlying business.

Outline of the Book

The structure of the book follows the progression of my investigation into what creates and sustains a headquarters economy. I start by describing an exemplar headquarters economy—the Minneapolis-St. Paul metropolitan area—in Chapter 2. The unique nature of this region's economy motivated my study of corporate headquarters. The Minneapolis-St. Paul region is home to a concentration of large corporate headquarters in a diverse set of industries. It has a sustained history of growing competitive and innovative companies rather than luring established companies to the region with business and tax incentives. However, the region's economy is not consistent with standard explanations for the geographic concentration of economic or headquarters activity. Moreover, it is a region considered to have a high quality of life and to be economically prosperous—suggesting a relationship between a headquarters activities and regional economic and social vitality. In this chapter, I describe the region and the concentration of headquarters activity that exists there. Based on these data, I demonstrate that well-established explanations for the geographic concentration of business and headquarters activity fail to explain Minneapolis-St. Paul's experience.

With existing explanations not up to the task, I advance a novel explanation for what drives the Minneapolis-St. Paul headquarters economy in Chapter 3. My explanation centers on three building blocks: *managers*; their *mobility* across companies in a region; and their *migration* into and out of a region. My explanation builds from the data I present in Chapter 2. I augment this data with additional data from interviews and other archival sources. These data highlight features about the business environment in the Minneapolis-St. Paul metropolitan area that are not the focus of other existing explanations.

The key elements of my explanation are: (a) there is a concentration of professional managerial talent in Minneapolis-St. Paul that is valuable in managing a wide array of companies. (b) Professional managerial talent is mobile and often moves between companies. When this talent moves between

9

companies, it often stays within the region yet moves into new industries. This has a cross-pollinating effect of bringing new practices and managerial skills to companies. This effect is magnified when talent moves across businesses from a variety of industries. (c) Professional managerial talent also moves from these headquarters to smaller firms and start-up companies, which in turn aids these companies' growth. Many of these companies evolve to become much bigger companies with a larger headquarters presence. (d) Although this flow between companies can happen anywhere, it is pronounced in a region where professional managerial talent does not leave. In other words, if talent is unlikely to leave a region, it is more likely to move across employers within a region. (e) Growing companies require additional talent, thus attracting more talent to the region. Although built from examples and experiences from Minneapolis-St. Paul, these underlying mechanisms of managerial talent and its mobility have general applicability to understand the growth of a head-quarters economy.

Because a key element of the explanation in Chapter 3 is the movement of managerial talent, Chapter 4 draws upon micro-level data to examine differences in the migration patterns of educated, high-earning individuals across the major metropolitan areas in the United States. These data reinforce my arguments of what sustains the Minneapolis-St. Paul headquarters economy. The region has the lowest out-migration rate of educated, high-earning individuals compared to the other major metropolitan areas in the United States. Although the migration rate into the region is relatively low, the net-migration rate shows the area adding to its existing talent base. These analyses provide a tool—The Talent Migration Map—to assess how regions fare in attracting and retaining talent that is vital to a headquarter economy (or other talent bases).

The migration patterns in Chapter 4 document an important way in which the Minneapolis-St. Paul region differs from other major metropolitan areas in the country. Although the analyses provide evidence as to what drives this migration pattern, it is only suggestive. In order to go beyond this, I draw upon proprietary survey data from approximately 3,000 professional head-quarter employees in the Minneapolis-St. Paul metropolitan area to see what affects employee mobility. Chapter 5 presents these data.

The survey data confirm many characteristics that I argue shape the choices of a professional managerial and administrative workforce. They are well-educated. They are well-compensated. They are predominantly in dual career situations. Many are in child-rearing stages of their lives. As a result, the key regional quality of life factors that this talent base demands revolve around economic opportunities and child-rearing. Moreover, the importance of economic opportunities has a relatively stronger impact on drawing talent to a region; whereas, other quality of life factors play a more important role in retaining talent. The survey data support my explanation for what drives a headquarters economy.

Chapters 6 and 7 build on the descriptions and data from the previous chapters to draw more formal implications for advancing economic and social vitality through a headquarters economy. Although building from the experiences of the Minneapolis-St. Paul region, I draw more universal applications. In Chapter 6, I discuss the benefits that accrue from a head-quarters economy—many of which are unique compared to other types of regional economies. I also demonstrate that policies to advance a headquar-ters economy and foster regional economic and social vitality must build from an understanding how individuals in this talent base make decisions of where to live and work. Although based on individuals' decisions, a set of interconnected actors affect these individuals' decisions. The set of actors include other individuals that comprise the talent pool, companies, govern-ments, and non-governmental organizations.

In Chapter 7, I present five insights from my research that advances current discourse about regional economic development and the role that businesses play in shaping it. These insights also provide novel implications for how companies can enhance their competitiveness by tapping the benefits of a headquarters economy.

First, there are regional advantages that stem from a talent base whose skills are applicable across many industries or sectors of the economy. In the case of a headquarters economy, this talent base is managerial and administrative talent. Because managerial talent is key to all companies, local access to a deep managerial talent pool with diverse skills can be a source of regional company competitiveness.

Second, different factors play prominent roles in attracting and retaining talent. For managerial and administrative talent, economic opportunities play the primary role for talent attraction. Quality of life factors play a prominent role for talent retention. Effective company strategies for building their talent base must consider the locational preferences and rigidities of the individuals that they wish to attract and retain. In addition, regional development efforts must consider the importance that managerial talent plays in fostering economic and social vitality, and how different forces affect the attraction and retention of managerial talent.

Third, talent is often more geographically bound than the companies that employ this talent. Therefore, talent can be a more effective anchor and foundation for economic growth compared to considering companies as that anchor and foundation. Strategically, companies have to consider how choices such as where they locate operations and what types of talent they wish to employ maps to local talent concentrations or to the underlying geographic preferences of the talent that they attempt to relocate.

Fourth, hidden headquarters comprise a significant amount of headquarters activity. These activities are often overlooked, yet they provide opportunities for economic development and can substantially contribute to regional economies. The prevalence of hidden headquarters also highlights that companies face important choices about where they locate different activities and how such choices affect the access to and retention of desired talent for their business units.

Fifth, there is often a difference in the quality of life factors that play an important role in attracting or retaining talent compared to a region's quality of life strengths. This means that what individuals value in a region and what they believe are a region's strengths can be very different things. Understanding this is important for corporate recruiting and retention policies and for regional development policies.

Overall, these insights point to policy levers and company considerations that are largely overlooked. These insights also suggest that current discourse with respect to corporate and regional strategies might be misaligned or misguided—especially if they build only from popular considerations such as industry clusters or creative talent.

Chapter 8 concludes the book. I discuss the broader implications of my research and what it means for companies, regions, and their role in the global economy. I highlight other regions that I consider to be headquarters economies; discuss how companies might strategically tap the advantages of these regions; and reinforce the important influence that corporate headquarters and professional managerial talent can have on a region.

Structure of the Book from a Research Design Perspective

As the previous section indicates, the structure of the book follows the chronological progression of a multi-year study. At many points in this process, I made purposeful decisions of how to proceed among viable alternatives. I walk through these decisions to be clear about my research design choices.

My investigation is phenomena driven, motivated by my efforts to understand the concentration of corporate headquarters in the Minneapolis-St. Paul metropolitan area. Adding to this motivation was the sense that existing academic explanations for the concentration of economic or headquarters activity were not consistent with the region's experiences. Moreover, better understanding this phenomenon had important implications because of the apparent connection between headquarters activities and regional economic and social vitality.

Confronted with this puzzle, my initial step was to gather data to describe the phenomenon. As a result, I familiarized myself with the history of the region and of many of its prominent businesses. I gathered data to more precisely understand the vitality of region and the level of headquarters activity—especially in comparison to other metropolitan areas in the United States and within the region over time. These data confirm that existing explanations in the literature are not up to the task of describing Minneapolis-St. Paul's headquarters economy and provide guidance as to what a novel account would have to explain. I initially envisioned that an important element of the book would be a lengthy historical account of the region. However, the nature of the data that I uncovered lead me to take a different course of action. As I document in Chapter 2, there is significant turnover in headquarters. These data reveal that understanding why a region sustains or grows a headquarters economy requires one to focus on the creation and reinvention of large companies rather than just describing historical foundations of a local economy.

Chapter 3 builds from the data in Chapter 2, and augments it with additional data, interviews, and discussions with managers in the region to build my theoretical arguments for what sustains the Minneapolis-St. Paul headquarters economy. The central insight is that to understand headquarters activities one must understand the talent that resides in headquarters—in particular, professional managerial and administrative talent. Although the theorizing is not directly derived from an existing theoretical base, the closest theoretical base is the growing field of strategic human capital. This literature assesses how firm competiveness stems from the talent that it employs. My theory development leads to the argument of how managers, mobility, and migration affect headquarters activities in a region.

Using the exemplar case of Minneapolis-St. Paul to derive these predictions, the next step in the research was to look beyond the exemplar case with different data than what I used to help build the theoretical insights. A key prediction from the arguments in Chapter 3 was the migration pattern of managerial talent. Regions with net inflows of talent and low levels of outward migration would be likely to create the beneficial dynamic central to my arguments. Rather than pair Minneapolis with another city and conduct a comparative case study as done in other studies of regional vitality (e.g., Saxenian, 1994; Storper et al., 2015), I chose to focus on this prediction and compare migration patterns of employed, educated, high-earning individuals (i.e., demographic characteristics of headquarters management talent) across the largest twenty-five metropolitan areas in the United States. This allows me to assess my argument across a wider set of metropolitan areas than with a case study approach and with using different data sources than what I used to develop the theory. These data confirmed my expectation.

Having developed a theory that was novel, consistent with the data describing headquarters activity Minneapolis-St. Paul, and predictive of the way in which the migration of employed, educated, high-earning individuals would differ from other major metropolitan areas in the United States, I wished to present additional evidence for the mechanisms underlying my theory. Isolating the mechanisms underlying my arguments is difficult using secondary sources like the data I employ Chapter 4. For this reason, I decided to pursue a large primary data collection effort where I would survey head-quarters employees in the Minneapolis-St. Paul region. Chapter 5 describes my efforts and presents primary data analyses that substantiate many mechanisms of the theory that I derive in Chapter 3.

Chapters 2 and 3 use archival and primary qualitative data to advance my theory; and Chapters 4 and 5 assess different data sources and provide confirmatory evidence of the theory. With this empirical support of the underlying mechanisms of my theory, the remaining chapters return to the theoretical arguments to advance implications for managers and for regions. The goal of these chapters is to highlight how the underlying mechanisms of the theory offer insights to many settings. In other words, although I ground and refine the arguments with data from Minneapolis-St. Paul, the underlying mechanisms can be universal. The final chapter directly makes many of these connections.

Notes

1. While I was finishing the book, Holiday was sold to Alimentation Couche-Tard Inc. of Canada. On announcement, Couche-Tard described their intentions to keep Holiday's headquarters operations as an operational base. My discussions with managers several months after the acquisition announcement confirmed this. At that time, the expectation was that approximately 95 percent of the employees and about half of the senior management would remain after acquisition. In addition, Couche-Tard would keep the Holiday name and use the Holiday operations as a regional headquarters. Thus, it appears that while Holiday's corporate headquarters would technically be in Canada after the acquisition, the Holiday unit will continue to be headquartered in Minneapolis-St. Paul and become what I describe as a 'hidden-headquarters' later in the chapter.
2. Important in my definition of a headquarters economy is the concentration of headquarters from diverse industries. Other sources use the term headquarters economy. Their usage, while related to my concept, often differs. Hitz, Schmid, and Wolff (1994: 171) describe the transformation of the Swiss economy (and Zurich, in particular) away from manufacturing to "a headquarters economy specializing in controlling and organizing multinational production as well as in the commanding international circuits of capital." Moreover, they discuss the change to the region's geographic footprint of industry based on this transformation. Chan and Poon (2012) use the term to describe the locational attributes and governmental

policies that attract headquarters to a region. Headquarters location choice was pronounced in the Chinese context as many companies separated headquarters from regional manufacturing as the Chinese government incented foreign firms to locate regional headquarters in China. They note that headquarters in many of these cities are not concentrated by industry clusters, as they argue is the case is western economies. Zhao (2013: 1026) describes the concentrations of regional headquarters in Shanghai, Beijing, and Hong Kong "as a reflective measurement for ranking and division of functions of financial centers since spatial concentrations of corporate regional headquarters constitute strategic control points and correspond to the upper tier of the financial system in China." These studies highlight geographic concentrations of headquarters but do not focus on the diversity of headquarters. In addition, they see headquarters related to financial functions as in the global cities literature (see Appendix). I do not make this connection.

3. Professional managerial and administrative headquarters jobs would be "traded-sector" jobs because, like technology jobs, they create services that are consumed outside of the region (Moretti, 2012). As Moretti (2010a) demonstrates, traded-sector jobs are not only more highly compensated than non-traded-sector jobs; they also have a greater multiplier effect on the local economy.

4. Card et al. (2010) highlight how headquarters affect regional charitable giving mainly through providing highly compensated jobs, rather than through direct corporate contributions.

5. Archer Daniels Midland Company, Press Release, Decatur, IL, Dec. 18, 2013.

2

What Does a Headquarters Economy Look Like?

Minneapolis-St. Paul—an Exemplar

United Healthcare. 3M. General Mills. Target. Cargill. US Bank. What do these companies have common? Many people will recognize their names. They are all large corporations with thousands of employees and billions of dollars in revenue. Beyond these attributes, most would struggle to find additional commonalities because these companies participate in very different businesses. For example, the many businesses these companies participate in include: health insurance (United Healthcare), adhesives (3M), breakfast cereal (General Mills), retail stores (Target), agricultural commodity trading (Cargill), and personal banking (US Bank).

But there is another commonality. All are headquartered in the Minneapolis-St. Paul metropolitan area.

Interestingly, these six companies are only a subset of the large corporate headquarters that reside within Minneapolis-St. Paul. With such a large and diverse set of corporate headquarters, I consider the Minneapolis-St. Paul region to be an exemplar headquarters economy.

In this chapter, I describe the Minneapolis-St. Paul region and its economic and social vitality. I then describe the nature of headquarters activity within this region. Based on these data, I show that existing explanations for the concentration of economic activity or for the concentration of headquarters activity do not explain the experience of Minneapolis-St. Paul. I then highlight the need for a novel explanation to understand what sustains a headquarters economy.

Minneapolis-St. Paul: A Primer

Halfway between the equator and North Pole and located along the Mississippi River lies the Minneapolis-St. Paul metropolitan area. There are separate city centers of Minneapolis and St. Paul, with St. Paul being about 15 miles downriver from Minneapolis. For this reason, those who live in the metropolitan area commonly refer to it as the "Twin Cities."

European settlement in this area accelerated with the creation of Fort Snelling, which is situated at the confluence of the Minnesota and Mississippi Rivers. The fort located between what would become the city centers of Minneapolis and St. Paul. St. Paul grew because it was the last navigable stop on the Mississippi River and river transport preceded rail as the region grew. St. Anthony, which would later become Minneapolis, grew because of its location at the only major natural falls on the Mississippi River. Early entrepreneurs in the region used the falls to power industry.

Minneapolis-St. Paul is the only major metropolitan area within a large geographic area of the United States. Some might call it isolated. It lies 350 miles northwest of Chicago and 250 miles south of the Canadian border. The closest city to the south is Kansas City, which is 400 miles away. And the closest major city due west is Portland, which is over 1,400 miles away.

As the regional center of this vast area, its initial economic growth primarily stemmed from being a transportation hub and servicing the hinterlands' agricultural, forestry, and mineral resources. These initial geographic factors shaped the growth and the nature of the area's economy and are still visible in some of region's economic activities. However, the region's economy has evolved from these initial roots.

Today the region is a metropolitan area with a population of approximately 3.5 million people spread out over eleven counties in Minnesota and two counties in western Wisconsin.[1] It is the sixteenth largest metropolitan area in the United States in terms of population.

Compared to other large metropolitan areas in the United States, Minneapolis-St. Paul is economically prosperous. Table 2.1 shows that the 2012 median household income—adjusted for regional price differences—ranks second among the largest metropolitan regions in the United States. The unadjusted median income ranks fifth with a value of just over US $66,000.

Table 2.2 presents per capita income for the same metropolitan areas. Minneapolis-St. Paul's per capita income for 2012—adjusted for regional price differences—ranks ninth, which is notably lower than the ranking of median household income. The difference in the ranking of median household income and per capita income can be the result of three factors. Regions will have higher median household incomes and lower per capita incomes if any of the following occur. The region has more households with children because children are considered in the denominator in calculating per capita income but included in households. The region has more dual-income (or multi-income) households because that increases household earnings,

17

Table 2.1 Median household income, 2012

Metropolitan Statistical Area	Median Household Income ($)[a]	Rank: Adjusted for Cost of Living[b]	Rank
Washington-Arlington-Alexandria, DC-VA-MD-WV	88,233	1	1
Minneapolis-St. Paul-Bloomington, MN-WI	66,282	2	5
Boston-Cambridge-Newton, MA-NH	71,738	3	3
San Francisco-Oakland-Hayward, CA	74,922	4	2
Seattle-Tacoma-Bellevue, WA	65,677	5	6
Baltimore-Columbia-Towson, MD	66,970	6	4
Denver-Aurora-Lakewood, CO	61,453	7	8
St. Louis, MO-IL	52,243	8	17
Atlanta-Sandy Springs-Roswell, GA	54,628	9	16
Portland-Vancouver-Hillsboro, OR-WA	56,978	10	13
Dallas-Fort Worth-Arlington, TX	56,954	11	14
Chicago-Naperville-Elgin, IL-IN-WI	59,261	12	11
Houston-The Woodlands-Sugar Land, TX	55,910	13	15
Philadelphia-Camden-Wilmington, PA-NJ-DE-MD	60,105	14	10
San Antonio-New Braunfels, TX	51,486	15	19
Pittsburgh, PA	50,489	16	21
New York-Newark-Jersey City, NY-NJ-PA	63,982	17	7
Phoenix-Mesa-Scottsdale, AZ	51,359	18	20
Detroit-Warren-Dearborn, MI	50,310	19	22
San Diego-Carlsbad, CA	60,330	20	9
Riverside-San Bernardino-Ontario, CA	51,695	21	18
Los Angeles-Long Beach-Anaheim, CA	57,271	22	12
Orlando-Kissimmee-Sanford, FL	46,020	23	24
Tampa-St. Petersburg-Clearwater, FL	44,402	24	25
Miami-Fort Lauderdale-West Palm Beach, FL	46,648	25	23

[a] *Source*: Bureau of Economic Analysis.
[b] Calculated by dividing Median Household Income by Regional Price Parity (source: Bureau of Economic Analysis).

everything else being equal. Regions with very high income disparities will tend to have higher average per capita income and lower median incomes. This is because income is bound by zero on the lower end and medians versus means are not as sensitive to an extended right tail of the distribution with very-high-earning individuals. In subsequent chapters, I describe the prevalence of dual-career professionals raising children in the Minneapolis-St. Paul region.

Another demographic attribute is that the level of educational attainment is high compared to other large metropolitan areas in the country. Table 2.3 ranks the major metropolitan areas in the United States in terms of percentage of the over-22 population that completed high school. Table 2.4 ranks the major metropolitan areas in the United States in terms of percentage of the over-22 population that completed four years of college. These data show that the Minneapolis-St. Paul ranks first in terms of the percentage of the over-22 population that completed high school at just under 94 percent. It ranks sixth in terms of the percentage of the over-22 population that complete college at just over 38 percent.

Table 2.2 Per capita income, 2012

Metropolitan Statistical Area	Per Capita Income ($)[a]	Rank: Adjusted for Cost of Living[b]	Rank
San Francisco-Oakland-Hayward, CA	68,029	1	1
Boston-Cambridge-Newton, MA-NH	61,258	2	3
Pittsburgh, PA	48,280	3	13
Washington-Arlington-Alexandria, DC-VA-MD-WV	61,907	4	2
Seattle-Tacoma-Bellevue, WA	54,590	5	5
St. Louis, MO-IL	45,346	6	17
Houston-The Woodlands-Sugar Land, TX	51,348	7	9
Baltimore-Columbia-Towson, MD	54,152	8	6
Minneapolis-St. Paul-Bloomington, MN-WI	50,825	9	10
Denver-Aurora-Lakewood, CO	51,432	10	8
New York-Newark-Jersey City, NY-NJ-PA	58,934	11	4
Philadelphia-Camden-Wilmington, PA-NJ-DE-MD	51,885	12	7
Dallas-Fort Worth-Arlington, TX	46,400	13	15
Chicago-Naperville-Elgin, IL-IN-WI	48,447	14	12
Sacramento-Roseville-Arden-Arcade, CA	45,493	15	16
Charlotte-Concord-Gastonia, NC-SC	41,436	16	21
Detroit-Warren-Dearborn, MI	42,539	17	20
Portland-Vancouver-Hillsboro, OR-WA	43,189	18	19
Miami-Fort Lauderdale-West Palm Beach, FL	44,814	19	18
Atlanta-Sandy Springs-Roswell, GA	40,738	20	22
San Diego-Carlsbad, CA	50,664	21	11
San Antonio-New Braunfels, TX	39,565	22	24
Los Angeles-Long Beach-Anaheim, CA	47,743	23	14
Tampa-St. Petersburg-Clearwater, FL	39,903	24	23
Phoenix-Mesa-Scottsdale, AZ	38,487	25	25

[a] *Source*: Bureau of Economic Analysis.
[b] Calculated by dividing Median Household Income by Regional Price Parity (source: Bureau of Economic Analysis).

Table 2.3 Over-22 population completing high school

Metropolitan Statistical Area	%[a]
Minneapolis-St. Paul, MN	93.99
Seattle-Everett, WA	93.21
Pittsburgh, PA	92.63
Portland, OR-WA	92.03
Boston, MA-NH	91.67
Washington, DC/MD/VA	91.11
St. Louis, MO-IL	90.71
Denver-Boulder, CO	90.44
Philadelphia, PA/NJ	89.96
Sacramento, CA	89.60
Baltimore, MD	89.56
Detroit, MI	89.39
Tampa-St. Petersburg-Clearwater, FL	89.19
Atlanta, GA	88.97
San Francisco-Oakland-Vallejo, CA	88.97
Chicago, IL	88.05
Charlotte-Gastonia-Rock Hill, NC-SC	87.73
Phoenix, AZ	87.65
San Diego, CA	87.60
New York-Northeastern NJ	86.31
Dallas-Fort Worth, TX	84.68
Houston-Brazoria, TX	82.03
Riverside-San Bernardino, CA	81.91
Miami-Hialeah, FL	81.88
Los Angeles-Long Beach, CA	80.88

[a] Data source: IPUMS-USA, University of Minnesota, http://www.ipums.org 2007–11, ACS five-year. Author's analysis.

Table 2.4 Over-22 population completing four or more years of college

Metropolitan Statistical Area	%[a]
Washington, DC/MD/VA	47.39
Boston, MA-NH	44.21
San Francisco-Oakland-Vallejo, CA	41.33
Seattle-Everett, WA	40.34
Denver-Boulder, CO	38.91
Minneapolis-St. Paul, MN	38.09
New York-Northeastern NJ	36.13
Baltimore, MD	34.98
Atlanta, GA	34.71
Portland, OR-WA	34.32
Chicago, IL	34.12
San Diego, CA	33.55
Philadelphia, PA/NJ	32.78
Charlotte-Gastonia-Rock Hill, NC-SC	31.08
Dallas-Fort Worth, TX	31.01
Los Angeles-Long Beach, CA	30.53
St. Louis, MO-IL	30.10
Pittsburgh, PA	29.74
Sacramento, CA	28.47
Phoenix, AZ	28.41
Houston-Brazoria, TX	28.22
Detroit, MI	26.63
Miami-Hialeah, FL	26.13
Tampa-St. Petersburg-Clearwater, FL	25.49
Riverside-San Bernardino,CA	19.04

[a] Data source: IPUMS-USA, University of Minnesota, www.ipums.org. 2007–2011, ACS 5-year. Author's analysis.

In addition to these demographics, the Minneapolis-St. Paul region also scores high on other economic indicators. The unemployment rate in the region was among the lowest of major metropolitan areas during the great recession.[2] At the peak of national unemployment in the United States from 2009 to 2011 Minneapolis had the lowest or second lowest unemployment rate among the large metropolitan areas in the US.[3]

The region also tends to perform very well on many quality of life rankings. These include rankings for healthiest city, best city for recent graduates, top food city, location for entrepreneurs, and friendliness.[4] *The Atlantic* magazine profiled Minneapolis-St. Paul as one of the few places with the potential for upward mobility and where housing is affordable.[5]

Although the region has many favorable characterizations, like most metropolitan areas it also faces challenges. Among the most pronounced are indications that prosperity has not been equally realized by the non-white population of the region.[6] A likely contributing factor is that academic achievement in the region differs by race, and this difference is among the most pronounced among major cities in the United States.[7]

Relatedly, the population in the region is relatively homogenous in terms of race. The region has the second highest proportion of the population that is white compared to other major metropolitan areas in the United States—behind Pittsburgh. Table 2.5 presents these data. The proportion of 78.6 percent of the population being white is similar in proportion to the metropolitan areas of Portland, St. Louis, and Boston. There is concern that this will constrain the region as the demographic profile of the United States evolves over the next several decades.

What Does Minneapolis-St. Paul Look Like in Terms of Headquarters Activity?

Having very briefly described the metropolitan area and its prosperity, I return to the focus of this chapter—the existence of a headquarters economy in the Minneapolis-St. Paul region. My approach is to use various data to highlight

Table 2.5 Breakdown of population by race and ethnicity by MSA[a]

Metropolitan Statistical Area	Non-Hispanic White %	Non-Hispanic Black %	Hispanic %	Asian %	Other %
Pittsburgh, PA	87.0	9.2	1.3	2.0	0.4
Minneapolis-St. Paul-Bloomington, MN-WI	78.6	8.4	5.4	6.4	1.2
Portland-Vancouver-Hillsboro, OR-WA	76.3	3.6	10.9	7.6	1.7
St. Louis, MO-IL	75.1	19.1	2.6	2.6	0.6
Boston-Cambridge-Newton, MA-NH	74.9	6.6	9.0	6.5	3.0
Seattle-Tacoma-Bellevue, WA	68.0	6.8	9.0	14.3	1.9
Detroit-Warren-Dearborn, MI	67.9	23.6	3.9	3.9	0.8
Tampa-St. Petersburg-Clearwater, FL	67.5	12.0	16.2	3.5	0.8
Denver-Aurora-Lakewood, CO	65.8	6.2	22.4	4.5	1.1
Philadelphia-Camden-Wilmington, PA-NJ-DE-MD	65.0	20.2	7.8	4.9	2.0
Charlotte-Concord-Gastonia, NC-SC	61.2	24.6	9.8	3.6	0.9
Baltimore-Columbia-Towson, MD	60.0	29.6	4.6	5.2	0.7
Phoenix-Mesa-Scottsdale, AZ	58.7	5.4	29.5	4.1	2.3
Sacramento–Roseville–Arden-Arcade, CA	55.7	8.3	20.2	14.2	1.6
Chicago-Naperville-Elgin, IL-IN-WI	55.0	17.6	20.7	6.2	0.5
Orlando-Kissimmee-Sanford, FL	53.3	15.9	25.2	4.6	1.0
Atlanta-Sandy Springs-Roswell, GA	50.7	32.9	10.4	5.3	0.7
Dallas-Fort Worth-Arlington, TX	50.2	15.4	27.5	5.9	0.9
New York-Newark-Jersey City, NY-NJ-PA	48.9	16.8	22.9	10.6	0.8
Washington-Arlington-Alexandria, DC-VA-MD-WV	48.6	26.5	13.8	10.4	0.8
San Diego-Carlsbad, CA	48.5	5.6	32.0	12.8	1.1
San Francisco-Oakland-Hayward, CA	42.4	9.1	21.6	25.9	0.9
Houston-The Woodlands-Sugar Land, TX	39.7	17.3	35.3	7.0	0.7
Riverside-San Bernardino-Ontario, CA	36.6	8.0	47.2	7.1	1.0
San Antonio-New Braunfels, TX	36.1	6.6	54.1	2.6	0.7

[a] Data source: 2010 Census, Data accessed from Racial Structures in the Social Sciences, Brown University, http://www.s4.brown.edu/us2010/index.htm

the nature and pattern of headquarters activity within the region. Although I allude to the experiences of individual companies, my goal is not to provide a detailed historical account on a company-by-company basis or a detailed description of the activities of the companies currently headquartered in the region. Corporate histories of many of the notable companies in the region exist and can provide such background.[8]

Every company has a unique story of how it came into existence and why it grew. And most of these stories have some connection to the geographic area in which the company was founded. As interesting and unique as these stories can be, if I focus on the specific stories and the unique attributes of each company, I might overlook the existence of more general forces that shape many of these individual stories.

Minneapolis-St. Paul's Fortune 500's

When assessing the concentration of large corporate headquarters, the place where many start is the Fortune 500.[9] Table 2.6 presents the list of the Fortune 500 firms headquartered in the Minneapolis-St. Paul region in 2011—the year I started compiling data for my inquiry. Another reason I present the 2011 Fortune 500 is because data from that year reflect company performance from 2010 and I will map these data to population data from the 2010 Census in some analyses.

Table 2.6 Fortune 500 companies in Minneapolis-St. Paul, 2011

Company	Sector	Rank
UnitedHealth Group	Healthcare: insurance and managed care	22
Target	General merchandisers	33
Best Buy	Specialty retailers: other	47
Supervalu	Food and drug stores	61
3M	Miscellaneous	97
CHS	Wholesalers: food and grocery	103
U.S. Bancorp	Commercial banks	126
Medtronic	Medical products and equipment	158
General Mills	Food consumer products	166
Land O'Lakes	Food consumer products	218
Xcel Energy	Utilities: gas and electric	237
Ameriprise Financial	Diversified financials	246
C. H. Robinson Worldwide	Transportation and logistics	265
Thrivent Financial for Lutherans	Insurance: life, health (mutual)	318
Mosaic	Chemicals	346
Ecolab	Chemicals	378
St. Jude Medical	Medical products and equipment	436
Nash-Finch	Wholesalers: food and grocery	449
Alliant Techsystems	Aerospace and defense	472

Source: 2011 Fortune 500 list.

The list of nineteen companies in Table 2.6 reflects all of the Fortune 500 companies headquartered in Minnesota except one. The one exception is Hormel, which is headquartered 100 miles south of Minneapolis-St. Paul in Austin, MN. As a result, Minneapolis-St. Paul is the hub for headquarters activity in the state.

In addition to the company names, I also present the main industry sector in which each company competes. Striking is the industry mix of this set of companies. Their primary industries include retail, distribution, industrial, insurance, and banking businesses.

To put this count into perspective, Table 2.7 ranks US metropolitan areas with the largest number of Fortune 500 headquarters in 2011. To define metropolitan areas, I use metropolitan statistical area (MSA) definitions from the Office of Management and Budget. Turning to the data in Table 2.7, one can see that other metropolitan areas in the United States have greater numbers of headquarters. Minneapolis-St. Paul is sixth on this ranking—tied with

Table 2.7 Fortune 500 companies by metropolitan area, 2011

Metropolitan Statistical Area	Number of Companies	Number of Sectors
New York-Northern New Jersey-Long Island, NY-NJ-PA	72	35
Chicago-Naperville-Joliet, IL-IN-WI	28	22
Houston-Sugar Land-Baytown, TX	22	10
Los Angeles-Long Beach-Santa Ana, CA	21	16
Dallas-Fort Worth-Arlington, TX	20	17
Minneapolis-St. Paul-Bloomington, MN-WI	19	15
San Francisco-Oakland-Fremont, CA	19	17
Washington-Arlington-Alexandria, DC-VA-MD-WV	17	12
Detroit-Warren-Livonia, MI	14	7
Philadelphia-Camden-Wilmington, PA-NJ-DE-MD	13	13
San Jose-Sunnyvale-Santa Clara, CA	12	6
Atlanta-Sandy Springs-Marietta, GA	12	11
Boston-Cambridge-Quincy, MA-NH	11	10
Cincinnati-Middletown, OH-KY-IN	10	10
Denver-Aurora, CO	10	8
Charlotte-Gastonia-Concord, NC-SC	9	9
St. Louis, MO-IL	9	9
Pittsburgh, PA	8	8
Seattle-Tacoma-Bellevue, WA	8	8
Bridgeport-Stamford-Norwalk, CT	7	6
Cleveland-Elyria-Mentor, OH	7	6
Phoenix-Mesa-Scottsdale, AZ	7	6
Richmond, VA	6	6
Milwaukee-Waukesha-West Allis, WI	6	6
Columbus, OH	6	6
Omaha-Council Bluffs, NE-IA	5	5
Hartford-West Hartford-East Hartford, CT	5	5
San Antonio, TX	5	4
Miami-Fort Lauderdale-Pompano Beach, FL	5	5

Source: 2011 Fortune 500 list.

San Francisco. However, this ranking outstrips the region's sixteenth ranking in terms of population. Moreover, the metropolitan area's count of nineteen Fortune 500 headquarters in 2011 is impressive in its own right and greater than metropolitan areas such as Washington, Detroit, Philadelphia, Atlanta, Boston, St. Louis, Seattle, and Denver.

To make this comparison more evident, I scale the number of Fortune 500s by metropolitan area population. In making this comparison, I first restrict the analysis to metropolitan areas that have more than four Fortune 500 Headquarters; I then divide by the population of the metropolitan area to calculate Fortune 500 headquarters per million people. I restrict my analysis to regions with more than four headquarters because I wish to focus on metropolitan areas where there is a notable concentration of large corporate headquarters. For example, in 2011 Decatur, Illinois was home to one Fortune 500 firm: ADM. With a population of just over 110,000, Decatur exhibits an extremely large per capita level of Fortune 500 headquarters. Although headquarters intensive in that almost all cities of this size do not have Fortune 500 headquarters, one Fortune 500 headquarter does not make this a headquarters economy. Panel A of Table 2.8 presents the rank of metropolitan areas by Fortune 500's per population.

In Panel A of this table, one can see that the Minneapolis-St. Paul region sits third in terms of headquarters per million people—behind Bridgeport and San José. Thus confirming the intensity of headquarters in the region—especially on a per capita basis. Moreover, Bridgeport and San José are MSAs that are contiguous with other MSAs. Bridgeport to New York City and San José to San Francisco. In light of this, Panel B of Table 2.8 combines those metropolitan areas with their neighboring metropolitan areas to make the comparison. If one considers San José as part of the greater Bay Area or Bridgeport as part of the greater New York City area, then the data in Panel B of Table 2.8 will be more appropriate. This ranking further highlights the concentration of the Fortune 500 companies in the Minneapolis-St. Paul region.

WHAT DID THE REGION'S FORTUNE 500's LOOK LIKE
SIXTY YEARS AGO?

Although current data show the intensity of headquarters activity in the Minneapolis-St. Paul region, a more complete picture emerges if I consider what it looks like over a longer period of time. To do this, I examine the Fortune 500 list from 1955, which is the year that the list was first published.

In 1955 nine Minneapolis-St. Paul companies appear in the Fortune 500 list. Table 2.9 presents these companies. Two other Minnesota companies made the list: Hormel in Austin and Marshall-Wells in Duluth. These data show a notable concentration of large corporate headquarters in the Minneapolis-St. Paul metropolitan over sixty years ago. In addition, examining these

Table 2.8 Fortune 500 companies per capita, 2011

Panel A: All Metropolitan Statistical Areas

Metropolitan Statistical Area	HQs per Capita	Number of HQs
Bridgeport-Stamford-Norwalk, CT	7.64	7
San Jose-Sunnyvale-Santa Clara, CA	6.53	12
Minneapolis-St. Paul-Bloomington, MN-WI	5.79	19
Omaha-Council Bluffs, NE-IA	5.78	5
Charlotte-Gastonia-Concord, NC-SC	5.12	9
Richmond, VA	4.77	6
Cincinnati-Middletown, OH-KY-IN	4.69	10
San Francisco-Oakland-Fremont, CA	4.38	19
Hartford-West Hartford-East Hartford, CT	4.12	5
Denver-Aurora, CO	3.93	10
Milwaukee-Waukesha-West Allis, WI	3.86	6
New York-Northern New Jersey-Long Island, NY-NJ-PA	3.81	72
Houston-Sugar Land-Baytown, TX	3.70	22
Pittsburgh, PA	3.40	8
Cleveland-Elyria-Mentor, OH	3.37	7
Columbus, OH	3.27	6
Detroit-Warren-Livonia, MI	3.26	14
St. Louis, MO-IL	3.20	9
Dallas-Fort Worth-Arlington, TX	3.14	20
Washington-Arlington-Alexandria, DC-VA-MD-WV	3.05	17
Chicago-Naperville-Joliet, IL-IN-WI	2.96	28
Boston-Cambridge-Quincy, MA-NH	2.42	11
San Antonio, TX	2.33	5
Seattle-Tacoma-Bellevue, WA	2.33	8
Atlanta-Sandy Springs-Marietta, GA	2.28	12
Philadelphia-Camden-Wilmington, PA-NJ-DE-MD	2.18	13
Phoenix-Mesa-Scottsdale, AZ	1.67	7
Los Angeles-Long Beach-Santa Ana, CA	1.64	21
Miami-Fort Lauderdale-Pompano Beach, FL	0.90	5

Panel B: Collapsing Greater New York and San Francisco Bay Area MSAs

Metropolitan Statistical Area	HQs per Capita	Number of HQs
Minneapolis-St. Paul-Bloomington, MN-WI	5.79	19
Omaha-Council Bluffs, NE-IA	5.78	5
Charlotte-Gastonia-Concord, NC-SC	5.12	9
Bay Area	5.02	31
Richmond, VA	4.77	6
Cincinnati-Middletown, OH-KY-IN	4.69	10
Hartford-West Hartford-East Hartford, CT	4.12	5
Greater NY	3.99	79
Denver-Aurora, CO	3.93	10
Milwaukee-Waukesha-West Allis, WI	3.86	6
Houston-Sugar Land-Baytown, TX	3.70	22
Pittsburgh, PA	3.40	8
Cleveland-Elyria-Mentor, OH	3.37	7
Columbus, OH	3.27	6
Detroit-Warren-Livonia, MI	3.26	14
St. Louis, MO-IL	3.20	9
Dallas-Fort Worth-Arlington, TX	3.14	20
Washington-Arlington-Alexandria, DC-VA-MD-WV	3.05	17

(continued)

Table 2.8 Continued

Panel B: Collapsing Greater New York and San Francisco Bay Area MSAs

Metropolitan Statistical Area	HQs per Capita	Number of HQs
Chicago-Naperville-Joliet, IL-IN-WI	2.96	28
Boston-Cambridge-Quincy, MA-NH	2.42	11
San Antonio, TX	2.33	5
Seattle-Tacoma-Bellevue, WA	2.33	8
Atlanta-Sandy Springs-Marietta, GA	2.28	12
Philadelphia-Camden-Wilmington, PA-NJ-DE-MD	2.18	13
Phoenix-Mesa-Scottsdale, AZ	1.67	7
Los Angeles-Long Beach-Santa Ana, CA	1.64	21
Miami-Fort Lauderdale-Pompano Beach, FL	0.90	5

Sources: 2011 Fortune 500 list, United States Census Bureau.

Table 2.9 Fortune 500 companies in Minneapolis-St. Paul, 1955

Company	Rank
General Mills	56
Pillsbury Mills	97
Minnesota Mining and Manufacturing	131
Minneapolis-Honeywell Regulator Co.	132
Archer-Daniels-Midland	155
Seeger Refrigerator	264
Minneapolis-Moline Co.	353
Minnesota & Ontario Paper	379
Gould-National Batteries	444

Source: 1955 Fortune 500 list.

companies demonstrates the diverse set of industries in which they participate. These industries include white-goods (Seeger Refrigerator), batteries
(Gould National Batteries), farm equipment (Minneapolis-Moline), pulp and
paper (Minnesota and Ontario Paper), and milling (Pillsbury). The diversity
might not look as great as the diversity of companies currently among
Minneapolis-St. Pauls' Fortune 500s. However, the Fortune 500 list initially
focused on industrial firms and did not consider the range of companies that
currently appear on the list.

WHAT DID THE PROCESS OF CHANGE LOOK LIKE?
Simple arithmetic shows that the region more than doubled its Fortune 500
headquarters count between 1955 and 2011—moving from nine to nineteen.
However, closer examination of the recent list and the 1955 list show that
only two companies from the 1955 list are on the list today. Those companies
are 3M and General Mills. Therefore, the evolution from nine to nineteen is

more complicated than adding ten companies to the nine headquartered in Minneapolis-St. Paul in 1955.

Tracing the firms that entered and left the Fortune 500 over these sixty years paints a picture of churn in the largest companies in the region. Tables 2.10 and 2.11, respectively, list the companies from the Minneapolis-St Paul region that entered and left the Fortune 500 between 1955 and 2011. It also

Table 2.10 Fortune 500 additions in Minneapolis-St. Paul, 1956–2011

Company	Year	Company	Year
Land O'Lakes Creameries	1963	Northwest Airlines	1995
International Milling	1964	Norwest Corp.	1995
Farmers Union Central Exch.	1964	St. Paul Cos.	1995
Bemis Bro. Bag	1965	Northern States Power	1995
Control Data	1965	First Bank System	1995
Hoerner Waldorf	1967	Supervalu	1995
Green Giant	1968	United Healthcare	1995
American Hoist & Derrick	1970	Best Buy	1995
Peavey	1973	Nash Finch	1995
Economics Laboratory	1976	Lutheran Brotherhood	1995
Midland Cooperatives	1978	U.S. Bancorp	1997
MEI	1983	Reliastar Financial	2000
Deluxe Check Printers	1984	Cenex Harvest States	2000
Pentair	1985	Xcel Energy	2001
H. B. Fuller	1985	C.H. Robinson Worldwide	2002
Jostens	1985	PepsiAmericas	2003
Medtronic	1985	Mosaic	2006
Cray Research	1987	Ameriprise Financial	2007
Toro	1988	Alliant Techsystems	2010
Dayton Hudson	1990	St. Jude Medical	2010

Source: Fortune 500 lists 1955–2011.

Table 2.11 Fortune 500 exits from Minneapolis-St. Paul, 1956–2011

Company	Year	Company	Year
Seeger Refrigerator	1956	Deluxe	1995
Minneapolis-Moline Co.	1958	Pentair	1995
Gould-National Batteries	1963	H. B. Fuller	1995
Minnesota & Ontario Paper	1963	Jostens	1995
Archel Daniels Midland	1970	Cray Research	1995
Hoerner Waldorf	1978	Toro	1995
Green Giant	1980	International Multifoods	1996
Peavey	1983	First Bank System	1997
Midland Cooperatives	1983	Norwest Corp.	1998
American Hoist & Derrick	1984	Northern States Power	1998
MEI	1987	Honeywell	2000
Pillsbury	1990	Reliastar Financial	2001
Farmers Union Central Exch.	1990	St. Paul Traveler's Co.	2007
Control Data	1992	Northwest Airlines	2009
Bemis	1995	PepsiAmericas	2011

Source: Fortune 500 lists 1955–2011.

documents the year that they entered or left the Fortune 500. From these data, I document that the process of moving from nine to nineteen Fortune 500 firms was by adding forty firms and seeing thirty drop out.

There are many interesting stories with the additions and deletions to the region's Fortune 500s. For example, Seeger Refrigerator dropped from the Fortune 500 in 1956 once Whirlpool acquired the company. This acquisition facilitated Whirlpool's entry into the refrigerator business. Reflecting this, Whirlpool renamed itself Whirlpool-Seeger for a short period of time after the acquisition before reverting to its shorter original name.

A careful read of these tables will highlight a lot of movement—both entry and exit—in 1995. This is the year that Fortune redefined the Fortune 500 to include a broader array of industries. Therefore, many of the firms shown as exiting did not cease being headquartered in Minneapolis-St. Paul. For example, Toro and H. B. Fuller are still headquartered in the region today. These companies were replaced on the Fortune 500 list by larger companies coming from other sectors of the economy.

One might suggest that this redefinition artificially magnifies the sense of change in the biggest firms in the region. I highlight that one of the reasons why we see so much entry *and* exit with the redefinition of the Fortune 500 is that it reflects of the diversity of the companies headquartered in the Minneapolis-St. Paul metro area. When the Fortune 500 expanded beyond industrial companies, a region gained headquarters counts only if large non-industrial companies were located there. Looking at Table 2.10, note that ten Minneapolis-St. Paul companies entered the Fortune 500 that year. The companies are in sectors such as banking (Norwest and First Bank System), insurance (St. Paul Companies and United Healthcare), and distribution (Nash Finch). This would not have happened if the region had companies concentrated in industrials—there would have been exit but little entry. Likewise, if the region's companies were concentrated in non-industrials, then there would have been entry but little exit.

The churn associated with the significant movement into and out of the Fortune 500 is not a revelation in its own right. There is an understanding of the significant change in any compilation of the largest companies in the United States economy over time (e.g., Stangler and Arbesman, 2012). Likewise, Klier (2006) shows that the net change in headquarters counts by metropolitan area between 1990 and 2000 is much smaller than the entry and exit of the firms that make-up this count. However, the degree of entry and exit among the Fortune 500—and among publicly traded firms in general—highlights an important element of a headquarters economy. Churn in the largest companies is going to occur and many companies will cease being Fortune 500 firms. A region is only able to sustain a headquarters economy if it is able to replace the inevitable loss of headquarters with new headquarters.

WHERE DID THE NEW HEADQUARTERS COME FROM?

The year 1995 is not the only year where the region saw additions to head-quartered firms on the Fortune 500. Therefore, the addition to the Fortune 500 over time does not simply reflect the movement from industrials to a broader array of companies. A closer examination of the list of companies that entered the Fortune 500 provides an interesting insight. Only one of the forty companies that entered the list was a Fortune 500 firm that was located elsewhere and moved its headquarters to the Minneapolis-St. Paul metropolitan area. All of the other companies were already headquartered in the region prior to joining the Fortune 500. The one exception is Bemis Corporation which moved to the Minneapolis-St. Paul region from St. Louis in 1965. The company dropped out of the Fortune 500 in 1995 and subsequently moved its headquarters to Wisconsin.

This almost complete reliance on homegrown companies to repopulate the Fortune 500 is unique. It is very different compared to other cities that increased Fortune 500 headquarters over the last several decades. For example, Atlanta shows a notable increase in Fortune 500 firms from zero in 1955—all three Georgia Fortune 500s in 1955 were outside of Atlanta—to eleven in 2011. A number of the additions come from headquarter relocations including well-known companies like Newell Rubbermaid, UPS, NCR, First Data, and Novelis.

Although the focus on Fortune 500 headquarters is informative when describing important headquarters activity, it misses two types of activity that are important when it comes to gauging headquarters activity. Moreover, both types of activity are prevalent in the Minneapolis-St. Paul region. The first is headquarters of privately held companies. The Fortune 500 does not track these companies; yet they can have operations that rival many Fortune 500 or Fortune 1000 companies.

Large Privately Held Companies

Anecdotally, when those who live in the Minneapolis-St. Paul area discuss the business environment they highlight that privately held companies play an important role in the economy. To aid in quantifying this sentiment, I turn to the Forbes list of the Largest Private Companies in the United States from 2011. The 2011 Forbes list includes 212 companies that Forbes estimates have over US$2 billion in sales. Sales of over US$2 billion would place all of these companies among the 1000 largest publicly traded companies in the United States as tracked by the Fortune 1000. As Table 2.12 shows, there are a number of large privately held companies headquartered in the Minneapolis-St Paul region. There are five companies from that list, including the largest privately held firm in the country—Cargill. Cargill describes itself as a provider of food, agriculture, financial and industrial products and services to the world. It has over 150,000 employees in sixty-seven countries. The other four companies are Carlson, which is a worldwide hospitality and travel company; Holiday, which operates gas station convenience stores; M. A. Mortenson, a construction company; and Anderson, which describes itself as the largest window and door manufacturer in North American.

Table 2.13 compares the Minneapolis-St. Paul region to other metropolitan areas in the country with respect to the number of large private firms that they have on the Forbes list in 2011. The table presents the fourteen metro areas with four or more headquarters in the Forbes list. Here one can see that Minneapolis-St. Paul ties for eighth place on the list, which is a higher rank than its population. Once again, many larger cities have fewer of these large private headquarters including San Francisco, Washington, Phoenix, and Detroit.

To make this relative comparison more transparent, I scale the number of headquarters by population and present headquarters per million people for the fourteen metropolitan areas presented in Table 2.13. Table 2.14 presents this

Table 2.12 Forbes large private companies in Minneapolis-St. Paul, 2011

Company	Rank
Cargill	1
Carlson	84
Holiday Companies	106
M. A. Mortenson	176
Andersen	206

Source: 2011 Forbes list of the largest private companies in the United States.

Table 2.13 Forbes large private companies by metropolitan area, 2011

Rank	Metropolitan Statistical Area	Companies
1	New York-Northern New Jersey-Long Island, NY-NJ-PA MSA	23
2	Chicago-Naperville-Joliet, IL-IN-WI MSA	11
2	Los Angeles-Long Beach-Santa Ana, CA MSA	11
4	Dallas-Fort Worth-Arlington, TX MSA	10
5	Philadelphia-Camden-Wilmington, PA-NJ-DE-MD MSA	9
6	Boston-Cambridge-Quincy, MA-NH MSA	7
6	St. Louis, MO-IL MSA	7
8	Atlanta-Sandy Springs-Marietta, GA MSA	5
8	Denver-Aurora, CO MSA	5
8	Houston-Sugar Land-Baytown, TX MSA	5
8	Miami-Fort Lauderdale-Pompano Beach, FL MSA	5
8	Minneapolis-St. Paul-Bloomington, MN-WI MSA	5
8	Omaha-Council Bluffs, NE-IA MSA	5
14	San Francisco-Oakland-Fremont, CA MSA	4

Source: 2011 Forbes list of the largest private companies in the United States.

Table 2.14 Forbes large private companies per capita, 2011

Metropolitan Statistical Area	HQs	HQ/Million
Omaha-Council Bluffs, NE-IA MSA	5	5.78
St. Louis, MO-IL MSA	7	2.49
Denver-Aurora, CO MSA	5	1.97
Dallas-Fort Worth-Arlington, TX MSA	10	1.57
Boston-Cambridge-Quincy, MA-NH MSA	7	1.54
Minneapolis-St. Paul-Bloomington, MN-WI MSA	5	1.52
Philadelphia-Camden-Wilmington, PA-NJ-DE-MD MSA	9	1.51
New York-Northern New Jersey-Long Island, NY-NJ-PA MSA	23	1.22
Chicago-Naperville-Joliet, IL-IN-WI MSA	11	1.16
Atlanta-Sandy Springs-Marietta, GA MSA	5	0.95
San Francisco-Oakland-Fremont, CA MSA	4	0.92
Miami-Fort Lauderdale-Pompano Beach, FL MSA	5	0.90
Los Angeles-Long Beach-Santa Ana, CA MSA	11	0.86
Houston-Sugar Land-Baytown, TX MSA	5	0.84

Sources: 2011 Forbes list of the largest private companies in the United States; United States Census Bureau.

ranking. In these data, Minneapolis-St. Paul ranks sixth highest in concentration of large private headquarters with a concentration similar to Dallas, Boston, and Philadelphia. Omaha, St. Louis, and Denver are the only metropolitan areas with a notably greater concentration of large private firms. I should note that only Minneapolis, Omaha, and Denver are among the top ten in ranking of headquarters per population for this list and the Fortune 500 list as presented in Table 2.8.

The other type of important headquarters activity that is not captured by focusing on the Fortune 500 or large privately held firms are what I refer to as "hidden headquarters."

Hidden Headquarters

Although the list of Fortune 500s and large private companies is impressive, it does not completely tell the story of headquarters activity in Minneapolis-St. Paul. Several companies have operational, divisional, or regional headquarters in the region, even though their corporate headquarters reside elsewhere.

Currently, two companies that would be Fortune 500 firms have their operational headquarters in the Minneapolis-St. Paul area, although they are technically headquartered in Europe because of corporate inversions. These companies are Medtronic and Pentair. Medtronic, which appears on the 2011 Fortune 500 list, completed a corporate inversion at the beginning of 2015 after its acquisition of Covidien. This resulted in its removal from the Fortune 500 because it became Medtronic PLC—an Irish company. Medtronic went to great lengths at the time of the acquisition announcement to assure local stakeholders that its operational headquarters would remain in

Minneapolis-St. Paul. Moreover, the company announced that it expected to increase its presence in the region as it consolidated its operations with Covidien.[10]

Pentair was founded in the Minneapolis-St. Paul area in 1966. Over time it grew to become a Fortune 1000 company that remained headquartered in the region. In 2012 it merged with Tyco's flow control and valve business. The combined entity was initially incorporated in Switzerland for tax purposes. However, its United States headquarters, and arguably its operational headquarters, are in the Minneapolis-St. Paul region. A look at its 2013 10-K demonstrates this. As stated in the 10-K: "Our registered principal office is located at Freier Platz 10, 8200 Schaffhausen, Switzerland. Our management office in the United States is located at 5500 Wayzata Boulevard, Suite 800, Minneapolis, Minnesota." Examining the financial statements show that Pentair's auditor is Deloite and Touche Minneapolis. Pentair subsequently moved its registration jurisdiction of organization from Switzerland to Ireland at the end of 2013.

Although the Medtronic and Pentair inversions are recent and high-profile examples of hidden headquarters within the region, they are not the only ones. To get a more complete picture of the hidden headquarters, I examined sources that listed employment in the region from non-Minnesota headquartered firms. Because I want to focus on hidden headquarters and not just companies with large operations in the region, I removed retailers and non-business entities. For example, Walmart has thousands of employees in the region that work in their retail operations. However, the company does not have a headquarters-type presence. Likewise, the Federal Government and the United States Postal Service are large regional employers. However, they do not have a headquarters-type presence as in the case of a business entity.

Table 2.15 presents five companies with the largest count of employees in the region, are headquartered elsewhere, and have a divisional or regional headquarters presence in the Minneapolis-St. Paul metro. A little background on these companies helps demonstrate where the region's hidden headquarters tend to come from. At the top of the list is Wells-Fargo. The data show that Well Fargo has over 20,000 employees in the region. I should note that this, in

Table 2.15 Hidden headquarters Minneapolis-St. Paul, 2014

Company	Minneapolis-St. Paul Employment Estimate[a]
Wells Fargo	20,000
Thomson Reuters	7,700
Boston Scientific	4,500
Honeywell	3,500
Cummins Power Generation	2,000

[a] *Source:* Compiled from Minneapolis-St. Paul *Business Journal* 2014 list of largest employers.

part, reflects employees in Wells Fargo's retail banking operations in the region. However, Wells Fargo has a very large presence in the region beyond retail bank branches. Minneapolis-St. Paul is a regional headquarters for many key operations like the retail business. It is also the headquarters location for over a dozen Wells Fargo national businesses including equipment financing and education financing. Minneapolis-St. Paul is a key location for the mortgage business in that several thousand employees in this business are situated in the region. In addition, individuals with enterprise-wide functions, who could well be located at the corporate headquarters in San Francisco, work out of the Minneapolis-St. Paul. The extent of these activities reflects that Norwest Bank of Minneapolis merged with Wells Fargo in 1998. The resulting entity kept the Wells-Fargo name and San Francisco corporate headquarters. Nevertheless, it kept significant operations in the Minneapolis-St. Paul region and has substantively added to these operations as the bank has grown post-merger.

Next on this list is Thomson Reuters. This hidden headquarters stems from the acquisition of West Publishing. West Publishing was founded in St. Paul in 1872 and its business evolved to be a large provider of legal, business, and regulatory reference materials. Thomson acquired West Publishing in 1996 and Thomson, in turn, merged with Reuters in 2007. The business that was West Publishing is now Thomson Reuters' Legal Solutions Business and is headquartered in the Minneapolis-St. Paul suburb of Eagan even though Thomson Reuters' corporate headquarters are in New York City. In 2013, Thomson Reuters' Legal Solutions Business recorded sales of US$3.4 billion.

The remaining firms on the list share similar experiences. Boston Scientific's operations in the region reflect acquisitions of local medical device firms. The company's two major business units in the region are cardiac rhythm management and interventional cardiology. Both businesses have their roots in local start-ups. The cardiac rhythm management business, which includes products like implantable pacemakers and defibrillators, traces back to Cardiac Pacemaker Inc. Cardiac Pacemaker was acquired by Eli Lily in 1978; then spun-off as part of Guidant when Lily divested its medical device business in 1994. Boston Scientific subsequently acquired Guidant in 2006. The interventional cardiology business in the region has its roots in SciMed Life Systems, which Boston Scientific acquired in 1995.

Honeywell too reflects operations whose corporate headquarters were previously in the Minneapolis-St. Paul area. Formed in 1927 by the merger of the Minneapolis Heat Regulator Company and Honeywell Heating Specialty Company, the resulting Minneapolis-Honeywell Regulator Company became an iconic Minnesota business. The company simplified its name to Honeywell in the 1960s and remained headquartered in Minneapolis until 1999 when AlliedSignal acquired Honeywell. AlliedSignal retained its headquarters in

Morristown, New Jersey, yet took the Honeywell name. Currently, the company's Automation and Control Solutions business unit's global head-quarters remain are in the Minneapolis-St. Paul region. This division recorded over US$14 billion in sales in 2014 (Honeywell 2014 10-K), which is larger than all of Honeywell's US$8.4 billion in sales pre-acquisition.[11] That US$8.4 billion figure in 1999 would be equivalent to US$11.9 billion in 2014 adjusting for price changes as reflected by the Consumer Price Index.

Cummins Power Generation—a division of Columbus, Indiana's Cummins Inc.—is also headquartered in the Minneapolis-St. Paul region. Again, the history of this division has its roots in the region as described on the company's website.

> In 1986, Cummins Engine Company, Inc. acquired Onan Corporation from Cooper Industries. Onan Corporation was founded in Minneapolis in 1920 by David W. Onan, initially to produce and market a line of automotive test equipment and tools. The first Onan electric generator set was designed in 1926, producing three hundred- (300) watts of electrical power. Onan was the leading supplier of generator sets to the U.S. military during World War II.[12]

In 2013 this business segment recorded over US$3 billion in sales as reported in the company's 10-K filing.

One can see why the operations of these companies are important to consider when assessing headquarters activity in the region. The employment total from the five companies in Table 2.15 is over 37,000 employees. Not to mention that all of these business units record yearly sales in the billions of dollars. These operational, regional, and divisional head-quarters activities share many commonalities to headquarters of companies compiled by Fortune or Forbes in terms of the level and nature of talent that they employ. Moreover, these companies are active in the community through corporate philanthropy and other forms of corporate engagement.

Although they are typically not discussed when making note of a region's headquarters, I believe that this is a mistake. They go hidden—and therefore the reason that I like to refer to these types of operations as the "hidden headquarters" of a region. However, their impact on the region is far from invisible. Policy makers and others who ignore these operations do so at their peril because of the important role that they can play with respect to regional economic and social prosperity.

The important role that hidden headquarters can play on a region's economic and social vitality is reinforced in when one considers the high level of entry and exit in the Fortune 500. Regions will fare differently if the Fortune 500 companies that cease to be headquartered there retain a headquarters-type presence in the form of a regional, divisional, or operational headquarters. In the case of Minneapolis-St. Paul, most exits from the Fortune 500 in the region are not from headquarters moves. Rather, they are changes in corporate control that stem from mergers and acquisitions where the resulting entity's corporate headquarters were elsewhere but where important business divisions remain in the region. In many of these cases, these hidden headquarters have thrived and the businesses are larger than when the corporate headquarters resided in the region.

Of course, this has not happened in every instance. For example, since Northwest Airlines was acquired by Delta Airlines its headquarters operations moved to Atlanta. Although there was initially discussion that some of these activities might stay in the Minneapolis-St. Paul region, Delta reassessed this in search of efficiencies.[13]

Describing the history of these hidden headquarters provides insight into where they come from. Therefore, a key element in understanding hidden headquarters is understanding why an acquiring company would keep the management of an acquired businesses in its previous location rather than consolidate it elsewhere with the rest of the company. The change in corporate control and the resulting change in corporate strategy that stems from an acquisition can provide an impetus to reassess many aspects of the acquired business. Seeing so many companies resisting such change and growing the acquired business in its pre-acquisition region suggests the importance of some regional factor.

Why is Minneapolis-St. Paul a Headquarters Economy?

The data paint a compelling picture that the Minneapolis-St. Paul area has a notable headquarters presence that is disproportionate to its size.[14] Although there are ebbs and flows from year to year, the data show that the region has sustained a substantial headquarters presence over a long period to time. My experience is that the nature of this economy is not well-understood outside the region. Moreover, as I compiled and presented these data to audiences in the Minneapolis-St. Paul region, I found that most people living in the region do not appreciate the magnitude of the headquarters activity that occurs in the region.

Seeing the data with respect to the level of headquarters activity in the Minneapolis-St. Paul region, almost everyone has the same question—why? Answering this question has much broader implications than resolving the curiosity surrounding Minneapolis-St. Paul's experience. It has important implications for corporate leaders and policy makers both within and outside of the region. The concentration headquarters activity provides many advantages to a region and is arguably a key factor in the region's economic and social vitality that I previously described. Understanding its determinants can provide knowledge of what fosters or dampens local headquarters activities.

To guide this inquiry I start with five factors used to explain why economic activity or headquarters activity concentrates within a region. All are potential candidates to describe the experience of Minneapolis-St. Paul. Armed with the data presented earlier in this chapter, I am in a better position to evaluate if these factors explain why the Minneapolis-St. Paul region has sustained a concentration of large diverse headquarters.

When confronted with the data, these explanations do not appear adequate to explain the experience of Minneapolis-St. Paul. The following sections describe arguments of why we see geographic concentrations of business or headquarters activity and assesses to what extent they garner support from the data with respect to the Minneapolis-St. Paul region. My approach is not to review or extensively survey these literatures because they do not appear consistent with the data. The Appendix discusses some of these perspectives in greater detail. The focus of the Appendix is to describe how the explanation I advance in the next chapter differs from these perspectives, despite there being similarities.

Geographically Tied Determinants of the Underlying Businesses

One reason why businesses geographically concentrate is the existence of geographically tied endowments. For example, forestry companies will have operations in forested areas and not in the desert. Transportation businesses will often concentrate around ports or on major transportation routes. The rationale is straightforward. Businesses are more mobile than these fixed geographic features; therefore, businesses will form and grow alongside these geographic features. Although geographic attributes of the region historically influenced many companies and the nature of the economy in the Minneapolis-St. Paul metropolitan area, this explanation is not consistent with the overall patterns in the data. There are three reasons why.

First, many of the companies headquartered in the region do not draw on geographically tied inputs. Consider the following observations. The businesses of the headquartered companies in the Minneapolis-St. Paul region are extremely diverse. With such diversity, it is difficult to find a geographic feature that would link all of these businesses to the region. Moreover, many of these businesses do not have a geographic anchor and presumably could be located anywhere in the country. For example, medical device companies such as St. Jude Medical or health insurance companies such as UnitedHealth could be located anywhere. There is not a geographically tied element of the region that would draw such companies here. Of course, there are historical reasons that link these particular companies to the region. However, this is very different from saying that these companies draw upon a geographically tied regional input. Although some businesses are tied to the region due to geographic factors, they could well locate in other locations and harness similar benefits. For example, there are many agribusiness firms in the region like Land O'Lakes. If these companies wish to be proximate to the mid-west agricultural bases upon which they were originally founded, it is not clear they would have to be Minneapolis-St. Paul versus other communities such as Chicago, St. Louis, or Kansas City.

Second, it is not appropriate to assume that a company's headquarters needs to be co-located with its operations that are geographically tied. In fact, as a company expands its geographic footprint, it is impossible to co-locate its headquarters with all of its operations. Take for example the surge in the oil and gas production in North Dakota in the 2000s and 2010s. The energy being harvested is geographically tied and many businesses involved in this process have operations in the area. Although these businesses have their operations in North Dakota, many are not headquartered in there. For example, their headquarters can be in Oklahoma City (Continental Resources), Houston (Marathon Oil), or Stavanger Norway (Stat Oil). Reinforcing this point, the large agribusiness companies headquartered in the Minneapolis-St. Paul region are multinational firms and their operations have an international footprint. They cannot headquarter proximate to all of their operations because their operations span many continents.

Third, even when geography has a compelling influence on company founding, there is no reason to believe that a company will remain headquartered in the region where it was founded over an extended period of time. Companies might move their headquarters as their operations disperse. Likewise, companies might change headquarter locations due to events like mergers and acquisitions. For example, Pillsbury was founded in 1872 in Minneapolis as a milling company taking advantage of the waterpower of the falls along the Mississippi River and access to wheat from the region. One can see the geographic imprinting in its founding. By 1955, Pillsbury was one of the Fortune 500 firms in the Minneapolis-St. Paul area. Pillsbury left the Fortune 500 in 1989 when the British company Grand Metropolitan acquired Pillsbury, and later changed the name of the combined entity to Diageo. Although Pillsbury was a hidden headquarters in the region because Grand Metropolitan kept Pillsbury's operations in Minneapolis, it did not appear in listings like the Fortune 500 because Grand Metropolitan's headquarters were in London. In this case, an acquisition trumped the initial geographic influence in affecting the headquarters location. When we consider the churn in the Fortune 500 from changes in corporate control like mergers and acquisitions, these events can have a large impact in de-linking headquarters from the geographic determinants of their businesses' origins.

For all of these reasons, geographically-tied inputs do not appear to be a prominent reason why the Minneapolis-St. Paul region has sustained a large concentration of corporate headquarters. A Fortune magazine article profiling the metropolitan area in 1936 predicted that the region was in an economic downward spiral because it had exhausted the primary natural resources of the region such as timber. Therefore, even by the late 1930's it was apparent that the region would stagnate if it relied only on the initial geographically-tied endowments to fuel its economy.[15]

I wish to reiterate that there exist historical reasons why each company in the region is geographically located there. However, this is different from concluding that geographically-tied resources lead to this concentration of headquarters activity—especially over an extended period of time.

Industry Clusters

When one discusses the economic vitality of a region, a recent focus is the existence industry clusters (e.g., Marshall, 1890; Porter 1990; Saxenien 1994). An industry cluster is a collection of companies in the same industry that are co-located. Notable examples include Silicon Valley as a hub of technology business; Detroit historically being a cluster of automobile business; and Los Angeles being a center of entertainment and media business.

The benefits of industry co-location are generally considered to come from three sources: pools of specialized labor, pools of specialized input providers, and information spillovers between companies (e.g., Marshall, 1890; Krugman, 1991). Pools of specialized labor and other inputs are beneficial because firms gain access to industry-specific skills or inputs that would not be available if they located in another region. For example, software engineers are not uniformly distributed across the country and a company requiring this skill set will often have to locate where this talent resides—versus having the talent move to where the company is located. Likewise, companies often need to draw on industry-specific inputs (i.e., upstream inputs) or distribution (i.e., downstream inputs). When those inputs are geographically proximate, it often makes them easier or less expensive to access. Information spillovers are best highlighted by the stories associated with the founding of Silicon Valley where information was shared between competing companies (e.g., Saxenian, 1994). Sometimes it was through the hiring of other companies' employees, other times it was from the informal exchange of information in social settings between rival companies' employees. Regardless of the source, companies often benefitted from the information and experiences of other companies in the region.

The notion of industry clustering is closely related, yet generally considered distinct from geographically tied inputs that I discussed in the previous section. Geographically tied inputs tend to be natural resources or geographical features such as water access. Clustering benefits could conceivably end up in many locations and are not tied to the geography. For example, electrical engineers could live in almost any place, provided there is demand for their skills. There is no reason to believe that it would have to be in a place like Silicon Valley. However, once there exists a concentration of electrical engineers in a region, this is a localized endowment that can affect businesses' location choices.

Notwithstanding it being a popular description for regional economic vitality and having many high-profile supporting examples, industry clustering does not appear to be a good explanation for the economy in Minneapolis-St. Paul metropolitan area. The diversity of companies in the region suggests that industry clustering is not the primary determinant of business activity in the region.

This is not to say that Minneapolis-St. Paul is devoid of industry clusters. For example, the region is home to large concentration of medical device firms. Important medical device players Medtronic, St. Jude Medical, Boston Scientific, and Smiths Medical all have headquarters or hidden headquarters within the region. Moreover, the region is also home to many mid-sized and start-up medical device companies. These include companies such as Cardiovascular Systems and Torax Medical. Nevertheless, this cluster and other industry clusters in the region (e.g., agribusiness) comprise only a fraction of the economic and headquarters activity when one considers the host of companies that I described in the first part of the chapter. Therefore, although industry clusters exist within the region, this is not a setting where a prominent industry cluster explains the bulk of economic and headquarters activity.

Geographic Movement of Population and Economic Activity within the United States

Another possible explanation for the concentration of headquarters activity in the Minneapolis-St. Paul metropolitan area is that it reflects the general pattern of movement in population and economic activity in the United States (Semple, 1973). Over the last sixty years, population and economic activity have spread to the west and south from its previous concentration in the industrialized north and east.

A look at the data on the dispersion of Fortune 500 headquarters over the last sixty years and the net change in population across states does not lend support for this explanation in the case of Minneapolis-St. Paul. Although the population of Minnesota increased over the past fifty years, its growth is not as large as many other states. Minnesota's population grew from 3.4 million in 1960 to 5.3 million in 2010. This increase of 55 percent ranked twenty-seventh among the fifty states. Minnesota saw its roster of Fortune 500 firms increase from eleven to twenty between 1955 and 2011, which ranks seventh in terms of net gain. This increase of 82 percent is much greater than the increase in population and ranks fourteenth in percentage increase for states that had at least one Fortune 500 firm in 1955.

Another way to see this is to map the states that increased and decreased the number of Fortune 500 companies between 1955 and 2011. Figure 2.1 provides this. The dark shaded states are states where the number of Fortune 500 headquarters increased between 1955 and 2011. The lighter shaded states are states where the number of Fortune 500 headquarters decreased between 1955 and 2011. The map reinforces the overall movement of economic activity to the west and south. However, it highlights three notable exceptions to this pattern: Minnesota, New Jersey, and Connecticut. In all three states, the increase in headquarters activity appears to run counter to the trend. New Jersey and Connecticut both benefitted from New York headquarters moving out of Manhattan to suburban locations in the neighboring states. The effect on the neighboring states was pronounced because New York saw a decrease of ninety-four Fortune 500 firms over this period of time. Minnesota had no such factor accounting for the growth in Fortune 500 headquarters, making the increase especially notable.

State and Local Public Policy Levers to Attract Business Activity

Another factor that could explain the concentration of headquarters activity revolves around public policy considerations. In particular, state laws and

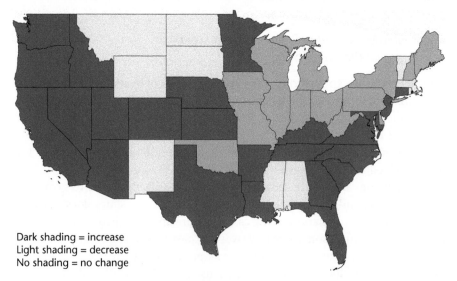

Dark shading = increase
Light shading = decrease
No shading = no change

Figure 2.1 Change in Fortune 500 headquarters, 1955–2011

incentives that are favorable to businesses—especially corporate headquarters. This would include policies that provide low taxes, favorable labor laws, and incentives for headquarters relocations.

Again, this explanation does not appear consistent with many patterns in the data. First, when looking at the map in Figure 2.1, most of the states that one would ascribe public policy commonalities with Minnesota have seen a reduction in Fortune 500 firms over this period of time. Minnesota appears to be an exception when compared to mid-western states in general and Wisconsin and Iowa in particular. Moreover, Minnesota's experience of increasing Fortune 500 headquarters differs from most northern industrialized states in the country over this period.

Second, in terms of policy levers like taxes or labor laws, Minnesota has policies that most would consider as unfriendly to attracting business to the state. Minnesota's tax rates tend to be higher than most states. For example, the Tax Foundation ranks Minnesota forty-seventh in their 2015 State Business Tax Climate Index.[16] Minnesota, however, taxes companies on their sales in the state.[17] This is advantageous for headquarters operations compared to tax regimes that also apportion based on payroll or property in making tax assessments. With respect to labor laws, Minnesota is not a right to work state and remains so, even as mid-western states such as Michigan and Wisconsin have changed their laws.

Third, Minnesota has not historically provided large incentives to attract businesses. A December 2012 *New York Time* article shows Minnesota as fortieth in terms of yearly businesses incentive spending across all states and forty-sixth in terms of per capita spending.[18] Reinforcing this is the observation that the increase in Fortune 500 firms in Minnesota is not driven by corporate relocations.

Overall, public policy considerations, such as low taxes, favorable labor laws, and business incentives relative to other regions in the country, do not appear to be the key driver of headquarters activity in the Minneapolis-St. Paul metropolitan region.

TWO IMPORTANT CAVEATS

First, I want to be clear that I am *not* concluding that taxes or similar public policy considerations are unimportant with respect to where a headquarters locate. The point I wish to highlight is that favorable tax and labor policies vis-à-vis the rest of the country do not appear to be the key factors in explaining Minneapolis-St. Paul's experience over this sixty-year period of time.

I would like to stress that the relationship between taxes, labor laws, and headquarters activity is not simple and that large sophisticated companies actively manage their operations taking into account these considerations. For example, in the early 2010s it was brought to light that General Electric was not paying any US income tax although it had record earnings.[19] It is clear that managing its tax liability is an important element of the company's operations. A company can strategically locate non-headquarters operations and the location of the headquarters need not play a large role in managing tax exposure. For example, Apple can keep its corporate headquarters in California, but manage its taxes through how it structures its operations in Nevada or Ireland.[20]

When one considers these points it reveals that an "informed" perspective is important when thinking about the role of such policy choices. There is substantial evidence that companies manage to these issues—they are important. However, just because a company manages to it does not mean that all of the company's operations will end up in the location that provides these advantages. At the same time, those who dismiss these issues as unimportant because other issues weigh on firm choice or that they will not necessarily affect headquarters' operations are being myopic. Left unchecked, these issues can become so pressing that they affect major corporate location decisions.

Second, I realize that other policy levers influence business—albeit more indirectly. For example, state policies fostering education might attract businesses looking for certain types of talent. I choose to focus on the direct business incentives because they are often the center in many discussions involving business attraction and retention. I will discuss the broader array of policy levers later in the book.

Co-location with Business Services

There is a body of research highlighting that corporate headquarters co-locate with business services (e.g., Henderson and Ono, 2008; Davis and Henderson, 2008; Straus-Kahn and Vives, 2009). Such services include accounting firms, consulting firms, law firms, banks, and other professional services. Naturally, there is a question of cause and effect with respect to this relationship. Is it that professional service firms locate near headquarters, headquarters locate near professional service firms, or both? When addressing the question of why headquarters have increased in the region, the question of do headquarters locate near professional service firms is most appropriate. There is evidence that this part of the relationship holds, although one can still question the completeness of the evidence. Nevertheless, this could be a potential explanation for the growth of headquarter activities in a region.

Data confirm that the Minneapolis-St. Paul region houses a concentration of business service providers. Some mid-sized professional service firms are headquartered in the region and many larger professional service firms have offices or operations in the region. For example, Accenture's tenth largest office in the United States is in Minneapolis. Therefore, the Minneapolis-St. Paul experience is consistent with the observations that headquarters and professional service firms co-locate.

However, this explanation does not provide much insight into why over time some metropolitan areas increase headquarters whereas other areas decrease headquarters. This explanation would suggest that regions with a significant headquarters presence—and the associated concentration of business services—would tend to see that presence consistently increase. It would not explain why regions with a large headquarters presence would lose them, or why regions with a negligible headquarters presence would gain them.

If one looks at the movement of headquarters within the United States—as highlighted previously in Figure 2.1, this explanation would suggest that there was a greater concentration of business service providers in the south and west compared to the north and east. I have seen no evidence of this. Alternatively, one would have to believe that first the business service providers left and then the headquarters followed. For example, professional services firms preceded the withdrawal of corporate headquarters from New York. I have also not seen evidence of this pattern of activity.

Although the observation that professional services and headquarters are co-located is undeniable, it appears not to be the key explanation of why the Minneapolis-St. Paul region has sustained and increased headquarters activities.

Two Regional "Folklore" Explanations

Five prevalent explanations for the geographic concentration of business and headquarters activity have little success explaining the concentration of headquarters activity in the Minneapolis-St. Paul region. In my discussions with local business and policy leaders, they raise two other explanations. Although I consider them local folklore and they are easy to dismiss with the data, I include them for completeness and because there are elements of fact in each explanation.

The first reason I hear is something along the lines of, "it is cold so we work really hard." It is true the climate is cold and most people will agree with the description of a work ethic in the region. However, Minneapolis-St. Paul is not the only cold-weather city in the country or the only place with a work ethic. Moreover, cold climates in the United States generally experienced a decrease in headquarters activity. As I previously highlighted, the concentration of Fortune 500 companies has migrated south and west over the last sixty years.

The second reason is something along the lines of "we come from hard-working Scandinavian heritage." It is true that the region's farmland was heavily settled by waves of immigrants from Sweden and Norway. Although there is a concentration of Scandinavian immigrants in the region, they were not the only immigrants. In fact, the wave of immigration from Scandinavia does not coincide with the general increase in headquarters activity over time. Then there is also the observation that many of the initial companies were founded and run by New Englanders who moved to the region.

Although I do not believe that these explanations provide a convincing rationale for the experience of the region, they share two attributes that I wish to highlight. First, both explanations center on ways in which the region differs from other areas of the United States. The weather in one case and the initial immigration makeup in the other. There is a logic here because the data I presented earlier in the chapter show that the concentration of headquarters activity in the Minneapolis-St. Paul region is unique; therefore, a valid explanation would try to identify something that is unique about the region when compared to the rest of the country.

Second, both explanations center on a work ethic or industriousness of the region's residents. Again, this makes sense when one considers the economic prosperity of the region—especially because prosperity is not driven solely by leveraging natural resource endowments. Businesses do not grow themselves, it is a reflection of the people who found, manage, and execute the day-to-day operations of those businesses. Therefore, industriousness and talent of a region's residents may well play an important role. Both of these elements have merit that I will leverage.

Need for a New Explanation

With common research-based explanations failing to account for the source of the Minneapolis-St. Paul headquarters economy and two folklore-based explanations also not up to the task, it suggests the need for a new explanation. In addition, the exercise of drawing together the data that I present in the chapter provides insight into what that explanation might look like. The benefit of examining general patterns in the data is that they offer a level of abstraction where I can begin to assess if there are commonalities in the pattern of business activity that I might otherwise miss if I focus on the intricacies of the individual cases.

I consider the following to be key patterns in the data that will have to be part of any explanation.

- Headquarters in the Minneapolis-St. Paul region come from a diverse set of industries.
  - It is not a reflection of a predominant industry cluster.
- The region has been a headquarters economy for a long period of time.

- There is a lot of turnover in the headquartered companies.
  - Many of the 1955 companies do not exist today.
  - Many of today's companies did not exist in 1955.
- Headquarters relocations play an unimportant role in adding to or replacing headquarters activity.
  - The addition of large corporate headquarters comes from companies previously headquartered within the region.
- Hidden headquarters play an important role in the economy.
  - Many regional companies that are acquired see their operations left in the region and they continue to grow.

In light of these patterns, it becomes clear that the explanation should not focus on the initial seeding of businesses or natural resource endowments. Although this is a tempting place to start, the dynamism of business headquarters is so pronounced that one will have to look beyond explanations related to initial endowments. A valid explanation will have to be one about creating and growing new businesses into large companies and sustaining or reinventing large established companies.

I have not yet discussed this last point of sustaining and reinventing companies in the region. However, over the extended period in which I have examined headquarters activities in the Minneapolis-St. Paul region, the companies that have persisted have evolved. Many look very different in terms of the businesses in which they participate and the processes that they employ.

Examining General Mills and 3M, which are the two Minneapolis-St. Paul companies that were present in the 1955 and 2011 Fortune 500 lists, demonstrates this point. Both of these companies retain iconic elements of their business from over sixty years ago. For example, Cheerios and Betty Crocker are still important brands for General Mills. 3M continues to make Scotch Tape and sandpaper. However, if one looks at the scope of their businesses and the footprint of their reach, these businesses have evolved significantly over the last sixty years.

Comparing General Mills' 1955 annual report with its 2015 annual report reveals significant changes in the company's portfolio of business. Out are businesses such animal feed, electro-mechanical products, and stratospheric research balloons. In are businesses such as yoghurt, frozen foods, and organic foods. In the intervening period, the company went through a series of moves that diversified the company and then a subsequent set of moves that undid these diversification efforts. For example, at one point General Mills owned Parker Brothers (toys and games) and FootJoy (footwear). General Mills developed the flight data recorder (i.e., black box) and a deep-diving submarine. All of these businesses were later sold. It is clear that the General Mills of today is not the exact same company it was thirty years ago and that was not the exact same company as it was thirty years prior to that. The company has evolved as consumer demands and the business environment has changed over time.

3M's businesses have also evolved. One of the most striking ways is that the international footprint of 3M's operations have grown immensely. In their 1955 annual report, 3M discussed moves to bolster their international presence through acquisitions in Germany. They also highlighted that 14 percent of the company's sales came from outside of the United States and they ran fourteen manufacturing plants in seven countries. By 2015, over 60 percent of the company's sales came from outside of the United States. 3M operated 127 manufacturing and converting facilities in thirty-seven countries outside of the United States. Again, one can see that the company has evolved and transformed as the international business environment has changed.

Summary

A headquarters economy boasts a concentration of large headquarters from companies in a diverse set of industries. It matches this economic might with high incomes and high quality of life for its residents. Because there is great churn in the largest companies, a vibrant headquarters economy replenishes the stock of headquarters or transforms these corporate headquarters to hidden headquarters. An exemplar of such an economy is the Minneapolis-St. Paul metropolitan area in the upper mid-west of the United States.

Although there are many well-established explanations for why economic activity concentrates in particular regions, these explanations are not up to the task of explaining the existence and evolution of a headquarters economy— in general—and the Minneapolis-St. Paul economy in particular. The data suggest that the key to understand a headquarters economy is understanding why a region would excel in creating and nurturing a diverse set of businesses to grow large, sustaining, and reinventing businesses as the economy evolves. I offer an explanation in Chapter 3.

Notes

1. Minneapolis-St. Paul-Bloomington, MN-WI MSA as defined by the United States Office of Management and Budget.
2. Bureau of Labor Statistics data. https://www.bls.gov/bls/news-release/metro.htm#2008
3. Washington, DC, had a lower unemployment rate than Minneapolis-St. Paul for parts on this time period.

4. Rankings are tracked by various agencies including: http://www.minneapolis.org/media/facts-amp-research/accolades

5. http://www.citylab.com/housing/2014/11/choose-one-millennials-upward-mobility-or-affordable-housing/382953/

6. https://www.theatlantic.com/business/archive/2015/02/minneapoliss-white-lie/385702/

7. http://www.startribune.com/minnesota-achools-not-closing-education-gaps-new-state-report-shows/368987671/

8. The following are examples of corporate and economic histories for the region: Hartsough (1925); Schmid (1937); Gray (1954); Marvin (1969); Minnesota Mining and Manufacturing Company (1977); Larson (1979); Powell (1985); Jefferey (1989); Rodengen (1995); George (2003); Hidy et al. (2004); Wills (2005); Bell (2007); Castle (1912); Misa (2012, 2013); El-Hai (2013).

9. The Fortune 500 includes firms that operate in the United States, are incorporated in the United States, and file financial statements with a government agency (e.g., 10-K). Most companies on the list are publicly traded. However, the Fortune 500 includes cooperatives, mutual insurance companies, and private companies that meet these requirements.

10. Medtronic buys Irish firm for US$42.9 billion: Fridley firm's executive headquarters will move to Dublin, but Medtronic said Minnesota would not lose any jobs (Schafer and Brunswick, 2014: A.1).

11. http://www.nytimes.com/1999/06/07/business/allied-signal-and-honeywell-to-announce-merger-today.html

12. Description from company website.

13. Up to 400 NWA operations jobs to shift to Atlanta: Workers at a closing Twin Cities facility would be offered relocation packages (Fedor, 2008).

14. Ono (2006) also documents the prevalence of standalone headquarters activity in major metropolitan areas in the United States using 2000 Census data. Those data present a similar picture of Minneapolis-St. Paul having among the highest count and a high concentration of headquarters activity.

15. *Fortune* (1936: 112).

16. http://taxfoundation.org/article/2015-state-business-tax-climate-index (accessed April 20, 2015).

17. Michael (2015).

18. http://www.nytimes.com/interactive/2012/12/01/us/government-incentives.html (accessed April 20, 2015).

19. http://www.nytimes.com/2011/03/25/business/economy/25tax.html

20. http://www.nytimes.com/2012/04/29/business/apples-tax-strategy-aims-at-low-tax-states-and-nations.html

3

What Creates a Vibrant Headquarters Economy?

Managers, Mobility, and Migration

My explanation for why the Minneapolis-St. Paul metropolitan possesses a headquarters economy centers on the insight that understanding headquarters activity requires understanding the professional managerial and administrative talent pool central to headquarters operations. A region with a concentration of headquarters will have a sizeable pool of professional managerial and administrative talent. Moreover, a vibrant headquarters economy reflects a virtuous cycle that deepens the regional professional managerial and administrative talent pool. Successful companies attract talent to the region, job opportunities and quality of life within the region retain this talent, and the movement of talent from company to company within the region spreads best practices and management skills—further reinforcing the success of these companies. Figure 3.1 summarizes this relationship.

In this chapter, I develop this explanation from three foundational building blocks. The first building block is the existence of a significant professional managerial and administrative talent pool in the region—*managers*. The second building block is understanding the dynamics of how these individuals move among companies in the region and the consequences of this—*mobility*. The third building block is understanding the dynamics of attraction and retention of this talent pool within a region—*migration*. Focusing on these building blocks aids in presenting my arguments and illuminates important mechanisms that underlie a headquarters economy. Being clear about these mechanisms is important to gauge empirical support for my arguments.

I ground my explanation from observing the experience of the Minneapolis-St. Paul region. This allows me to develop a novel explanation for what leads to and sustains a headquarters economy. My arguments relate to existing academic literatures and approaches; however, they differ. The Appendix

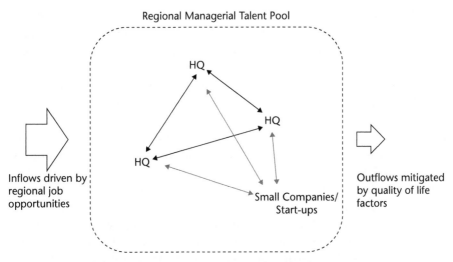

Figure 3.1 The virtuous cycle of a headquarters economy

discusses these literatures and the way in which my arguments differ. Although I present many examples in this discussion from the Minneapolis-St. Paul region, the underlying mechanisms are widely applicable. Namely, understanding the pool of managerial and administrative talent, their mobility, and their migration are factors that can affect headquarters operations anywhere in the world. Chapters 6, 7, and 8 describe how understanding these mechanisms can provide insight for regions and companies—including those outside of Minneapolis-St. Paul.

Managers

The first building block stems from the realization that any explanation about corporate headquarters will have to revolve around human capital—or what I will refer to as talent. In other words, the important element in understanding headquarters is not the physical infrastructure such as the buildings or amenities. It has to do with the people who occupy these buildings and the skills that they leverage in their employment. Although the activities that take place within headquarters vary across companies, there is one type of talent—broadly defined—in every headquarters: professional managerial and administrative talent.

Companies vary in the nature and level of managerial and administrative activities they house at their headquarters. Nevertheless, all headquarters house some. That is, after all, the definition of a headquarters. The fact that other types of talent might be resident at headquarters does not invalidate this. For example, some companies house research and development (R&D) activities at their headquarters. However, I know of no companies where their headquarters house only R&D activities and nothing else. Such locations are not headquarters; they are R&D facilities. Likewise, some companies have production activities co-located with their headquarters. Again, these locations will also have managerial and administrative talent resident. A location that houses only production facilities is not a headquarters. I should be clear, the fact that a headquarters has to have managerial and administrative talent does not mean that this will be the only location within a company houses such talent. For example, regional or divisional headquarters will house this talent. Likewise, production facilities and R&D facilities will house managers and administrators.

With the observation that all headquarters house managerial and administrative talent, it then follows that a region with a large headquarters presence will have a sizeable pool of managerial and administrative talent. This is not exclusive of other types of talent such as research scientists, computer programmers, or skilled manufacturing workers. However, when examining headquarters activities, it is important to focus on managerial and administrative talent.

The observation that a headquarters economy has a sizable pool of managerial and administrative talent is consistent with the many types of headquarters activities that I highlighted in the previous chapter. Publicly held companies, privately held companies, regional headquarters, divisional headquarters, and operational headquarters will all house this type of talent. It is also important to highlight that all companies require managerial and administrative talent, regardless of the activities they undertake or the industries in which they participate. Furthermore, many non-business entities will employ this type of talent. This includes governmental agencies and not-for-profit organizations.

What Does the Managerial and Administrative Talent Pool Look Like?

It is important to describe this talent pool because of the central role that it plays in a headquarters economy. Initially, let me draw attention to two important generalizations. First, the women and men who make up this talent pool tend to be well-educated. Most will have college degrees and many will have graduate degrees. Although many will have degrees from business schools, it is misleading to define the talent pool so narrowly. The managerial and administrative workforce that corporations employ comes with many skill sets enhanced by work experience. For this reason, managerial and administrative professionals will often have degrees from non-business professional schools such as law and engineering. Likewise, many will have degrees in the humanities, liberal arts, and sciences. Within the context of the Minneapolis-St. Paul metropolitan area, this is consistent with the data showing that a large proportion of the population holds college degrees.

Second, professional managerial and administrative talent within a company is dispersed across many levels of the organization. This includes entry-level, junior, mid-level, and senior management. I make this point to stress the importance of not defining professional managerial and administrative talent as only the most senior executives of a company. Although I provide examples in this chapter that draw on the experiences of senior-level management, senior-level talent comprises only a small fraction of the managerial and administrative talent pool. Although senior management plays an important role in shaping the direction and outcomes of a company, the other managerial and administrative talent within the company also plays an important role.

To see this, take for example, the marketing function in a company. Many companies, especially those that sell directly to consumers, will have a senior executive in charge of marketing, often with a title such as a chief marketing officer. He or she will typically oversee the marketing function, its alignment with the company's overall strategy, and its integration with the other functions in the organization. Reporting to this person are often directors who oversee different product lines. Reporting to these directors are often managers who have responsibility for various products within these lines. These managers will often have a staff with specific roles in developing and implementing the marketing plan at a more refined level. The company requires the talent and effort of all of these individuals to bring marketing plans to fruition—especially within the context of aligning with the company's overall strategy. No one person can complete the task in isolation, although some might have more power, experience, and impact relative to others. Therefore, considering talent across all of these levels is necessary to get a picture of the company's marketing capabilities. For example, the more skilled an individual at any level, the better the company's capabilities, and more likely that the company will be successful in its marketing efforts.

Another reason why it is important to consider managerial and administrative talent beyond the most senior levels is because the typical career path of senior executives has them spending time in non-senior roles as they progress in their careers. The women and men who will be the senior executives and leaders of these companies in the future are likely to not currently be in such roles. For these reasons, broadly defining the management and administrative talent pool provides insight into current capabilities and future potential.

First Building Block: Managers
A pool of managerial and administrative talent is the foundation of a headquarters economy. All headquarters draw upon managerial and administrative talent, regardless of the industries in which they participate.

Mobility

The second building block centers on the movement of individuals within the managerial and administrative talent pool from company to company within a region as their career progresses. Movement to different employers is common in the career path of managerial and administrative professionals. As managerial and administrative professionals advance in their careers, they are promoted and take on additional responsibilities. This reflects that work experience augments their skills over time. It can also reflect additional investments in education and training.

An individual's career progression within one company can be interrupted for a host of reasons, requiring that they look for opportunities in another company. First, there might not be opportunities at the higher level in the organization when a person is ready to be promoted. This reflects the pyramidal or hierarchical structure of most organizations. This is also why some see progression to the executive ranks of a company—where there are few positions—as a tournament (e.g., Lazear and Rosen, 1981). Second, political reasons or personality conflicts can hamper an individual's advancement even if they are ready to be promoted. Third, companies might face difficulties and seek to reduce headcount, thus negating any chance for promotion. Fourth, talent developed within the company might not be appreciated. For example, a person's ability when they entered the organization might overly anchor the assessment of their capabilities even though their abilities have increased over their tenure. Fifth, skilled employees are often approached with attractive job opportunities from outside of their current employer. These, and other reasons, can preclude the possibility that an individual advances in their career within the same organization.

Although many managerial and administrative jobs have industry-specific components and individuals have industry-specific experiences, the skills that underlie most managerial and administrative jobs are applicable in a wide array of settings and transferable. Therefore, when faced with the aforementioned obstacles or opportunities, employees often look for employment in other companies even if they not do have experience in that industry. When there exist other headquartered companies in a region, we see movement of managerial and administrative talent between companies. Moreover, we see career transitions for managerial and administrative employees that often involve moving between companies in different industries.

The ability to apply skills in many different industries is not equally viable across occupations. For example, the ability of managerial and administrative talent to apply their skills in almost any industry is more pronounced than for other types of talent such as scientists and engineers. Therefore, mobility across companies and industries is expectedly more pronounced for managerial and administrative talent.

Although managerial and administrative skills can be leveraged in many industries, the fact that industry-specific characteristics shape individuals' and companies' experiences means that industries tend to adopt certain norms, practices, or points of view. I will often hear managers tell me "this is how things are done in our industry," "our industry is unique," or "we are unlike other industries." When industries develop strong norms or become locked into set ways of doing things (i.e., when industry-specific skills are strong), they might become myopic.

Hiring individuals with experiences outside of their industry is one way that they bring skills and best practices that are not currently adopted or well-known in their industry. This can be beneficial in that it brings new insights or uniqueness to a company relative to its industry competitors. It shakes companies out of commonly accepted patterns of behavior or from industry inertia.

One can consider this akin to cross-pollinating managerial practices. As individuals move to companies in different industries, they can aid their new employers by bringing skills and practices that are novel to the industry.

This is why having a diverse set of companies in a region is key to fostering a headquarters economy. With a diverse set of companies, it is more likely that companies benefit from this cross-pollination of managerial and administrative practices compared to the situation where all companies are in the same industry—as would be the case in an industry cluster. Therefore, this key benefit of a headquarters economy is distinct from that of an industry cluster; even though the movement of talent across companies is important in both contexts.

There are many high-profile examples this type of managerial and administrative talent movement and cross-pollination of managerial practices within the Minneapolis-St. Paul region. I highlight three moves by senior level executives.

The first case is Wintson Wallin's appointment as chief executive officer (CEO) at Medtronic. By the mid-1980s, Medtronic had grown to become one of the major medical device companies in the world. Yet by the middle of the decade, the company had stagnated and was facing difficulties. Its stock price had dropped by 50 percent, it faced a major product recall, a couple of acquisitions failed, and it was losing its technological lead in pacemakers. As a result, Medtronic laid off 15 percent of its workforce in 1985.

Later in 1985, Medtronic hired Winston Wallin as CEO. Wallin came to Medtronic from Pillsbury, where he was a president and chief operating officer. Pillsbury was headquartered in Minneapolis-St. Paul and operated a diversified set of food-related businesses at the time, ranging from the iconic flour business to restaurants such as Burger King. Wallin left Pillsbury, in part, because he was passed over for the CEO position. Having worked at Pillsbury for thirty-seven years after graduating from the University of Minnesota, Wallin's experience was not in medical devices or the healthcare industry. He was, however, on the Medtronic board prior to taking the job.

Under Wallin's guidance as CEO from 1985 to 1991, Medtronic entered a period of remarkable growth and profitability. Over this time, the company acquired eleven companies, tripled its earnings, and saw its stock price rise over 800 percent (rising from US$14 to US$117 a share). Medtronic's founder Earl Bakken credited Wallin with saving the company. He also considered it an advantage that Wallin had come to Medtronic from outside of the industry.[1]

When interviewed about his role guiding Medtronic—especially with his managerial experiences from outside of the company and industry—Wallin discussed several ways in which he applied his previous experiences.[2] First, he viewed his role as a senior executive as managing people and employing their skills in the organization—he needed not be a technical expert in the underlying business. As he stated, "If you're at the top level, that's more of an organizational thing and it's more of identifying the people that you think can do it and then get out of their way and let them do it." Second, Wallin alluded to the skills that he brought to the job from his experiences at Pillsbury and how they complemented the medical device technical skills in the company at the time. He noted,

> They had been short on management that had a lot of knowledge about other things that the company would need, including everything from financing to the management processes and so forth, and that's really kind of the role that I played.

Third, he talked of implementing a strategic planning process in the company upon his arrival. When asked if Medtronic was doing strategic planning prior to his arrival, he responded, "The company had done strategic planning, but not anywhere near to the extent of the effort that we undertook." This is consistent with Wallin bringing managerial practices into the company that it had not previously implemented.

Fourth, Wallin discussed how he brought other practices from Pillsbury that were new to the medical device industry. The following exchange between Wallin and an interviewer about his efforts to secure Medtonic's salesforce exemplifies this point.

> WIN WALLIN: Well, everyone was always raiding each other's sales force, for one thing, and we kind of pretty much put an end to that, as far as Medtronic was concerned, by giving stock options to the sales force. So they became tied to the company, and the more the stock went up, the more it cost them to leave.

DAVID RHEES: Was that a new idea, or had other companies tried that?

WIN WALLIN: Not that I know of in this industry.

DAVID RHEES: Were you familiar with that from—

WIN WALLIN: I had done that with Pillsbury, an entirely different industry, where we had one certain business where we had employees that could sell their services to the competitors, and would try to tie them together.

Win Wallin's experience at Medtronic highlights a couple of key issues. The first is that there are general managerial skills that were applicable in both Medtronic and Pillsbury. To the extent that industry-specific knowledge and skills are important, it is not vital that all employees be versed in the industry-specific skills, as long as they are able to bring some form of expertise to the task at hand. Or it might be more accurate to state that these industry-specific skills need not be required at the time of hire. Skilled employees will develop industry-specific knowledge and skills over time. Second, there was benefit for Medtronic to look outside the organization and industry and bringing a set of skills that were likely lacking in the relatively nascent medical device industry. Wallin's experience demonstrates how importing managerial skills and experiences from outside of the industry were beneficial when applied at Medtronic.

Interestingly, Wallin's successor at Medtronic shared a similar change in career path of coming from a different industry when he entered the company. Bill George succeed Win Wallin as CEO. George was president of Honeywell's space and aviation business prior to joining Medtronic in 1989. Once again, Honeywell was headquartered in the Minneapolis-St. Paul region and was a company in a different industry.

Another case of such movement at the senior level within Minneapolis-St. Paul is the experience of Richard Anderson. Richard Anderson was CEO of Northwest Airlines between 2001 and 2004. In 2004 he stepped down from his role as CEO at Northwest to become executive vice president at UnitedHealth. The movement from a CEO to a non-CEO position is unusual. At the time of the announcement, Anderson's responsibilities were not described. However, an analyst noted that "It's not unusual for UnitedHealth to hire high-priced executives without immediately giving them a clear set of duties . . . It's almost like a football team that drafts players for their talent, not necessarily to fill an open position."[3] Because Northwest Airlines was considered a leader in the airline industry in the use of information technology (IT), many thought that would be Anderson's role. And that appeared to be the case. He oversaw UnitedHealth's Ingenix Division, which employed IT to mine health-claims data. In 2007, Anderson left UnitedHealth to become CEO of Delta Airlines.

A final case is that of Hubert Joly. Joly was the CEO of privately held Carlson whose businesses were in the travel and hospitality industry and headquartered in the Minneapolis-St. Paul region. In the fall of 2012, he left Carlson to become CEO of Best Buy, one of the Fortune 500 firms in the Minneapolis-St. Paul region. At that time, Best Buy was facing difficulties due to changes in the way that customers were purchasing electronics and required a turnaround. When assessing his aptitude for the role, many observers noted Joly's experience in corporate turnarounds from his previous positions as an executive at Carlson, Vivendi, and Electronic Data Systems. Carlson's chair, Marilyn Carlson Nelson, noted the following skills that Joly would bring to Best Buy when interviewed about his departure and new role.[4]

> "One of his skills is diagnosis," Nelson said. "He's very fact-based (and) very detail-oriented. He will diagnose the problem and come up with a plan to revive their vitality."

> Carlson Wagonlit's technology platform, some of which was developed under Joly's direct supervision of that unit and some of which came after he was promoted to CEO of Carlson, gives him the background to tackle Best Buy's challenge with Internet-based retailers like Amazon.com, she said.

One can imagine the application of these skills in efforts to lead the turnaround of Best Buy. Nevertheless, not all observers believed that these experiences would be transferable and believed that industry-specific experiences in retail would be more important.

> "We find Mr. Joly's résumé unimpressive, and believe he lacks sufficient experience to engineer a turnaround at Best Buy," Michael Pachter of Wedbush Securities wrote in a research note on Monday. "Mr. Joly's experience in U.S. retail is virtually nonexistent, with all of his experience in the media, technology and hospitality sectors."

> The Joly appointment "puzzles me," said Jim McComb, president of the McComb Group, a retail and real estate consultancy in Minneapolis. He too expected someone with a stronger retail background. While Best Buy is making an international push and Joly has global experience, "their problems are in the U.S.," McComb said.

By the summer of 2015, many observers noted progress in Best Buy's turnaround with many analysts giving positive stock recommendations. The company's stock price was trading in a range approximately double compared to the time of Joly's appointment. One commentator even stated, "the turnaround at Best Buy is one of the most impressive in the history of retail."[5] It is clear that the Best Buy board was relying on managerial skills in turnaround and not industry-specific experiences in retail. And there is reason to believe that these skills from outside of the retail industry were effectively employed at Best Buy. I have heard that Joly's approach to restructuring the business at Best Buy has many parallels to his actions at Carlson when I have talked with people who worked at both companies.

These three examples of high-profile senior managers are indicative of the movement of talent among companies and across industries in the Minneapolis-St. Paul region, and the skills that they bring to their new employer. This is especially noteworthy because there are relatively few executive-level managers within a company and we are less likely to observe talent movement at this level. Similar movements are pronounced at lower levels within a company.

For example, when I run into my former Master's of Business Administration (MBA) students in the Minneapolis-St. Paul area five to seven years after graduation and ask about their career progression, I will generally hear that many of them have worked in many different companies within the region. For example, my students will have had marketing jobs in companies such as Northwest Airlines and UnitedHealth, General Mills and 3M, Medtronic and 3M.

Although these movements do not create the same attention as the executive-level movements, there are similarities. First, these movements do not occur unless the hiring company believed that my former students' skills are useful to their organization. This reinforces my point that many professional managerial and administrative skills are readily transferable across industries. Second, in addition to their general skills, all of these individuals brought their past work experiences to their new job. For this reason, their movement was an important element in the cross-pollination of business practices in the region, as they brought experiences from one industry to bear on the managerial and administrative tasks they faced with their new employer.

Talent Flows from Large Companies to Smaller Companies and Start-ups

The flow of managerial and administrative talent among large companies headquartered within the region is not the only important movement of talent. Also important is the flow of talent between large headquartered companies and smaller companies in the region, including start-ups.

Smaller companies and start-up companies require skilled managerial and administrative talent in order to grow. Starting, sustaining, and growing a business takes more than the underlying idea or technology. I assert that one of the reasons why the Minneapolis-St. Paul metro has had success in growing businesses is because of the access to the regional pool of managerial and administrative talent. Likewise, moving a company from an established entity and scaling it up often requires skills beyond those that the company currently possesses (e.g., Smith et al, 1985; Boeker and Wiltbank, 2005). With a skilled managerial and administrative talent pool within the region, there is a ready talent base to tap.

The experiences of Bruce Beckman, reflect this type of talent movement. Beckman graduated from the Carlson School at the University of Minnesota and took at position at General Mills. Over the next twenty years Beckman rose through the ranks within the company. At the end of 2014 he was finance vice president of a billion dollar division.

In the spring of 2015 Beckman became vice president of finance at Entegris—a "worldwide developer, manufacturer and supplier of yield-enhancing materials and solutions for advanced manufacturing processes in the semiconductor and other high-technology industries"—as stated in their 10-K. Entegris, which was founded in the Minneapolis-St. Paul metropolitan area, merged with Mykrolis, which was founded in the Boston metropolitan area. The merged entity took the Entegris name; however, it kept the Boston-area headquarters. Although the combined entity's official corporate headquarters are in Boston, in 2015 some of the corporate positions resided within the Minneapolis-St. Paul area—including the chief financial officer (CFO) and IT.

As a result of this merger and a subsequent acquisition in 2014, Entegris surpassed annual sales of US$1 billion. My conversations with Beckman informed me that this is a size where many companies have to refine the processes that they use to meld financial reporting information with strategic planning. These were skills and experiences that Beckman had from General Mills and Entegris was looking to add this type of expertise. As Beckman said to me, "you might think that the food businesses of General Mills and the semiconductor business of Entegris have no relationship—but that would be incorrect." They face similar issues when creating forward-looking forecasts for strategic planning and use the same type of financial information systems. Of course there are differences in the businesses and each company has a different culture—Entegris being very engineering-driven and General Mills being very brand-driven. However, he found that his professional skills and experiences were especially valuable as he transported them from the much larger General Mills to the growing Entegris.

Another area in which I see a related flow of talent but to even smaller and startup firms is in a technology-based industry that has a fair amount of start-up activity in Minneapolis-St. Paul—the medical device industry. Here, a start-up firm often needs a novel technology in order to realize success in the marketplace. However, possession of this technology is necessary but alone is no guarantee of success—even if the technology is useful and economically viable. The regulated nature of this industry means that technologies have to be managed in terms of documenting their performance and getting governmental approval. Doing so starts to look more like managerial and administrative tasks—broadly defined—than more narrow engineering tasks. After product approval, managers must address issues such as market launch, manufacturing, quality control, and staffing. Having a pool of professional talent in the region with these skills aids small and start-up companies. I see individuals step out of their headquarters jobs at large companies and move into these small and medium sized companies with the intention of helping them grow. Many of these moves are by individuals with experience in the medical device industry. However, not all are. Many have experiences in unrelated industries, yet have experience in the underlying managerial and administrative skills that are necessary to launch or scale a business.

The experiences of Peter Horwich's career trajectory demonstrate this. Horwich moved to the Minneapolis-St. Paul region in 2002 having recently completed an MBA at the Olin School at Washington University in St. Louis. His motivation to relocate centered on his wife's employment opportunities. She landed an attractive job opportunity at one of the Fortune 500 firms in the Minneapolis-St. Paul region.

Horwich's background, before getting an MBA, was in chemical process engineering of new technologies. He had gained broad technical and managerial experiences at Zoltek—a start-up enterprise in pursuit of full-scale commercialization of carbon fiber as an everyday building material. After moving, Horwich started a job search and accepted a position in an industry where he did not have experience—medical devices. His role was a senior market analyst at Guidant (which is now Boston Scientific). His job responsibilities included market forecasting, competitive intelligence, and strategic analyses.

After a couple of years at Guidant, Horwich left to take a leadership role at a smaller company looking to expand their business in the biomedical arena. This was the first of four stops at relatively small companies. Although all of these companies participated in the biomedical industry—broadly defined, they focused on different markets, provided different therapies or services, and employed different technologies. At each stop, Horwich's role revolved around managerial and other professional-management activities. Often this involved aiding or developing growth strategies, understanding market segments, and engaging customers in the design of new offerings. At each of these companies, Horwich applied his skills and experiences with the goal of facilitating these smaller companies' growth.

Through this journey, Horwich not only brought his skills to each company; his experience at each company augmented his skillset as he worked in new markets, applied new technologies, and collaborated with new colleagues. This enhanced skillset made Horwich an attractive candidate at many companies. After working at the smaller companies, Horwich returned to a larger company when he accepted a position at Medtronic. His journey is one I have seen in the region—from large headquarters, to smaller companies, to large headquarters. Horwich's career path highlights the applicability of managerial skills across a spectrum of company sizes and ages.

Some might wonder why individuals would leave secure jobs in large head-quartered companies to move to start-ups and small firms—especially because the latter are seen as being more risky. When I have talked with many people who have made these moves, most mention that they are intrigued with the possibility of having a larger impact, and a smaller organization provides that possibility. Therefore, with the risk comes reward. A number of individuals tell me that they are willing to take on this risk because their spouse is a working professional with a steady income. Many will also mention that if things do not go well with the move, they believe there is the potential to move back to their previous company and reclaim a similar position.

However, another facet of the economy in the Minneapolis-St. Paul region—the collection of headquarters jobs—appears to facilitate this movement of talent. In addition to having their previous employer as a possible safety net if things do not progress in a small organization, many will note the overall market for their skills within the metropolitan area. I will hear the following, for example:

> Although I have moved from a large medical device firm to a medical device start-up, I am really a marketing person. If I have to find I job, I am qualified to work at the large medical device companies in town such as Medtronic, St. Jude, or Boston Scientific. However, I could just as easily see myself working in a related function at General Mills, UnitedHealth, or Ecolab.

With a large set of options given their managerial and administrative skill set, many see the risk of moving to a start-up firm manageable.

An example of this is one of my former MBA students at the Carlson School of Management, Brent Carlson-Lee. Prior to graduate school, Carlson-Lee worked in the branding and professional services industries. After finishing his MBA in 2007, he took a position with Conagra in their snack division, which had a product development group in the Minneapolis-St. Paul area. Incidentally, Conagra's Minneapolis-St. Paul snack division came from the acquisition of Golden Valley Microwave Foods in 1991, which was headquartered in the Minneapolis-St. Paul region. Golden Valley Microwave Foods was the inventor of shelf-stable microwave popcorn. Carlson-Lee considered this a dream job. He was associate manager of innovation marketing where he was involved in developing new snacks and trying to make the business case for the potential new products.

In 2010 ConAgra announced it was going to close the Minneapolis-St. Paul facility to consolidate operations in Naperville, Illinois. Although ConAgra offered to relocate Carlson-Lee, he chose to leave ConAgra and start his own company. Asked why, he said that he wanted to stay in the region. He also said that he had always been thinking of starting a new venture and this was the impetus to try it.

When I talked to him five years after leaving ConAgra, he described the fits and starts of being an entrepreneur and his latest endeavor, developing a frozen appetizer for restaurants. Given the substantial start-up costs and long product development cycle, he took on a part-time position in the business development function with one of the hidden headquarter companies in the health-care industry in the region. His ability to find such a role—in an industry where he had not previously worked—while continuing to invest in his own business reinforces the applicability of managerial and administrative skills across industries. Moreover, it demonstrates how the availability of these jobs in the region facilitates talent looking for opportunities with smaller or start-up endeavors.

These arguments and examples highlight how managerial and administrative talent is mobile across industry. More importantly, these examples show the benefits that companies receive when they hire talent from another industry that possess skills that their employees do not possess.

First Building Block: Managers
A pool of managerial and administrative talent serves is the foundation of a headquarters economy. All headquarters draw upon managerial and administrative talent, regardless of the industries in which they participate.

Second Building Block: Mobility
As this talent moves between companies—especially across industries—it becomes a resource that aids the receiving companies' growth and performance.

Why the Movement of Managerial Talent among Companies
in Minneapolis-St. Paul is Pronounced

My arguments hinge on the mobility of managerial and administrative talent among companies in the region—and especially the benefits when mobility brings insights and practices across industries. At the same time, it raises the question: why does this not happen in all regions that have concentrations of headquarters activity? Many metropolitan areas have concentrations of head-quarters and the requisite talent to run these organizations. However, not all are headquarters economies.

I wish to highlight two distinguishing factors. The first element—as I have previously described—is the importance that the diversity of businesses plays in cross-pollinating management practices across industries. Many regions with a concentration of headquarters activity do not have a diverse base of companies. These regions are built around an industry cluster. Although they derive many benefits as talent moves across companies in the region, they do not capture the same cross-pollinating benefits of managerial and administrative practices central to my arguments.

The second and related element that distinguishes the experiences of Minneapolis-St. Paul from many other regions is the propensity of talent to move across industries. A statement that I hear from many executive recruiters and human resource professionals in the region I believe enhances the likelihood that talent moves across industries. That statement is, "it is hard to get people to move to Minneapolis . . . but it is almost impossible to get them to leave." This leads to the third building block: migration.

Migration

If the regional talent pool that is central to Figure 3.1 is not static but changing, then migration to and from a region can have an important effect on the previous dynamic of professionals' mobility across companies within a region. As a result, the way in which migration patterns differ across regions can explain why not all regions with managerial and administrative talent pools form a headquarters economy. For this reason, the third building block of my argument reflects the dynamic of migration to and from a region with respect to the managerial and administrative talent pool.

To assess migration carefully, it is important to consider separately inflows to and outflows from a region. Doing so demonstrates that there are important differences when considering migration to a region (i.e., talent attraction) versus migration from a region (i.e., talent retention).

Managerial and Administrative Talent Retention

Let me start with the latter part of statement, "It is hard to get people to move to Minneapolis . . . . But it is almost impossible to get them to leave," because I believe this has especially important consequences in building and sustaining a headquarters economy. If true, it suggests a factor that varies across metropolitan areas. I first describe the effect that a high talent retention rate (i.e., low levels of outward migration) has on the previously discussed building blocks: managers and mobility. I then discuss what affects talent retention—especially with respect to managerial and administrative talent.

EFFECT OF STRONG RETENTION
To see the effect of migration, it is important to revisit the career path of professional managerial and administrative talent. As I previously discuss, the resources that professional managerial and administrative employees invest in their career and the nature of their career path make it common for them to look outside of a current employer as they progress in their careers. To understand the role that migration plays here, it is important to consider the

choices that an individual considers when leaving a company for career advancement. I highlight choices along two dimensions: whether or not to search for employment in the same industry and whether or not to search for employment in the same geographic location.

In a frictionless employment market, an individual would assess their best option across industries and geographies when looking for opportunities outside their current employment. However, this choice becomes more complicated when one considers the realities of changing industries or changing geographies. There are frictions in making such employment changes.

Consider the frictions of changing industries. An individual's skills might not be fully applicable or they have to make investments in order to effectively to apply their skills in a different industry. As I argue, professional managerial and administrative skills are often applicable in many industries—and especially more applicable than many technical and skills. Nevertheless, there are often adjustment costs when switching industries. These costs include understanding a new regulatory environment, learning about new competitors, learning the jargon of a new industry, among others. Moreover, such switches might require an individual to initially take a lower level position because of their lack of industry expertise.

Likewise, there are often significant frictions associated with changing geography (i.e., relocating). This includes the tangible costs of moving. It also includes the transaction costs of moving such as finding housing in a new location and selling housing in the previous location. There can also be significant but less tangible costs of moving away from friends and family, or moving to a location that they perceive as a less desirable place to live.

In light of the frictions of moving industry or geography, the most straightforward transition is when an individual can leverage their industry skills and experiences within the same geographic region. Although they would have to adjust to a new company, this allows the most direct application of their skills and minimizes the disruption of having to relocate.

However, this is not always possible nor is it necessarily desirable. For example, depending on the industry and geography there might be few or no such companies. If such companies are present, whether or not they are hiring and whether or not an individual can find a job at their appropriate skill level cannot be certain. Switching industry or geography might be advantageous if the change allows for better opportunities. Therefore, individuals often look to opportunities in new industries or new geographies even when frictions do not exist.

If the prevailing preference were to look for opportunities in the same geography, we would observe relatively low migration rates from a region. This would be the expected outcome when business activity in a region centers on an industry cluster. Individuals would desire to build on their industry experiences, they would have local options, they would not have to endure relocation costs, and, as a result, outward migration rates would be low.

However, an interesting dynamic occurs when regions have low migration rates and when business activity does not center on an industry cluster. Here, low migration rates indicate the movement of talent across industries. If talent does not leave the region when it moves employers, then it likely switches industries. As a result, I expect talent movement among industries to be pronounced in a region with a high retention rate and when the businesses are in diverse industries (i.e., not focused on an industry cluster). In other words, high talent retention within a region with a diverse company base magnifies the dynamic that I described in the previous section.

For regional economies not based on industry clusters, if individuals seek opportunities in the same industry then there would be high migration rates out of the region due to the lack of same-industry opportunities. In addition, high migration rates out of a region can indicate that talent seeks to live elsewhere, regardless of the nature of employment within a region.

WHAT AFFECTS RETENTION?

Because high retention rates magnify the beneficial dynamic of talent move-ment in a diverse economy, it is important to identify factors that affect retention of managerial and administrative professionals. When a region has a very high retention rate, it means that local opportunities are more abun-dant, relocation frictions are more significant, or both. In the case of the Minneapolis-St. Paul region, both factors are present.

With respect to opportunities across industries, I previously discussed two important elements. First, there is a significant pool of managerial and admin-istrative talent and individuals with these skill sets are more able to look for local opportunities in different industries compared to those with technical skill sets that are very industry-focused. Second, the region is home to many companies in a diverse set of industries. This provides the variety of destin-ation points that allow for the movement of talent across industries.

There are also important frictions that relate to the managerial and admin-istrative talent pool and thus make it more likely that individuals consider switching industries rather than relocating outside of the Minneapolis-St. Paul region. The frictions that I present below draw on my experiences and inter-actions with business professionals, corporate recruiters, and human resources executives in the Minneapolis-St. Paul region.

To best illustrate these frictions that I wish to discuss, it is worthwhile to make additional observations and generalizations about the managerial and adminis-trative talent pool. I already note that their skills are applicable in many industry contexts, they are professionals, and they have made investments in their human capital through education and other professional experiences. I also note that professional managerial and administrative talent within a company exist across many levels of the organization—with a small minority at the most senior level (i.e., in the C-suite).

In addition to these generalizations, I would add the following. First, if these individuals are married or in relationships, their partners will be likely have similar educational attainment. United States data show that college degree holders are extremely likely to marry other college degree holders (e.g., those with a college degree who marry, marry a spouse with a college degree 71 percent of the time).[6] Second, many managerial and administrative professionals are at child-rearing times in their life. Because these individuals made human capital investments in college and possibly in graduate school, many enter into long child-rearing windows not long after entering their professional careers.

These attributes of the managerial and administrative talent pool highlight a number of frictions—beyond an individual's job opportunities—that discourage them from relocating and increase the likelihood that they consider jobs in new industries. Many refer to these as quality of life factors. I note that these quality of life factors also have economic components. Let me discuss three.

Dual Career Considerations

Consider first the observation that a high proportion of individuals within the managerial and administrative talent pool are college educated and, therefore, will be in relationships with well-educated partners. This makes it likely that individuals in this talent pool will be in dual career situations. Recall from the previous chapter that Minneapolis-St. Paul's ranking in terms of median household income is much higher than its ranking in terms of per capita income. Regions with more dual career households—all else equal—have higher household incomes compared to per capita incomes.

A vibrant headquarters economy, as exemplified by Minneapolis-St. Paul, has a number of opportunities to accommodate couples with dual careers. Of course, with the large concentration of headquarters there are many managerial and administrative jobs. However, a vibrant headquarters economy provides other career opportunities for an educated workforce. There are industry-specific jobs because many companies have technical operations and R&D labs located close to corporate or hidden headquarters. In Minneapolis-St. Paul this includes companies like Ecolab, 3M, Medtronic, Boston Scientific, General Mills, Land O'Lakes, Thomson Reuters, and St. Jude Medical, among many others. In addition, a vibrant economy has jobs in sectors such as healthcare, education, and other ancillary services. Therefore, the Minneapolis-St. Paul region provides a host of opportunities for those with dual career considerations. Although economies centered on an industry cluster will have a host of jobs and employment opportunities for dual careers, the diversity of professional opportunities will be less.

Dual careers can be an important friction that increases talent retention. When faced with the need to switch employers, the extent to which a partner is in a favorable career situation can be an important impediment to moving— especially if there are local opportunities for the partner looking to switch employers. Even if relocation advances one partner's career, what it means for the other partner can often negate these benefits. As a result, career opportunities for one's spouse or partner are often an important quality of life factor that affects retention for professional managerial and administrative employees.[7]

Environment to Raise Children

In light of the observation that many in the professional managerial and administrative talent pool are in child-rearing stages of their lives, quality of life aspects that revolve around raising children become an important friction. In the context of Minneapolis-St. Paul, the region has many amenities that benefit families raising children. It has quality public and private schools. It has many outdoor recreational activities—both summer and winter—that families with children value. Moreover, there exist amenities targeted to families such as family-focused arts (e.g., children's theaters) and museums. For this reason, the metropolitan area (or the state, depending on the geographic focus of the study) often rank very high in assessments of places to live. For example, Minnesota ranked first in the well-being of children in the Annie E. Casey Foundation, Kids Count Data Book. In addition, regions with more children will tend to have higher household incomes compared to per capita incomes, which is the case for Minneapolis-St. Paul.

I should note that there are frictions to relocating children, independent of the quality of life factors in a region. These include the emotional costs of leaving friends and logistical costs of switching schools and finding child-related services like healthcare and childcare in the new location. However, the quality of life factors that I describe above are in addition to these costs. For example, leaving a region with many child-targeted amenities.

My contention is that quality public education—in particular—is an important driver of talent retention. To see this, consider the typical alternative to public education—private schooling. A counter argument to the importance of quality public education for talent retention is the observation that almost every location provides the possibility of high quality education through access to high quality private schools. However, the observation that private schooling can provide quality education in almost all regions actually highlights the importance of public education in retaining talent—rather than invalidating it.

To see this, consider under what conditions schooling is a friction in the relocation of managerial talent. Take, for example, a family with two children that go to high quality public schools. They consider relocating to a region where they must rely on private schools for quality education. With access to high quality schooling, one might argue that this is not a friction. However, I do not agree with this statement. Moving from public to private education often has a tangible economic impact. Assume for the moment that private school tuition in the new location costs US$25,000 per year per child (and many might think that this underestimates the true cost). A family with two school-aged children face a yearly economic impact US$50,000—*after taxes*. This is a large economic impediment to relocating. Notice that this impediment does not exist for a family relocating from a region where they had been unable to send their children to quality public schools, because they would already be paying private school tuition.

Of course, this economic impact might be overstated because areas with high quality public schools often have higher taxes in order to fund these schools. Therefore, tax differentials can mitigate the friction. Nevertheless, that tax burden would have to be substantial as the economic impact in the above example highlights. Another way the friction might be overstated is that in areas where there is high variation in public school quality, house prices arbitrage part of the tuition savings. That is, in an area where there are few good public schools lower housing prices capture at least part of the cost saving that a buyer would realize from purchasing a house and sending a child to school (e.g., Chiodo et al., 2010).

In the Minneapolis-St. Paul region, I observe two factors that dampen this effect. First, to the extent that many school districts in a region offer high quality education, the housing market is less segmented. Contrast this to the situation where one public school district in a region is of high quality. With limited options, it is more likely that the economic benefits of living there and sending children to public school are arbitraged through house prices. Second, state policies for mandatory inter-district open enrollment—as exist in Minnesota—mitigate these housing price effects. These policies provide public school choice by allowing students to enroll in public schools outside of their district—with some provisions. Upon the adoption of these policies, differences in house prices across school districts declined in the Minneapolis area (Reback, 2005). Even in locations with open enrollment policies, housing prices differ by quality of school district because inter-district open enrollment is limited by capacity in the target district. Nevertheless, such policies mitigate these effects.

Another reason why the availability of quality private schools in a region might not eliminate this friction is that private schools might not have the capacity to take all students that wish to enroll. This is evidenced by the efforts that parents make to get their children into private schools in places like Manhattan.[8] Such capacity constraints can be especially binding for individuals relocating to a region. This is because many schools have targeted grades in which they accept more students and this might not coincide with a relocating family's need. Likewise, to the extent that schools give admission preference to families that have previously attended the school, this places relocating families without ties to the region at a relative disadvantage. In addition, private school access might be an issue for children with special needs because not all regions have private schools with high quality special needs education.

To summarize, I expect that access to high quality public education plays an especially important role in talent retention. A family with children in high quality public schools face greater frictions to relocating than those who do not. A region with high quality public schools will have a greater proportion of its talent utilizing those schools. As a result, that region's workforce will have higher frictions in relocating.

Critical Mass Demanding Similar Amenities

Another factor is that a region with a large proportion of professional educated individuals is better able to make investments in public goods and other institutions that they value. Although individuals' preferences will not all be the same, with a large proportion of the population sharing similar education status and being business professionals, it is likely that they will share desires for similar regional amenities. Such amenities include good public schools, a clean environment, safety, and recreational amenities such as arts, sports, or outdoor activities. Having a critical mass desiring these amenities makes it more likely that the political will to make these investments exists.

An example from the Minneapolis-St. Paul region is the Legacy Amendment to the Minnesota Constitution in 2008. As described by its website:

> In 2008, Minnesota's voters passed the Clean Water, Land and Legacy Amendment (Legacy Amendment) to the Minnesota Constitution to: protect drinking water sources; to protect, enhance, and restore wetlands, prairies, forests, and fish, game, and wildlife habitat; to preserve arts and cultural heritage; to support parks and trails; and to protect, enhance, and restore lakes, rivers, streams, and groundwater.

> The Legacy Amendment increases the state sales tax by three-eighths of one percent beginning on July 1, 2009 and continuing until 2034. The additional sales tax revenue is distributed into four funds as follows: 33 percent to the clean water fund; 33 percent to the outdoor heritage fund; 19.75 percent to the arts and cultural heritage fund; and 14.25 percent to the parks and trails fund.[9]

In order to have been adopted by the state constitution, this amendment required that a majority of the electorate valued these amenities.

Political clout is not the only reason why a region with such a workforce is likely to see investments in the amenities that they desires. Not all amenities come from government-funded public goods. Therefore, having a critical mass creates sufficient demand to support the provisions of these amenities from non-governmental sources. For example, Minneapolis-St. Paul has an extremely high concentration of theater seats—second only to New York on a per capita basis. This would not be sustainable unless the local population demanded this amenity.

Ability to Fund Amenities

Desiring amenities is one thing—but having the ability to fund or support them is another. Because a professional managerial and administrative talent pool is relatively well-compensated, they have the resources to support these amenities. In the case of Minneapolis-St. Paul, they are willing to pay a dedicated sales tax, they are willing to purchase tickets, and they are willing to fund many philanthropic activities. All of these would be less likely if the talent pool earned lower wages.

To summarize, in the case of Minneapolis-St. Paul, many of the quality of life factors map to the desired amenities of the professional workforce in the region. When these individuals look for career opportunities outside of their current employer, this tips the balance towards looking for opportunities that do not require relocation. Thus, employment opportunities in concert with desired amenities are an important force for talent retention.

I recognize that a counter argument for quality of life factors being an important force for talent retention is that compensation can overcome many of the frictions related to quality of life factors. Moreover, this would be especially relevant because I argue that managerial and administrative talent are well-compensated. I agree that compensation can mitigate or remove many frictions that prevent relocation. Nevertheless, it is important to assess under what conditions this is more or less likely to occur.

This counter argument is most relevant for managerial and administrative talent at the most senior levels of an organization. For example, if a company wants to attract a CEO or CFO, they can generally provide an incentive package that will compensate for many if not all of these frictions. Yet, an important element of the managerial and administrative talent pool is that only a relatively small percentage of the pool is at that level. The likelihood that a prospective employer offers excess compensation to offset the frictions of relocating tends to decrease at lower levels in the organization. Therefore, the ability of compensation from relocating to offset the frictions is not likely a solution for the mass of the managerial and administrative talent pool.

Managerial and Administrative Talent Attraction

In a vibrant headquarters economy, it is unlikely that hiring firms will be able to satisfy their needs by drawing only on talent from other companies in the region. As a result, an indication of a vibrant headquarters economy is that it will experiences a growing managerial and administrative talent base resulting from inward migration.

EFFECT OF TALENT ATTRACTION

Beyond the need to fill specific positions, the influx of talent into a region is important to the dynamic of sharing new experiences across companies. This is because the influx of talent will tend to increase the pool of skills and capabilities in the local managerial and administrative talent pool. Absent this, the cross-pollination of management practices can cease.

To see this, consider the situation where a there is little outflow in the region's talent and there is even lower inflow of migrants to a region. If this dynamic persists, two effects occur. With low talent outflow, but with even lower inflow, the talent pool shrinks. Exacerbating this negative effect is that a shrinking talent pool will tend to be less diverse and it will be less likely to generate the beneficial cross-pollination of business practices. Thus, sustained net out-migration of this talent pool interrupts the positive dynamic of talent across companies.

WHAT AFFECTS TALENT ATTRACTION?

To understand what is key to talent attraction, it is again important to consider the characteristics of the managerial and administrative talent pool that are critical to a headquarters economy. In the case of Minneapolis-St. Paul what attracts this talent? The main reason is quality employment opportunities. Quality of life factors, although often important and a focal part of my discussion on talent retention, appear secondary. The decision-making process is generally: 'Where are there good opportunities for my skill set? Given this, will I be happy and comfortable living there?' It tends not to be: 'Where is a great place to live? I will move there and look for a job.'

Again, the reason that economic opportunities are of paramount importance relates to this talent pool's investment in human capital. Having made these investments, individuals look to earn returns from their investments or pay off their investments. With a set of successful companies—many of which are premiere companies in their industries—Minneapolis-St. Paul is a good region for individuals to look for a return on their investment. To the extent that individuals in this talent pool face dual career situations with college-educated partners, the same considerations apply to their partner who has made previous investments in their human capital. The variety of opportunities in a headquarters economy provides an array of opportunities to find returns to human capital investment.[10]

Recapping the Building Blocks

Thus, retention and attraction of a region's professional managerial and administrative workforce has the potential to amplify the effects of talent mobility across companies. For this reason, it is the third building block to my explanation of what drives a headquarters economy.

First Building Block: Managers
A pool of managerial and administrative talent serves is the foundation of a headquarters economy. All headquarters draw upon managerial and administrative talent, regardless of the industries in which they participate.

Second Building Block: Mobility
As this talent moves between companies—especially across industries—it becomes a resource that aids companies' growth and performance.

Third Building Block: Migration
The beneficial dynamic of mobility is pronounced when regional talent retention is strong and when overall there exists regional talent attraction.

A powerful example of this dynamic comes from a conversation that I had at the end of a trans-Atlantic flight with a manager who worked for one of the large firms headquartered in Minneapolis-St. Paul. This person was a French national running a business in China for his company and who was transferring to the headquarters.

As we chatted, I mentioned my experiences moving to the region and that I enjoyed living there. He mentioned that he was looking forward to the move. One particular reason was that when he was working in China, his family had stayed in France. However, with the upcoming transfer he planned to move his family to Minnesota. He joked that the winters did not scare him and that in fact he enjoyed being in the region in the winter—I should add that the winters in the region is a common point of discussion for many people relocating to the area. On a more serious note, he said that he had spent time investigating what it would be like moving his family to the region. To aid him, he had talked with about a dozen other expatriates who worked at headquarters.

He mentioned that the reason he talked with a dozen co-workers was that he was only hearing one report back—all of them enjoyed living there. In fact, he noted that about half of the co-workers he talked to expressed their desire to remain in the region if the company should decide to transfer them out of Minneapolis-St. Paul. They said that they would look for other opportunities in the region and would seriously consider leaving the company. Their motivation was that they enjoyed living in the region, it worked very well for their families, their skills were employable in many other companies in the region, and they thought they would have little difficulty finding a suitable position in another company.

Two Complementary Factors

Two complementary factors play a role in reinforcing the dynamic that I describe above. The first is the existence of high quality post-secondary education in the state—especially in the form of professional schools and a strong research university. The second is the existence of institutions that promote cross-sectoral partnerships. I discuss each in turn.

Post-secondary Education

Consistent with the previous description, many students come to Minnesota to attend college and graduate school. The attraction is the quality of education that they can obtain. Because the local economy is large and vibrant, local companies are looking for college graduates to enter their workforce. An advantage of recruiting from local schools is that they do not have to convince people to relocate. Indeed, the extent to which college and graduate school students—like the managerial talent pool—appreciate the quality of life factors in the region, they are more likely to look for and accept local employment than to look for opportunities elsewhere. In other words, retention forces play a role in capturing the talent attending college and graduate school in the region.

An example of this would be a recent MBA graduate from the Carlson School of Management, Alyssa Callister. Callister grew up in Los Angeles. After high school, she started a non-profit organization and lived in East Africa where she developed a program to bring technology to children. While in Africa, she attended college remotely through Utah State University. After four years in Africa, Callister moved back to the United States and worked for Goldman Sachs Gives. After some time with Goldman Sachs Gives, Callister switched jobs within the company and worked in structured equity derivatives.

Motivated by a career opportunity for her husband that required relocation to the mid-west and her desire to attend graduate school, she moved to the Minneapolis-St. Paul region and entered the MBA program at the University of Minnesota. During the summer after her first year in the MBA program, she completed an internship at Gallop in Chicago. As she entered the second year of her MBA program, she started her job search. Having lived and worked in many places and with her husband considering returning to graduate school, there was little geographical constraint in her job search. Nevertheless, she wanted to remain in the Minneapolis-St. Paul region.

When I asked her why she wanted to stay in the Minneapolis-St. Paul region, she highlighted two factors: it was "a great place to grow one's career" and she enjoyed the quality of life in the region. With respect to the former, she mentioned how there were many attractive career opportunities in Minneapolis-St. Paul and having attended graduate school in the region she had created a strong network of business professionals. Most of these professionals took jobs in the region and most she expected would stay in the region over the course of their careers. Therefore, in addition to specific career opportunities, she valued having a professional network that was strong and stable. She talked about how such a network would provide her with long-term benefits, compared to building a network in a more transient region.

In addition to the career aspects, Callister highlighted two quality of life factors that factored into her decision. First was the set of friends that she formed while living here—some of whom were also part of the business network that she created. Second, she enjoyed living in her neighborhood—the "North Loop" district in downtown Minneapolis. She compared this neighborhood in feel to neighborhoods in New York, the west coast, and Scandinavian capitals. However, she noted the affordability of living in such a neighborhood in Minneapolis compared to the other cities that she had mentioned.

As her job search ran to conclusion, Callister ended up with many job opportunities outside of the Minneapolis-St. Paul region. However, she decided to take a job with McKinsey and Company in their Minneapolis office. The job choice reflected her desire to stay in the region in more than one way. Not only did she decline jobs elsewhere, but having landed a job at McKinsey and Company, candidates have a fair amount of leeway in choosing the office from which they work because there is often travel involved in their consulting efforts. She chose Minneapolis.

When I talked to Callister a couple of months into her job, she was happy with her job and being able to stay in the Minneapolis-St. Paul area. In fact, she mentioned a couple of benefits of the region in her current position. With a large business community, her first project was within the region and she did not have to travel. She also noted that for many people in her office who travelled, it was often more convenient to do so from the middle of the country than to travel between the coasts.

Cross-sectoral Institutions

Another complementary factor is institutions that promote cross-sectoral partnerships in the region. These institutions bring together participants such as businesses, non-profit organizations, and government. Often, their goals are to address regional concerns or facilitate regional investments—especially in quality of life amenities.

Many point to the existence of such institutions a unique aspect of the Minneapolis-St. Paul region that fosters the region's successes. For example, Brainerd et al. (1983) describe the Itasca Project. This is a collective of business, government, and non-profit leaders that seek to address common regional problems. Likewise, Ouchi (1984) devotes a chapter of his book to discuss the Minneapolis-St. Paul region, which he considers a prime example of the M-Form Society. This is a society where teamwork between businesses and other sectors leads to economic success. Other notable examples of such institutions in the Minneapolis-St. Paul's history include the 5 percent and 3 percent clubs. These were designations given to companies that agreed to donate 5 or 3 percent of their pretax profits to philanthropic causes. This recognition for corporate giving for regional companies exists today as the Keystone Program.[11]

I consider such institutions a complementary force because they reinforce the dynamic that I describe above—especially in the provision of regional quality of life factors. However, I do not consider this as a key building block of the region's headquarters economy. Likewise, such institutions are not the central force that leads to the creation or reinvention of new headquarters. To the extent that such institutions motivate investments in quality of life factors, they aid the dynamic that I describe above. In addition, although such institutions aid the region's ability to address regional issues or make investments, they tend not to be formal economic development activities.[12]

Another reason why I consider such institutions a complementary factor is that the dynamic that I describe helps create and sustain such institutions. If talent comes to the region and tends not to leave, then it has greater incentive to invest in the region. Individuals are more willing to invest in activities that better their community and go beyond the specific business or sector in which they work. For example, Galaskiewicz (1991, 1997) shows that personal networks of business professionals influence corporate giving in the Minneapolis-St. Paul region. Moreover, participation on the boards of non-profits or charities is an important element of business executives' social networks. When management moves between companies and industries it is more likely that executives will have such connections.

When These Building Blocks Work in Tandem

Virtuous Cycle

In tandem, these building blocks create a reinforcing system. They create a virtuous cycle with respect to economic and social vitality. To summarize, the virtuous cycle consists of the following elements: (a) Minneapolis-St. Paul houses a concentration of professional managerial and administrative talent that is valuable for managing companies. (b) Professional managerial and administrative talent is mobile and often moves between companies. When this talent moves between companies, it often stays within the region yet moves into new industries. This has a cross-pollination effect of bringing new practices and managerial insights to companies. (c) Professional managerial and administrative talent also moves from these headquarters to smaller and start-up companies, which in turn aids these companies' growth. Many of these companies evolve to become companies with a larger headquarters presence. (d) Although this flow between companies can happen anywhere, it is more pronounced in a region where professional managerial and administrative talent does not leave. In other words, if talent is unlikely to leave a region, it is more likely to move across employers within a region. (e) Growing companies require additional talent, thus attracting more talent to the region.

Detailing the building blocks of this dynamic helps illuminate under what conditions the virtuous cycle is likely to take hold in other regions. An important element is the movement of skills across companies and the resulting cross-pollination of management practices. This is facilitated in the Minneapolis-St. Paul region because of the concentration of professional managerial and administrative talent and the diversity of the businesses located there. In regions with a concentrated or focused economy, the effect is muted because there are fewer opportunities for cross-pollination. In regions populated by talent that stays within its industry silos, the effect is muted because talent flows do not allow for cross-pollination.

The diversity of a regional economy has a further effect that facilitates the transfer of talent across companies and industries. Because industry cycles of expansion and contraction are not perfectly aligned, regions with a diverse set of businesses experience greater variation in companies looking to expand and contract than in regions where all of the companies face the same industry-specific business cycle. Therefore, diverse regions are less likely to experience waves where most companies are looking to hire or downsize at the same time. To the extent that some companies are looking to expand and others are looking to contract within a region, this facilitates a movement of talent across firms as one feeds the other. Moreover, it also makes it more likely that talent can stay in the region even if their companies are victims of unfavorable industry economic trends.

For example, in the spring of 2015 Target reduced its corporate headquarters staff in Minneapolis-St. Paul in two waves. The first stemmed from the company's decision to close its operations in Canada. The second stemmed from restructuring plans to simplify and refocus the company. These reductions affected over 2,000 local headquarters employees. However, many observers commented that with this occurring in the spring of 2015—when the economy was in an upturn and many other sectors were hiring, it lessened the impact on individuals and the region.[13]

In addition, the diversity of the local economy makes it more likely that talent can be absorbed in the region if there are changes in the ownership of the company such as a change in headquarters. This occurred when Allied Signal acquired Honeywell. Although several operations remained in Minneapolis-St. Paul, some corporate functions consolidated at the headquarters of the combined entity in New Jersey—including human resources. With the consolidation, many senior human resource professionals from the former Honeywell stayed in the region, taking their skills to other Minneapolis-St. Paul companies. In particular, a concentration of this talent moved to two of the large privately held companies in the region: Andersen and Carlson.

Also key to the dynamic is that the positive effect of talent movement between companies becomes pronounced when regional talent retention forces are strong. In regions where out-migration rates are higher, we would be less likely to observe the dynamic. What limits out-migration of this talent is the combination of job opportunities and quality of life factors—especially quality of life factors that map closely to the demands of the underlying talent base. As I argue in the next section, quality of life factors can play a particularly meaningful role in retaining talent.

Quality of Life Factors Weigh More Heavily on Talent Retention than Talent Attraction

The previous discussion focuses on two factors that are central to the attraction and retention of professional managerial and administrative talent: employment opportunities and quality of life factors within the region. Although important in both attracting and retaining talent, the relative importance differs for these distinct talent flows. Specifically, quality of life factors play a relatively more important role retaining talent than they do attracting talent in a headquarters economy.

Let me illustrate this with a couple of examples. The first is from a senior human resources executive at a large company headquartered in Minneapolis-St. Paul that was in the processes of downsizing. She described that the need to reduce employment costs required reductions in headcount at all levels of the organization, including senior management. She reflected on the experiences of a senior manager who was affected and who the company had expended a lot of effort recruiting and relocating to Minneapolis-St. Paul about a year prior. Although attracted by the job opportunity, the recruiting process had been difficult because of the expected impact that relocation would place on this person's family. At one point the individual commented that they feared divorce if they pursued this opportunity. After an extended courting process and substantially improving the economics of the job offer, they had been able to attract the individual to the Minneapolis-St. Paul region.

Fast-forward a year to where corporate restructuring now eliminated this person's position. The one request from this individual to their employer was that the employer provide as many local employment contacts as possible. Having moved, their family was captivated by the quality of life in the region and did not want to relocate—even back to the place they had been so hesitant to leave. Because this person's skills were transferable to other businesses, their primary goal was to look for opportunities in the region.

In this case, I see that job-related factors played the central role in the decision to move to the region. Initially there had been concern that their quality of life would suffer relative to where they had previously lived. However, after relocating and experiencing the quality of life in the Minneapolis-St. Paul, the region's amenities became an anchor affecting further relocation.

This is also consistent with the experiences of Bruce Beckman, whose movement from General Mills to Entegris I described previously. The reason Beckman left General Mills was, with a downturn in the demand for many of its products, General Mills had gone through a restructuring at its headquarters that resulted in the reduction of several hundred positions, one of which had been Beckman's.

Beckman did not want to search for a new position outside of the region because he enjoyed living in the area. Part of this reflected some of the specific quality of life factors that are key to managerial and administrative talent. His children were in public schools and he was happy with their education. His wife, a business professional, worked for one of the large companies headquartered in the region. These and the other amenities of living in Minneapolis-St. Paul were strong pulls for him to focus his job search in that region so that he would not have to relocate. Moreover, he viewed his experiences at General Mills as providing him skills that would be valuable in many other businesses—in particular, the ability to provide strategic financial leadership. Because of the wide applicability of these skills, he was confident that he could find something without having to relocate. After only a few months of search, Beckman landed the position of vice president of finance at Entegris.

These vignettes reflect several experiences that I have observed. First, the most considered motivation for relocation of professional and managerial talent is employment opportunities. Although I see counter-examples, quality of life considerations play a secondary role. Jobs—especially good jobs—attract this type of talent. Moreover, for couples with dual careers, job opportunities for one spouse can be a key motivator to move, as was the case with Peter Horwitz.

Quality of life factors are relatively more important in preventing managerial and administrative talent from relocating—especially when there are employment opportunities in the region. I believe that this occurs for two reasons. First, many of the quality of life factors that I describe earlier in the chapter are frictions that can require substantial compensation or job opportunity to overcome. Take for instance, the availability of dual career options.

Second, many quality of life factors are experiential in nature. Not until someone lives in a region do they fully understand how the region's quality of life factors affect their day-to-day living. I recognize that there are many publicly available quality of life indicators or rankings; and other information sources attempt to quantify and make transparent regional quality of life factors. Nevertheless, how one's lifestyle interacts with these features is often not fully understood in advance of living in a region. In this situation, quality of life factors become more tangible once someone lives in a region and experiences them. Therefore, they play a different perceptual role in decision making for talent retention—they are more tangible, compared to talent attraction—they are more abstract and uncertain.

I would like to highlight two points with respect to the conclusion that although both career opportunities and quality of life factors are important, career opportunities play a relatively more important role in talent attraction and quality of life factors play a relatively more important role in talent retention. First, I focus on professional managerial and administrative talent. The investments in their human capital, their career path, and their demographics make this relationship more pronounced compared to other subsets of the population. Second, the importance of quality of life factors on retention is pronounced only if there are job opportunities in the region. Quality of life factors play a less significant role in a region with little opportunity outside of an individual's current employer.

Downsides to this Dynamic

My explanation of what drives the Minneapolis-St. Paul headquarters economy presents a positive force for regional economic and social vitality. However, there are potential negative effects of this dynamic. Of the four I present, I see evidence of the first two: insularity and regional anonymity. I have heard many express concerns about the third: complacency. There is no evidence of the fourth: the virtuous cycle becoming a vicious cycle. Nevertheless, it is a property of the underlying building blocks that I highlight and thus warrants discussion.

INSULARITY
When retention is a powerful force, it can lead to insularity. If people are unlikely to leave a region, it reinforces the status quo. In turn, attachment to the status quo can stymie adoption of new ideas and different ways of

doing things. A region can be slow to import and adopt trends that originate from outside.

Compounding this is that high retention forces can make non-natives' entry into the region difficult. I have heard many accounts that Minneapolis-St. Paul is a difficult location for people to move to and to break into social circles outside of their employment. A key element is that long-time residents have deep social connections from school or college friendships and draw on these relationships for a lot of their social activity. The effect of insularity does not end there. To the extent that insularity makes entry into the region difficult, it negatively affects talent retention. If those who move and cannot integrate, then they will not stay. This is in contrast to more transient communities. For example, expatriate communities in many global cities. Here, social networks are very fluid and tend to be very inclusive because there is so much turnover.

Relatedly, insularity can have a negative effect on the broader virtuous cycle. A key aspect of my explanation is that managerial expertise and experiences are shared across sectors (i.e., cross-pollination). To continue this positive dynamic, it is important that new ideas and talent continue to be introduced in the region. If new experiences are not brought into the region, then at some point only existing ideas circulate. Cross-pollination becomes inbreeding if there is no variety.

REGIONAL ANONYMITY

When retention rates are strong, most of a region's population stays for extended periods of time. This can dampen knowledge and understanding of the region outside of its boundaries, relative to regions that are more transient. For example, one is less likely to run into a neighbor or a colleague who used to work in the region. As a result, informal information exchange about the region occurs far less frequently.

Going beyond anonymity, when regional retention forces are strong, they can lead to negative information exchange about a region outside of its boundaries. When overall retention forces are strong, it means that those who leave often have exceptionally poor experiences in the region or exceptionally good opportunities elsewhere. The larger the proportion of ex-residents who have this view, the more negative the perception of the region that is spread by ex-residents. This can poison outside views of the region.

An example would be associated with ex-residents' perception of the weather in the Minneapolis-St. Paul region. I have met many people from warm climates who move to the region and adapt to the winter weather. Yet I have also met people from warm climates who used to live in Minneapolis-St. Paul and found the winters intolerable. As a result, they moved. Living outside of the region, you would be more likely to have a neighbor or colleague with the negative experience rather than the positive experience because a higher proportion of those with the positive experiences stayed.

COMPLACENCY

Another potential concern is that past success in keeping a vibrant headquarters economy leads residents to believe that its vibrancy will continue into the future. Admittedly, describing the underlying dynamic as a virtuous cycle can reinforce this assessment.

However, my motivation in identifying the underlying mechanisms that create this virtuous cycle is to highlight the determinants of this positive dynamic. Knowing this, one is better able to assess how the positive dynamic might be susceptible to changes. Although the dynamic that I describe occurs organically and not through the guiding hand of any one actor, this does not mean that it will continue to its own devices.

A large concern about complacency is that unintended consequences of other actions might unravel the positive dynamic because no one considers the sensitivity of this dynamic to change. For example, policy changes that affect mobility or the retention of talent have the potential to stall the beneficial dynamic. Likewise, company decisions can have similar effects. Therefore, policy and corporate choices have the potential to bring the virtuous cycle to a halt. Especially worrisome is that changes to the underlying factors of this virtuous cycle can do more damage than halting them. This is the final potential downside, which I describe below.

VICIOUS CYCLE

The same underlying set of interdependencies that give rise to a virtuous cycle can also give rise to a vicious cycle. That is, rather than being a positive reinforcing system, it can become a negative reinforcing system. If there is an adverse change in any of the elements of this dynamic, it has the potential to not only unravel but also precipitate negative cascading consequences.

Although it could initiate in any element, take for example, adverse changes in the quality of life within a region. If quality of life factors that retain talent wane, then talent increasingly looks for opportunities outside of the region rather than looking for opportunities among regional companies. If that happens, local firms have difficulty attracting talent from other local firms and they cease to benefit from bringing new ideas and skills into their company. If the difficulty in hiring talent or the lack of new skills thwarts growth, then these companies are less attractive and less likely to lure new talent to the region. Moreover, if these companies cannot find talent and move operations outside of the region, then this further precipitates the decline. Having fewer companies or opportunities decreases the pool of talent and this can hurt investments in quality of life amenities in the region. We now have a vicious cycle—rather than a virtuous cycle.

Consistency with the Data Regarding Minneapolis-St. Paul's Headquarters Activity

At the end of Chapter 2, I highlight a number of empirical observations about Minneapolis-St. Paul's headquarters economy that a valid explanation would have to provide. Those empirical facts guided my research as it progressed. Therefore, I wish to make clear the connections between the explanation I advance in this chapter and the key empirical observations I summarize at the end in Chapter 2. I address each one in turn.

Headquarters in the Minneapolis-St. Paul Region Come from a Diverse Set of Industries

The observation that there exist headquarters in many different industries is a central part of my explanation. The fact that there exist headquarters in many industries leads to the benefit derived from sharing managerial practices across companies. This in turn, leads to an advantage for the region's companies.

Although my explanation is not the standard industry clustering explanation, it shares some commonalities—in a multi-industry setting. A key element of what drives industry clusters is that regional companies benefit as talent moves between industry competitors. My arguments highlight that the key talent in headquarters—managerial and administrative talent—possesses skills that are transferable across industries. When this talent shares insights or moves across companies, it is similar to the industrial clustering mechanism. However, the ability to bring diverse practices that are often industry-bound to light outside of their context is unique—and a central element of my explanation. The Appendix provides a more detailed discussion.

The Region has been a Headquarters Economy for a Long Time

My explanation that managers, mobility, and migration create a virtuous cycle is consistent with the region sustaining a notable headquarters presence over a long period of time. This does not deny or invalidate the historical circumstance that sowed the seeds for the initial economic activity in the region. However, if the historical seeds had been the only factor, then it would not be clear why the region had continued to be a headquarters economy. The virtuous cycle offers an explanation why the region has sustained its

81

headquarters economy that is also consistent with the data about how the headquarters activity changed overtime—as described below.

There is Substantial Turnover in the Headquartered Companies

In Chapter 2, I discuss many reasons why headquarters leave a region over time. Therefore, key to sustaining a headquarters economy is stemming the loss of or replenishing headquarters. My explanation provides insight into both.

With respect to stemming the loss of headquarters, the existence of the professional managerial and administrative talent pool—and the cross-pollination of business practices as it moves between companies—better allows companies to reinvent themselves as the marketplace and competitive arena changes over time. Moreover, harnessing skills that are not widely held or disseminated within an industry provides companies a competitive advantage vis-à-vis other companies in locations where this does not occur. Therefore, regions that lack this talent pool dynamic either (a) lack the ability to draw on expertise and must try to recruit it to the region or (b) do not to benefit from the cross-pollination of management practices across industries and are less likely to look outside their current method of operating and to benefit from such practices.

With respect to replenishing headquarters, I address this with the next empirical observation.

Headquarters Relocations Play an Unimportant Role in Adding to or Replacing Headquarters Activity

In terms of replacing headquarters, there is a notable pattern in the Minneapolis-St. Paul region. Growing companies into the Fortune 500—rather than attracting them via headquarters moves—is the way that all but one Minneapolis-St. Paul company has entered the Fortune 500. My discussion of managerial talent movement can explain why organic growth occurs and why headquarters relocations are not a large element of explaining what is occurring.

Especially noteworthy is the role that a managerial and administrative talent plays in growing a company. For example, many conclude that it takes a very different set of skills to move an entrepreneurial venture from inception to a growing and viable entity (e.g., Smith et al., 1985; Boeker and Wiltbank, 2005). The same could be said in growing a small company into a mid-sized company or a mid-sized company into a large company. In each of these transitions, a new set of managerial skills are relevant so that the organization can function. For this reason, access to a talent base with a very broad set of managerial skills is important input that allows companies to grow. As I previously describe, the movement of managerial and administrative talent in the Minneapolis-St. Paul region is not just between large companies. It often moves from large companies to start-ups, small, and mid-sized companies. The influx of managerial and administrative skills into small and medium-sized companies is an important resource to grow these companies.

Hidden Headquarters Play an Important Role in the Economy

Another striking factor of the Minneapolis-St. Paul region is the extent to which there are hidden headquarters. As I describe in Chapter 2, these tend to be companies that retain a headquarters-type presence after a formerly headquartered company has been sold or acquired. Why would this tend to persist within the region? Answering this question is especially important because so many headquarter departures are actually changes in corporate control where a local company has been acquired by a company from outside of the region.

My explanation offers an answer. One of the reasons why acquired operations remain in the Minneapolis-St. Paul region is that these operations employ a skilled managerial and administrative workforce reflecting the regional talent pool. The acquiring company often fears losing this talent should it relocate operations post-acquisition. They would be especially wary of this if their employees were more included to stay in the region and work in a different industry rather than relocating with their new employer. For example, Boston Scientific considered talent and their unwillingness to relocate a key reason for keeping Guidant's former operations in the Minneapolis-St. Paul region.[14]

In addition, access to a talent base with a broad set of managerial skills is valuable if the acquiring company plans to expand or alter the operations. Access to such talent exists if the operations remain in the Minneapolis-St. Paul region. In fact, this can be a motivation for the acquiring company to not only keep the acquired operations in the region, but to consolidate operations from other regions with the operations in Minneapolis-St. Paul.

For example, in January 2015 Post Holdings acquired Minneapolis-St. Paul-based MOM Brands. MOM Brands was a large provider of private-label cereals whose original product was the hot breakfast cereal Malt-O-Meal. At the time of the acquisition, MOM Brands was the fourth largest cereal producer in the country and Post was the third largest. Four months after the acquisition announcement, in May of 2015, Post announced that it was moving the headquarters of its cereal operations from Parsippany, New Jersey, to the Minneapolis-St. Paul regional and consolidating them with MOM Brands' headquarters operations.[15] Although the Minneapolis-St. Paul area lost a corporate headquarters with Post Holding's acquisition of MOM Brands, the decision to consolidate the combined entity's cereal operations in Lakeville created a hidden headquarters. This hidden headquarters operations are larger than the MOM Brands headquarters due to the larger size of the new Post cereal business.

Summary

My explanation that managers, mobility, and migration create a headquarters economy is consistent with the observations that I present at the end of Chapter 2. In addition, it is consistent with the two key factors that I highlight that any valid explanation would have to draw upon. First, because businesses do not do grow themselves, the industriousness and talent of a region's residents should play an important role. The argument I present centers around talent. I focus on managerial and administrative talent, because all headquarters draw on these skills. Second, the experiences of the Minneapolis-St. Paul region differ from many regions; therefore, any valid explanation should offer a reason why the region differs from the norm. I propose that the important way in which the Minneapolis-St. Paul region differs reflects the make-up of the talent base, how the talent moves between companies, and the way in which the talent migrates to and from a region.

Notes

1. "CEO, philanthropist 'helped humanity'; The former Pillsbury and Medtronic executive raised millions to send thousands of poor students to college." *Star Tribune*, December 21, 2010.
2. The following quotes are from an interview with Winston Wallin by David Rhees on April 3, 1998, at the Metropolitan Center in Minneapolis Minnesota as part of the Pioneers in the Medical Device Industry in Minnesota Oral History Project of the Minnesota Historical Society. http://collections.mnhs.org/cms/largerimage.php?irn=10216222&catirn=10445347&return=
3. "Northwest Airlines CEO leaves for lesser post at UnitedHealth." By Mike Hughlett and Leslie Brooks Suzukamo, *St. Paul Pioneer Press*, October 2, 2004.
4. The following quotes from Nelson, Pachter, and McComb are drawn from, "Best Buy hires Carlson Cos. Joly as new CEO," by John Welbes and Leslie Brooks Suzukamo, *St. Paul Pioneer Press*, August 19, 2012.
5. http://www.fool.com/investing/general/2015/08/31/best-buys-turnaround-is-one-for-the-ages.aspx
6. https://www.theatlantic.com/sexes/archive/2013/04/college-graduates-marry-other-college-graduates-most-of-the-time/274654/

7. Costa and Kahn (2000) show that college-educated couples have increasingly chosen to locate in large metropolitan areas over time. Presumably, in part, to sustain dual careers.

8. http://www.nytimes.com/2011/09/06/nyregion/at-elite-new-york-schools-admissions-policies-are-evolving.html

9. http://www.legacy.leg.mn/about-funds

10. Although Molloy et al. (2014) present evidence that inter-state mobility has decreased over time, they document that the primary reason for inter-state mobility is job reasons. With similar data, Kaplan and Schulhofer-Wohl (2017) document the same effect.

11. http://www.mplschamber.com/pages/MinnesotaKeystone

12. The institutions differ from the more direct role that the regional government played in shaping the San Diego economy over time as described by Walshok and Shragge (2014).

13. For a discussion of how these workers landed new opportunities, see http://www.startribune.com/a-year-after-target-s-layoffs-life-is-brighter-for-many-of-the-thousands-that-the-retailer-let-go/373609231/

14. http://www.mprnews.org/story/2009/07/10/boston_scientific_ceo

15. http://www.twincities.com/localnews/ci_28122899/post-moving-cereal-headquarters-lakeville

4

What Creates a Vibrant Headquarters Economy?

Evidence from Migration Data

Using the Minneapolis-St. Paul metropolitan area as an exemplar, Chapter 3 builds an explanation that managers, mobility, and migration are key to understanding a headquarters economy. With this explanation in hand, I turn to additional data to assess its validity. In particular, I assess how the Minneapolis-St. Paul region compares to other major metropolitan areas in the United States. Because I demonstrate that Minneapolis-St. Paul's economy differs from other metropolitan regions in the country, it is important that I show that key elements of my explanation also differ when compared to other metropolitan regions in the country.

My explanation highlights two key ways that Minneapolis-St. Paul differs from many other metropolitan areas. The first is managerial and administrative talent mobility among companies within the region. The second is the migration pattern of managerial and administrative talent into and out of the region. Unfortunately, the difficulty to obtain comprehensive data on job switches across industries by managerial and administrative employees and how it varies across metropolitan areas precludes analyzing that characteristic directly. Nevertheless, in Chapter 5, I present data from the Minneapolis-St. Paul region that more directly addresses this issue.

Comprehensive data on migration patterns by metropolitan area, however, are available for the United States. I draw upon these data to compare the migration pattern of talent to and from Minneapolis-St. Paul to the other large metropolitan areas in the United States. This chapter presents these analyses.

Based on the arguments in Chapter 3, I expect that increased mobility across companies and industries occurs when a metropolitan area exhibits a low rate of talent out-migration. Therefore, a vibrant headquarters economy will possess a low rate of talent out-migration; and will exhibit net inflows of talent (i.e., in-migration minus out-migration).

Data

I base my analyses on the Integrated Public Use Microdata Series (IPUMS) Data, maintained by the Minnesota Population Center at the University of Minnesota (Flood et al., 2017). The data that I initially present are from five years of the American Community Survey (ACS; 2007–11). I draw on these years for the following reasons. Examining a five-year period helps smooth any random yearly variation in the data. These years were also the most recent data available when I conducted the analysis. Moreover, the end year of 2011 is close to the 2010 Census and I will refer back to Census data to make comparison to migration rates in 2000, 1990, and 1980 later in the chapter.

The ACS is a yearly survey conducted by the United States Census Bureau. It is sent to approximately 3.5 million addresses each year, which is a small subset of all households in the country. The survey asks questions about the household and individuals within the household. For households that receive the survey, participation is mandatory.

The ACS is well-suited to informing migration patterns within the United States. One of the survey questions asks whether each individual within the household lived at the same address in the previous year. If the individual did not, it asks where that person lived. With this information it is possible to map migration patterns. In addition, the ACS collects other demographic information about respondents, which is important for reasons that I discuss later. Because the ACS only samples a fraction of the population each year, it weights each response to better represent the underlying population.

In order to map migration patterns for metropolitan areas, I need to define what addresses fall into different metropolitan areas. I use the metropolitan area definitions in the IPUMS data, which are based on Metropolitan Statistical Area (MSA) definitions. MSA's are geographic areas defined by the Office of Management and Budget. They identify counties that form the urban core of a metropolitan area and the adjacent counties with a high degree of social and economic integration with the urban core. Social and economic integration is determined by assessing work commuting patterns.

To capture migration rates I take the following steps. First, I assess the survey responses of where each individual lived. I then compile these by metropolitan area in order to assess each metropolitan area's population.[1]

Second, to calculate in-migration I do the following. For the individuals in each metropolitan area, I assess their response to the question of where they lived in the previous year. If they respond that they lived at a different address, I examine where they previously lived. For respondents who indicate that their previous address was outside of their current metropolitan area, I consider them as having migrated to the metropolitan area. I scale the total inflow by the metropolitan area's population to calculate the in-migration rate.

For example, I analyze the responses of current residents of Minneapolis-St. Paul and note those who did not live at the same address in the previous year. I then examine where they lived in the previous year. If they moved to Minneapolis-St. Paul from outside of the metropolitan area, then I consider them in-migrants for Minneapolis-St. Paul. If they moved and their previous address was within the Minneapolis-St. Paul metropolitan area, I do not consider this as in-migration.

Third, to measure out-migration I do the following. First, I assess all survey respondents in the country who indicate that they lived at a different address in the previous year. I note the metropolitan area in which they previously lived. If they currently live outside of that metropolitan area, I consider them out-migrants from the metropolitan areas in which they previously lived. I scale the total outflow by population of the metropolitan area to calculate out-migration rate.

For example, to calculate the out-migration from Minneapolis-St. Paul I analyze all responses in the ACS except current residents of Minneapolis-St. Paul and note those who did not live at the same address in the previous year. I then assess where they lived. I compile all respondents who previously lived in Minneapolis-St. Paul metropolitan area, and use this to measure out-migration for Minneapolis-St. Paul.

I do not consider international migration in my analyses. The reason is that with the ACS data I can only measure migration from foreign countries to a United States metropolitan area. I cannot measure migration from a United States metropolitan area to foreign countries. This is because someone who moved from the United States to somewhere else in the world (i.e., out-migration) will not complete this survey because it is only sent to households in the United States. Someone who lived in the United States, having moved from a different country (i.e., in-migration), potentially completed the survey.

I collect these data for twenty-five large MSAs in terms of population. Table 4.1 lists these metropolitan areas. In the following analysis I drop three of the metropolitan areas from my analysis. The IPUMS data do not identify respondents who previously lived in Denver or Miami. Therefore, I am not able to effectively measure migration for these metropolitan areas. In addition, as I compiled the data for the other twenty-three metropolitan areas I noticed that the in-migration and out-migration rates for Pittsburgh appear exceptionally large and out of line with the other regions. Therefore, I chose not to present these data out of caution.

My arguments of a headquarters economy focus on the pool of professional managerial and administrative talent. Ideally, I would like to capture only this talent in my analysis. However, capturing this directly is difficult. Nevertheless, the demographic data collected in the ACS allows me to focus my inquiry.

Table 4.1 Metropolitan areas examined in
Chapter 4

Metropolitan Areas Examined in this Chapter

Atlanta
Baltimore
Boston
Charlotte
Chicago
Dallas
Denver
Detroit
Houston
Los Angeles
Miami
Minneapolis-St. Paul
New York-Northeastern NJ
Philadelphia
Phoenix
Pittsburgh
Portland
Riverside
Sacramento
San Diego
San Francisco
Seattle
St. Louis
Tampa
Washington, DC

I focus my inquiry on individuals with the following characteristics. They
must (a) have completed four or more years of college, (b) be currently
employed, (c) have a household income of over US$100,000, and (d) be over
22 years of age. These restrictions come from the generalizations of the professional managerial and administrative talent pool that I present in the
previous chapter. Restriction (a) reflects that they have made investments in
education by completing college or graduate school. Restriction (b) reflects
that they are actively employed. Restriction (c) reflects that they are well-
compensated because of their expertise. I chose a household income of US
$100,000 because this is approximately double the median household income
in the United States in 2011. Restriction (d), the restriction of being over 22 is
almost never binding, because of restriction (a). However, being over 22 is a
restriction that I used in Chapter 2 to compare education levels across metropolitan areas. Therefore, I retained it for consistency.

To assess the face validity of this restriction, Table 4.2 ranks metropolitan areas in terms of what percentage of the over-22 population has four
or more years of college education, is employed, and is in a household
with over US$100,000 annual income. The top five metropolitan areas are

Table 4.2 Percentage of population that is highly educated, employed, and high-earning[a]

Metropolitan Area	%[b]
Washington, DC	23.22
Boston	19.27
San Francisco	17.62
Baltimore	15.40
New York-Northeastern NJ	15.37
Seattle	15.16
Minneapolis-St. Paul	14.81
Philadelphia	13.81
Denver	13.77
Chicago	13.29
Atlanta	12.44
San Diego	12.19
Dallas-Fort Worth	12.12
Houston	11.43
Los Angeles	11.29
St. Louis	10.81
Charlotte	10.53
Portland	10.47
Sacramento	10.13
Detroit	9.82
Pittsburgh	9.79
Phoenix	9.09
Miami	7.37
Tampa	7.02
Riverside	6.70

[a] Data source: IPUMS-USA, University of Minnesota, www.ipums.org 2007–11, ACS five-year. Author's analysis.
[b] Percent of over-22 population with (a) four-plus years college, (b) employed, and (c) household income US$100,000+.

Washington, DC, Boston, San Francisco, Baltimore, and New York. Minneapolis-St. Paul ranks seventh, just behind Seattle. There are several metropolitan areas with a concentration of high-earning individuals. In the case of Minneapolis-St. Paul, the regional cost of living is lower than all of the metro areas ranked higher in this table. Therefore, this measure might suppress its relative ranking. Although I could adjust the household income cut-off based on regional cost of living, I choose to keep it constant for ease of comparison.

Migration Patterns of highly educated, employed, high-earning individuals

Table 4.3 ranks the twenty-two metropolitan areas that are the focus of my analysis by their outward migration rates. The metropolitan area with the lowest out-migration rate is Minneapolis-St. Paul at 1.57 percent. The low

Table 4.3 Outward migration of highly educated, employed, and high-earning[a]

Metropolitan Area	%[b]
Minneapolis-St. Paul	1.57
New York-Northeastern NJ	1.66
Chicago	2.06
Houston	2.18
Los Angeles	2.19
Dallas-Fort Worth	2.23
Detroit	2.26
Philadelphia	2.26
Seattle	2.26
St. Louis	2.30
Boston	2.33
Portland	2.38
San Francisco	2.53
Washington, DC	2.70
Sacramento	2.74
Baltimore	2.78
Atlanta	2.90
Riverside	2.91
Tampa	2.93
San Diego	3.21
Charlotte	3.46
Phoenix	3.47

[a] Data source: IPUMS-USA, University of Minnesota, www.ipums.org. Author's analysis.
[b] Percent of over-22 population with four-plus years college, employed, and household income US$100,000+, that report living in the metropolitan area in the previous year; and report living outside of the metropolitan area in the current year.

outflow rate is consistent with my expectations. To gauge the magnitude of this rate, note that it is less than half the outflow rate of the metropolitan areas with the highest rates: Phoenix (3.47 percent) and Charlotte (3.46 percent). Moreover, it is notably smaller than most metropolitan areas with New York the only other metropolitan area with an outflow rate below 2 percent.

Although my arguments highlight the importance of a small outflow rate, realizing the positive dynamic that I discussed is contingent on there being a net inflow of talent into a region. To assess this I calculated the net-migration rate. Table 4.4 ranks cities by the net-migration rate.

Minneapolis-St. Paul ranks ninth highest with net-migration rate of 0.22 percent. This net-migration rate is above the median for the twenty-two metropolitan areas in my analysis. These data reaffirm that the overall migration pattern is one that is consistent with the dynamic that I presented in Chapter 3. There is an overall inflow of employed, educated, high-earning talent, and the outflow rate is very low.

Table 4.4 Net-migration of highly educated, employed, and high-earning[a]

Metropolitan Area	%[b]
Riverside	0.96
Portland	0.73
Houston	0.65
Seattle	0.64
Tampa	0.55
Dallas-Fort Worth	0.51
Washington, DC	0.29
Baltimore	0.23
Minneapolis-St. Paul	0.22
Charlotte	0.20
San Francisco	0.20
Atlanta	0.10
Boston	0.10
Phoenix	0.06
St. Louis	0.05
San Diego	−0.08
Sacramento	−0.12
Chicago	−0.25
New York-Northeastern NJ	−0.41
Philadelphia	−0.43
Los Angeles	−0.44
Detroit	−0.54

[a] Data source: IPUMS-USA, University of Minnesota, www.ipums. org 2007–11, ACS five-yr. Author's analysis.
[b] Net-migration of over-22 population with four years college, employed, and household income US$100,000+ to a metropolitan area divided by the over-22 population with four-plus years college, employed, and household income US$100,000+.

The cities with the highest net-migration rates are Riverside, Portland, Houston, Seattle, and Dallas. The cities with the lowest net-migration rates are Detroit, Los Angeles, Philadelphia, New York, and Chicago. All of these cities show negative net-migration. Interestingly, of the cities with the lowest out-migration rates (Minneapolis-St. Paul, New York, Chicago, Houston, and Los Angeles) only Minneapolis-St. Paul and Houston show net-migration.

Table 4.5 presents the in-migration rates for the twenty-two metropolitan areas. Minneapolis-St. Paul is among the lowest, ranking nineteenth out of the twenty-two metro areas, ahead of only New York, Detroit, and Los Angeles. These data, when assessed with the other data, prove that the adage that "it is difficult to get people to move to Minneapolis-St. Paul... but almost impossible to get them to leave" rings true. The cities with the highest in-migration rates are Riverside, Charlotte, Phoenix, Tampa, and San Diego. Interestingly, these five metro areas are also the ones that have the highest out-migration rates. For highly educated high-earning individuals, these are the most transitory metropolitan areas among the most populated metropolitan areas in

Table 4.5 Inward migration of highly educated, employed, and high-earning[a]

Metropolitan Area	%[b]
Riverside	3.87
Charlotte	3.67
Phoenix	3.53
Tampa	3.48
San Diego	3.14
Portland	3.11
Baltimore	3.00
Atlanta	3.00
Washington, DC	2.99
Seattle-Everett	2.90
Houston-Brazoria	2.83
Dallas	2.73
San Francisco	2.73
Sacramento	2.62
Boston	2.43
St. Louis	2.35
Philadelphia	1.83
Chicago	1.81
Minneapolis-St. Paul	1.78
Los Angeles	1.75
Detroit	1.72
New York-Northeastern NJ	1.25

[a] Data source: IPUMS-USA, University of Minnesota, www.ipums.org 2007–11, ACS five-yr. Author's analysis.
[b] Percent of over-22 population with four-plus years college, employed, and household income US$100,000+, that report living in the metropolitan area; and report living outside of the metropolitan area in the previous year.

the United States. They have high levels of inflow and high levels of outflow of this talent base.

Talent Migration Map

I summarize the different dynamics of talent migration by plotting metropolitan areas on two dimensions: out-migration and net-migration. I plot net-migration on the vertical axis, so that metropolitan areas with higher net-migration place higher on this axis, those with lower net-migration (or greater net out-migration) place lower of this axis. On the horizontal axis I plot out-migration with values increasing from left to right.

I choose these two dimensions rather than plotting out-migration against in-migration for the following reasons. First, I argue that an important dynamic occurs when out-migration is low and when there is positive net-migration. Therefore, plotting these two dimensions directly captures my argument. Second, different locations on this plot reflect different dynamics. In Figure 4.1, I identify four quadrants that reflect different migration dynamics. The upper left quadrant is one where Minneapolis-St. Paul lies. These are metropolitan areas that have relatively low levels of out-migration and experience net-migration. These metropolitan areas are building their talent base by expanding the pool of talent. I use the term expanding because the existing talent tends not to leave. In this quadrant, a metropolitan area retains its current talent and adds new talent to this base.

The upper right quadrant area identifies metropolitan areas that experience net-migration and have relatively high levels of out-migration. These metropolitan areas are also building their talent base—more people arrive than depart. However, talent is more transient in these metropolitan areas. There are big flows in and out. Thus they are building their talent base, but more so by churning. An example in these data is Charlotte.

To the lower right are metropolitan areas with relatively high out-flows of talent and with net out-migration. I consider these metropolitan areas as decaying. These are losing talent in net and have a high outflow rate. Interesting, they might be bringing a lot of talent to the region if the inflow is also high; therefore, the rate of decay can vary a lot in this group. A metropolitan area that falls in this quadrant is San Diego.

In the lower left quadrant are metropolitan areas with relatively low out-migration with net out-migration. Although their out-migration rates are low, this means that their in-migration rates are even lower. I label these metropolitan areas as atrophying. The relatively low outflow of talent cannot

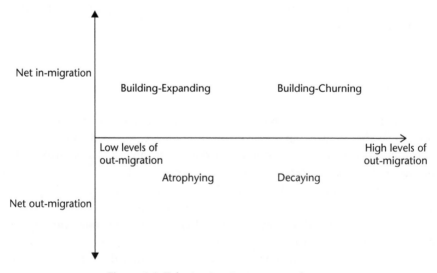

Figure 4.1 Talent migration map quadrants

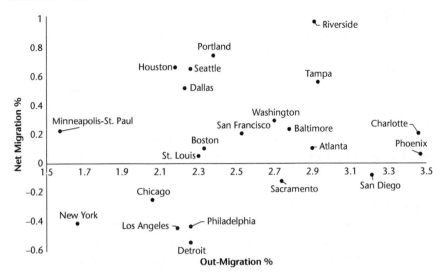

Figure 4.2 Talent migration map: highly educated, employed, and high-earning

overcome the even lower level of talent attraction. New York is an example of such a metropolitan area.

Figure 4.2 maps the twenty-two metropolitan areas on these dimensions.

Migration Patterns for Other Segments of the Population

My arguments for what drives the Minneapolis-St. Paul headquarters economy revolves around the mobility and migration of a professional administrative and managerial workforce. To assess the migration patterns of this workforce across major metropolitan areas in the United States, I restricted my analysis to the workforce that (a) has completed four or more years of college, (b) is currently employed, (c) has a household income of over US$100,000, and (d) is over 22 years of age.

I assess the sensitivity of this migration pattern to alternative definitions of the talent pool. The following sections address two alternative subsets of the population that aid my interpretation of the pattern of talent migration.

Educated, Employed, High-earning Individuals with School-aged Children

In Chapter 3, I highlight that many accounts of managerial and administrative talent retention in Minneapolis-St. Paul revolve around quality of life factors associated with raising children. If this is correct, then the pattern that I previously document should be as strong or stronger if I focus only on individuals that have school-aged children in their household. Therefore, I added an additional restriction to data. That there be at least one child between the ages of 5 and 19 in the respondent's household.

I revisit the previous analysis with this further-restricted demographic. I first assess the percentage of the over-22-year-old population that fits this new restriction for the largest twenty-five metropolitan areas in the United States. Table 4.6 presents these data. Overall, the rankings are fairly consistent between this table and Table 4.2, which do not include the restriction of a school-aged child in the household. However, there are some notable exceptions.

Minneapolis-St. Paul moves up four places and is third in this ranking compared to seventh in Table 4.2. This higher concentration of educated, high-income talent with school-aged children is consistent with the observation that child-rearing is important in the region—compared even to other regions in the United States. Washington, DC, and Boston remain in the top

Table 4.6 Percentage of population that is highly educated, employed, high-earning, with a school-aged child[a]

Metropolitan Area	%[b]
Washington, DC/MD/VA	5.68
Boston, MA-NH	5.15
Minneapolis-St. Paul, MN	4.37
Baltimore, MD	4.15
San Francisco-Oakland-Vallejo, CA	4.15
Seattle-Everett, WA	4.02
Philadelphia, PA/NJ	3.79
Denver-Boulder, CO	3.67
New York-Northeastern NJ	3.64
Chicago, IL	3.46
Atlanta, GA	3.34
St. Louis, MO-IL	3.22
Dallas-Fort Worth, TX	3.22
San Diego, CA	3.05
Charlotte-Gastonia-Rock Hill, NC-SC	2.97
Detroit, MI	2.94
Sacramento, CA	2.90
Houston-Brazoria, TX	2.85
Portland, OR-WA	2.85
Pittsburgh, PA	2.84
Los Angeles-Long Beach, CA	2.53
Phoenix, AZ	2.31
Tampa-St. Petersburg-Clearwater, FL	1.90
Miami-Hialeah, FL	1.76
Riverside-San Bernardino,CA	1.64

[a] Data source: IPUMS-USA, University of Minnesota, www.ipums.org 2007–11, ACS five-yr. Author's analysis.
[b] Percent of over-22 population with (a) four-plus years college, (b) employed, (c) household income US$100,000+, and (d) with a child aged between 5 and 19 in the household.

two places. New York and Los Angeles, respectively, drop four and six places. Educated, high-income talent is less likely to be raising children in these two metropolitan areas.

To examine the migration patterns of this subset of the population, I present analyses that parallel the previous section. Table 4.7 presents the out-migration data. The out-migration rates are lower in this table that in Table 4.3. This is intuitive. People with school-aged children are less likely to move compared to those without school-aged children. I will note, however, that although moving is less likely among this subset of the population, there is still variation in the migration rates across metropolitan areas. The rankings reflect this variation.

Once again, the Minneapolis-St. Paul metropolitan area has the lowest out-migration rate among the twenty-two metropolitan areas with an out-migration rate of 0.8 percent. Rounding out the top five are New York, Philadelphia, Los Angeles, and Chicago. This is the same top five as before, with the loss of Houston and the addition of Philadelphia. The metropolitan areas with the highest

Table 4.7 Outward migration of highly educated, employed, high-earning, with school-aged child[a]

Metropolitan Area	%[b]
Minneapolis-St. Paul	0.82
New York-Northeastern NJ	0.85
Philadelphia	1.00
Los Angeles	1.06
Chicago	1.08
Boston	1.09
Dallas	1.26
Seattle	1.27
Detroit	1.35
Baltimore	1.40
San Francisco	1.40
Houston	1.41
San Diego	1.43
Portland	1.44
Sacramento	1.48
Washington, DC	1.61
St. Louis	1.63
Charlotte	1.67
Atlanta	1.72
Tampa	1.74
Phoenix	1.86
Riverside	2.32

[a] Data source: IPUMS-USA, University of Minnesota, www.ipums.org 2007–11, ACS five-yr. Author's analysis.
[b] Percent of over-22 population with four-plus years college, employed, household income US$100,000+, and child in the household aged between 5 and 19, that report living in the metropolitan area in the previous year; and report living outside of the metropolitan area in the current year.

97

out-migration rate for this segment of the population are Riverside, Phoenix, Tampa, Atlanta, and Charlotte. The out-migration rates of 2.3 percent for Riverside and 1.8 percent for Phoenix are of much greater magnitude than the out-migration rate for Minneapolis-St. Paul.

Table 4.8 presents the net-migration for this segment of the population. Minneapolis-St. Paul once again shows net inward migration in this demographic of 0.3 percent. It continues to rank above the median within this group as it ranks ninth among the twenty-two metropolitan areas. The cities with the largest net inflows are Phoenix, Atlanta, Charlotte, San Diego, and Seattle. Those with the lowest are New York, Chicago, Boston, St. Louis, and Los Angeles.

For completeness, Table 4.9 presents the in-migration rates. Minneapolis-St. Paul's ranks fifteenth at 1.15 percent, which is once again below the median. Nevertheless, its ranking is higher than the demographic that did not contain the additional restriction of there being a school-age child in the household. The metropolitan areas with the highest inward migration ranks

Table 4.8 Net-migration of highly educated, employed, high-earning, with school-aged child[a]

Metropolitan Area	%[b]
Phoenix	0.65
Charlotte	0.58
Seattle	0.44
Dallas	0.40
San Diego	0.39
Riverside	0.39
Houston	0.33
Atlanta	0.32
Minneapolis-St. Paul	0.32
Baltimore	0.30
Tampa	0.30
Sacramento	0.26
Washington, DC	0.23
Portland	0.12
Philadelphia	−0.01
St. Louis	−0.03
Boston	−0.08
Chicago	−0.18
Los Angeles	−0.19
San Francisco	−0.33
New York-Northeastern NJ	−0.47
Detroit	−0.51

[a] Data source: IPUMS-USA, University of Minnesota, www.ipums.org 2007–11, ACS five-yr. Author's analysis.
[b] Net-migration of over-22 population with four-plus years college, employed, household income US$100,000+, and child in the household aged between 5 and 19 to a metropolitan area divided by the over-22 population with four-plus years college, employed, household income US $100,000+, and child in the household aged between 5 and 19.

Table 4.9 Inward migration of highly educated, employed, and high-earning, with school-aged child[a]

Metropolitan Area	%[b]
Riverside	2.71
Phoenix	2.51
Charlotte	2.25
Atlanta	2.04
Tampa	2.04
Washington, DC	1.85
San Diego	1.82
Sacramento	1.74
Houston	1.73
Seattle	1.72
Baltimore	1.70
Dallas	1.66
St. Louis	1.60
Portland	1.56
Minneapolis-St. Paul	1.15
San Francisco	1.07
Boston	1.00
Philadelphia	0.99
Chicago	0.90
Los Angeles	0.87
Detroit	0.85
New York-Northeastern NJ	0.38

[a] Data source: IPUMS-USA, University of Minnesota, www.ipums.org. 2007–11, ACS 5-yr. Author's analysis.
[b] Percent of over-22 population with four-plus years college, employed, household income US$100,000+, and child in the household aged between 5 and 19, that report living in the metropolitan area; and report living outside of the metropolitan area in the previous year.

are Riverside, Phoenix, Charlotte, Atlanta, and Tampa. Again, these are the same five metropolitan areas with the highest outward migration rates. The metropolitan areas with the lowest inward migration rates are New York, Detroit, Los Angeles, Chicago, and Philadelphia.

Finally Figure 4.3 presents the talent migration map for this demographic. The map has many commonalities to Figure 4.2. Key examples in the northwest, northeast, and southwest quadrants of the figure remain Minneapolis, Charlotte, and New York—respectively. There is only one metro area in the southeast quadrant, which is St. Louis. San Diego and Phoenix, which were in this quadrant in Figure 4.2, are no longer there. This indicates that the out-migration rate is higher in these cities for individuals without school-aged children.

The Entire Population

Instead of looking at a specific subset of the population, in this section, I examine the migration patterns for overall population. Table 4.10 presents

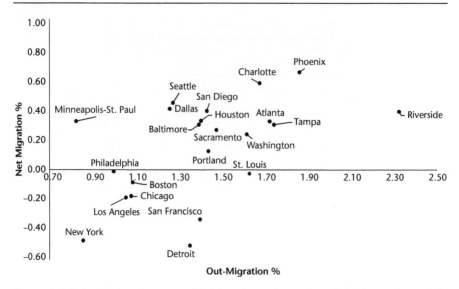

Figure 4.3 Talent migration map: highly educated, employed, high-earning, with school-aged child

Table 4.10 Outward migration of entire population[a]

Metropolitan Area	%
New York-Northeastern NJ	2.39
Philadelphia	2.74
Chicago	2.83
Los Angeles	3.01
Houston	3.02
Minneapolis-St. Paul	3.10
Detroit	3.16
St. Louis	3.17
Dallas	3.27
Boston	3.42
Baltimore	3.55
San Francisco	3.65
Portland	3.69
Charlotte	3.76
Riverside	3.82
Tampa	3.92
Atlanta	4.12
Washington, DC	4.14
Seattle	4.15
Sacramento	4.18
Phoenix	4.26
San Diego	4.52

[a] Data source: IPUMS-USA, University of Minnesota, www.ipums.org 2007–11, ACS five-yr. Author's analysis.

the out-migration rates, Table 4.11 presents the net-migration rates, and Table 4.12 presents the in-migration rates. Let me first describe the results for the Minneapolis-St. Paul metropolitan area.

The results share some semblance to the high-earning, educated population; nevertheless, there are also notable differences. The out-migration rate is relatively low compared to the other metro areas, but not as low as for the sub-samples of the population that I previously examined. The ranking for the entire poulation is sixth lowest. I terms of overall migration, there is a notable difference. Unlike the other segments of the population that I examined, overall there is net out-migration from the Minneapolis-St. Paul region. The net-migration rate is an outflow of 0.03 percent, which ranks fifteen among the twenty-two metropolitan areas. In light of the negative net-migration flow, the inflow is also relatively small. It ranks sixteenth among the metropolitan areas.

These data do not share the same pattern as the focused segments I previously analysed. Recall, the reason I focused on the previous segments of the population is that these are the individuals that I expect to most likely exhibit the dynamics that I described in Chapter 2. Because the population that is central to my argument exhibits the migration pattern that I expect and because the entire population does not, this lends further supports to my arguments. Namely, the dynamic that I describe is not universal for the Minneapolis-St. Paul region but

Table 4.11 Net-migration of entire population[a]

Metropolitan Area	%
Charlotte	1.08
Portland	0.88
Riverside	0.61
Houston	0.28
Dallas	0.26
Phoenix	0.24
Tampa	0.20
Sacramento	0.10
Seattle	0.10
Atlanta	−0.06
San Diego	−0.14
Boston	−0.17
Washington, DC	−0.22
Baltimore	−0.23
Minneapolis-St. Paul	−0.32
San Francisco	−0.43
St. Louis	−0.44
Philadelphia	−0.47
Chicago	−0.93
New York-Northeastern NJ	−1.02
Los Angeles	−1.04
Detroit	−1.35

[a] Data source: IPUMS-USA, University of Minnesota, www.ipums.org 2007–11, ACS five-yr. Author's analysis.

Table 4.12 Inward migration of entire population[a]

Metropolitan Area	%
Charlotte	4.84
Portland	4.57
Phoenix	4.50
Riverside	4.43
San Diego	4.38
Sacramento	4.28
Seattle	4.25
Tampa	4.12
Atlanta	4.06
Washington, DC	3.91
Dallas	3.53
Baltimore	3.33
Houston	3.30
Boston	3.25
San Francisco	3.22
Minneapolis-St. Paul	2.78
St. Louis	2.73
Philadelphia	2.27
Los Angeles	1.97
Chicago	1.90
Detroit	1.81
New York-Northeastern, NJ	1.37

[a] Data source: IPUMS-USA, University of Minnesota, www.ipums.org 2007–11, ACS five-yr. Author's analysis.

pronounced in the subset of the population whose demographics best match the talent that is central to my arguments.

Returning to the overall results, the following metropolitan areas exhibit the lowest out-migration rates: New York, Philadelphia, Chicago, Los Angeles, and Houston. These are fairly consistent with the rankings for the educated, employed, high-earning population with New York, Chicago, Houston, and Los Angeles being among the metropolitan areas with the lowest five outflows. Philadelphia was ranked eight for the educated, employed, high-earning population.

The metropolitan areas with highest out-migration rates are San Diego, Phoenix, Sacramento, Seattle, and Washington, DC. Interestingly, the metropolitan areas with the highest overall out-migration rates do not share as many similarities to the educated, employed, high-earning demographic. Although San Diego and Phoenix were among the metropolitan areas with the highest out-migration rates, the others were not. Sacramento was ranked fifteenth instead of twentieth. Washington, DC, was ranked fourteenth instead of eighteenth. Seattle was ranked ninth instead of nineteenth. It appears that Seattle and Washington, DC, are significantly more effective in retaining their educated, employed, high-earning workforce compared to their population in general. Alternatively stated, these metropolitan areas are seeing greater exit of the population is that is not highly educated, employed, and high-earning.

With respect to net-migration, the metropolitan areas with the highest rankings of net-migration are Charlotte, Portland, Riverside, Houston, and Dallas. Riverside, Houston, and Portland were in the top five ranked for the educated, employed, high-earning demographic. Charlotte was ranked tenth and Dallas was ranked sixth. Overall, this appears generally consistent across demographics. The lowest five ranked metropolitan areas are Detroit, Los Angeles, New York, Chicago, and Philadelphia. These are the same five metropolitan areas that have the lowest net-migration for the educated, employed, high-earning demographic.

In terms of in-migration, the metropolitan areas with the highest rankings are Charlotte, Portland, Phoenix, Riverside, and San Diego. All but Portland, which ranked sixth, are in the top five for the educated, employed, high-earning demographic. In terms of the lowest ranked inflows the five lowest are New York, Detroit, Chicago, Los Angeles, and Philadelphia. These were all among the six lowest ranked for the educated, employed, high-earning demographic.

Figure 4.4 presents the Talent Migration Map for the overall population, rather than a subset of the population as in the previous two graphs.

Differences in Migration between the Entire Population and the Employed, Educated, and High-earning

Although many metropolitan areas exhibit a relatively stable migration patterns with respect to the overall population compared to the educated,

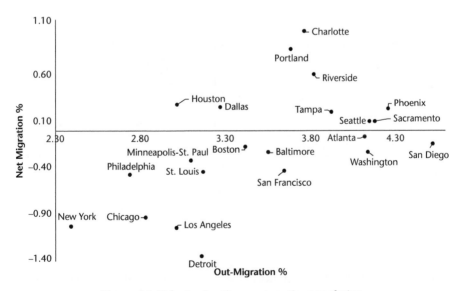

Figure 4.4 Talent migration map: entire population

employed, high-earning demographic, some do not. To see the difference in migration patterns for the entire population versus the educated, employed, high-earning demographic I generate Figure 4.5. Here I graph the difference in the out-migration rate on the horizontal axis and the difference in the net-migration rate on the vertical axis. In both cases, greater values indicate relatively better talent retention or net-migration for the educated, employed, high-earning population. A close examination of the data show that the overall migration rates for educated, employed, high-earning population are lower than for the entire population. Therefore, I place the axes at the median levels of the difference in out-migration and the difference in net-migration.

With this placement of the axes, there are now four quadrants that group metropolitan areas. In the top left quadrant are the metropolitan areas where the out-migration of the educated, employed, high-earning population is lower than out-migration of the overall population and where the net-migration of the educated, employed, high-earning population is greater than net-migration of the overall population. This quadrant includes Seattle, Minneapolis-St. Paul, Washington, DC, and San Francisco.

The top right quadrant includes metropolitan areas where the out-migration of the educated, employed, high-earning population is higher than out-migration of the overall population and where the net-migration of the educated, employed, high-earning population is greater than net-migration of the overall population. These metropolitan areas include Detroit, New York,

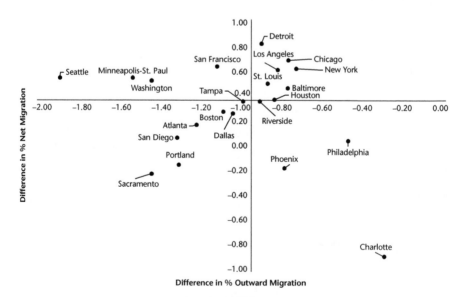

Figure 4.5 Migration map: difference between highly educated, employed, high-earning, and entire population

Chicago, Los Angeles, St. Louis, Baltimore, and Houston. Interestingly, many of these metropolitan areas have negative migration in both populations, meaning that they are losing fewer of the educated, employed, high-earning population than they are the population in general. These metropolitan areas include Detroit, New York, Chicago, and Los Angeles.

The bottom right quadrant includes metropolitan areas where the out-migration of the educated, employed, high-earning population is higher than out-migration of the overall population and where the net-migration of the educated, employed, high-earning population is lower than net-migration of the overall population. These metropolitan areas are building and retaining their overall population at a greater rate compared to the educated, employed, high-earning population. The metropolitan areas that exhibit this pattern include Charlotte, Philadelphia, Phoenix, and Riverside.

The bottom left quadrant includes metropolitan areas where the out-migration of the educated, employed, high-earning population is lower than out-migration of the overall population and where the net-migration of the educated, employed, high-earning population is lower than the net-migration of the overall population. These metropolitan areas include Boston, Dallas, Atlanta, San Diego, Portland, and Sacramento.

Historical Consistency of the Talent Migration Pattern

The data I present of educated, employed, high-earning individuals is consistent with my arguments of what drives the Minneapolis-St. Paul headquarters economy. Nevertheless, the 2007 to 2011 time period might not be indicative of the migration pattern over a longer period of time—and this is important to assess the validity of my arguments. Not only might there be temporal fluctuations in migration patterns for metropolitan areas, the 2007 to 2011 time frame captures a period of time when the economy was in the "Great Recession."

For this reason, I wish to examine migration patterns looking further back. To gather these data I again draw on the IPUMS Data maintained by the Minnesota Population Center at the University of Minnesota (Flood et al., 2017). For census years prior to 2010, the long form of the Census contained a question about migration that is similar to the question I use from the ACS. This question asks if an individual moved in the past five years; and if so, from where they moved.

I gathered data on this question for the Census years 2000 (which measures migration between 1995 and 2000), 1990 (which measures migration between 1985 and 1990), and 1980 (which measures migration between 1975 and 1980). I examine each set of Census data separately and undertake the same analysis that I did previously.

I present detailed tables and figures of out-migration, net-migration and in-migration for each decade in Tables 4.13–4.15 and Figures 4.6–4.8. These data are for the educated, employed, high-earning segment of the population. The data restrictions with respect to employment, age, and education are constant for all of the data. I do, however, change the cut-off for household income in order to account for inflation. Based on the consumer price index, I alter the cut-offs to the following: 2000 (US$77,000), 1990 (US$58,000), and 1980 (US$37,000).

I should note one issue when comparing migration rates from the Census data to those from the ACS. The migration rates are five-year rates in the Census data. The underlying question is whether an individual moved in the five years prior to responding to the census. This reflects that the Census data are collected every decade. The migration rates computed from the ACS are five years of one-year migration data. In other words, the compilation of the 2007, 2008, 2009, 2010, and 2011 surveys. The underlying question was whether an individual moved in the last year and the ACS was fielded in each of the five years.

Table 4.16 presents the rank of Minneapolis-St. Paul relative to the other twenty-two metropolitan areas on the migration measures that I examined previously: out-migration rate, net-migration rate, and in-migration rate.

Table 4.13 Migration data for highly educated, employed, and high-earning population, 2000[a]

Metropolitan Area	Outward Migration %	Inward Migration %	Net-Migration %
Atlanta	14.89	20.64	5.75
Baltimore	14.47	15.08	0.61
Boston	13.02	11.30	−1.72
Charlotte	14.62	25.42	10.80
Chicago	11.20	9.76	−1.43
Dallas	12.71	18.42	5.70
Detroit	10.29	10.58	0.29
Houston	13.21	15.73	2.53
Los Angeles	11.97	9.62	−2.35
Minneapolis-St. Paul	10.18	11.97	1.79
New York	8.50	7.01	−1.49
Philadelphia	11.82	10.88	−0.93
Phoenix	11.77	21.79	10.02
Portland	12.05	18.35	6.30
Riverside	17.39	18.70	1.31
Sacramento	12.59	17.78	5.19
San Diego	15.24	17.89	2.65
San Francisco	11.58	17.18	5.60
Seattle	12.00	16.16	4.15
St. Louis	14.53	10.84	−3.69
Tampa	16.71	20.44	3.73
Washington	13.99	14.63	0.64

[a] Data source: IPUMS-USA, University of Minnesota, www.ipums.org 2000 5% sample. Author's analysis.

Table 4.14 Migration data for highly educated, employed, and high-earning population, 1990[a]

Metropolitan Area	Outward Migration %	Inward Migration %	Net-Migration %
Atlanta	14.98	22.98	8.00
Baltimore	12.44	16.35	3.91
Boston	15.58	12.05	−3.53
Charlotte	15.15	25.06	9.91
Chicago	11.45	11.30	−0.15
Dallas	18.31	20.69	2.37
Detroit	9.73	10.99	1.26
Houston	19.61	17.11	−2.50
Los Angeles	11.40	12.23	0.83
Minneapolis-St. Paul	11.85	13.26	1.41
New York	9.34	6.57	−2.77
Philadelphia	11.32	13.24	1.92
Phoenix	16.26	22.36	6.09
Portland	12.80	16.79	3.99
Riverside	15.00	33.55	18.55
Sacramento	15.40	21.18	5.77
San Diego	14.21	21.12	6.90
San Francisco	13.05	16.96	3.90
Seattle	11.28	18.42	7.14
St. Louis	15.66	14.32	−1.34
Tampa	16.83	23.27	6.44
Washington, DC	13.04	17.03	3.99

[a] Data source: IPUMS-USA, University of Minnesota, www.ipums.org 1990 5% sample. Author's analysis.

Table 4.15 Migration data for highly educated, employed, and high-earning population, 1980[a]

Metropolitan Area	Outward Migration %	Inward Migration %	Net-Migration %
Atlanta	10.16	11.57	1.41
Baltimore	8.89	7.99	−0.91
Boston	16.76	6.33	−10.43
Charlotte	6.91	10.51	3.60
Chicago	6.63	5.98	−0.65
Dallas	7.50	10.72	3.22
Detroit	5.14	5.33	0.19
Houston	5.83	12.30	6.47
Los Angeles	5.54	6.00	0.45
Minneapolis-St. Paul	5.75	7.45	1.70
New York	5.83	3.75	−2.08
Philadelphia	7.82	7.22	−0.60
Phoenix	7.95	12.20	4.25
Portland	6.78	8.14	1.36
Riverside	10.31	12.56	2.25
Sacramento	9.09	8.85	−0.25
San Diego	8.04	12.09	4.05
San Francisco	7.16	8.12	0.96
Seattle	5.86	7.98	2.12
St. Louis	9.45	7.03	−2.41
Tampa	8.79	13.18	4.39
Washington, DC	7.65	9.45	1.80

[a] Data source: IPUMS-USA, University of Minnesota, www.ipums.org 1980 5% state sample. Author's analysis.

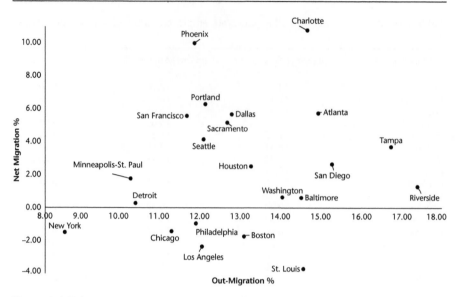

Figure 4.6 Talent migration map: highly educated, employed, and high-earning, 1995–2000

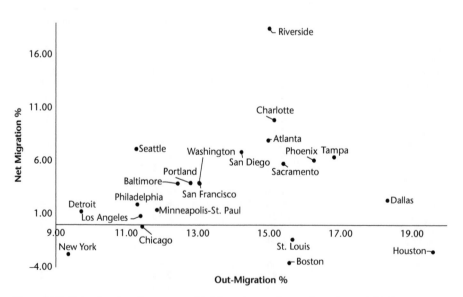

Figure 4.7 Talent migration map: highly educated, employed, and high-earning, 1985–90

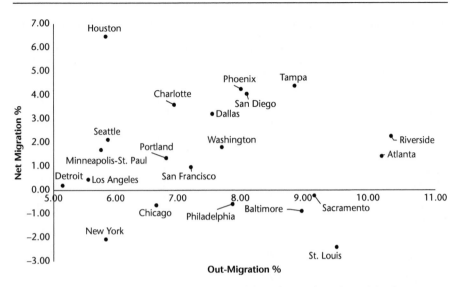

Figure 4.8 Talent migration map: highly educated, employed, and high-earning, 1975–80

Table 4.16 Historical comparison on migration of highly educated, employed, and high-earning population for Minneapolis-St. Paul[a]

Years	Rank Net-Migration	Rank Inward Migration	Rank Outward Migration[b]
2007–11	9	19	1
1995–2000	12	15	2
1985–90	15	16	7
1975–80	10	15	3

[a] Data source: Tables 4.3, 4.4, 4.5, 4.13, 4.14, and 4.15.
[b] Lowest outward migration assigned rank 1, second-lowest assigned 2 rank, . . .

Overall, the data for Minneapolis-St. Paul in Table 4.16 are very consistent with the pattern of data from 2007–11. The out-migration rate is among the lowest among the metropolitan areas that I assess. Moreover, the net-migration rate is positive in all cases and above the median for the twenty-two metropolitan areas that I examine. It is clear why the adage of being hard to attract talent but it staying once it arrives is well-ingrained in the Minneapolis-St. Paul region. It is pervasive over a long time span.

To get a sense of how metropolitan areas compare to each other over this time period, I average the rankings across the four data periods in Table 4.17. The reason that I average the ranking is to get a sense of the typical relative placement of a region at each point in time. Alternatives such as averaging the

Table 4.17 Migration rank for highly educated, employed, and high-earning population[a]

Metropolitan Area	Average Outward Migration Rank[b]	Average Inward Migration Rank	Average Net-Migration Rank
Atlanta	17.25	5.25	7.5
Baltimore	14.25	11.75	13.25
Boston	15.75	17	19.25
Charlotte	15.75	3.25	4.5
Chicago	5	19.5	18
Dallas	12.5	8.25	7.5
Detroit	3.25	20.5	17.25
Houston	11.25	9	8.75
Los Angeles	5	19.5	18.25
Minneapolis-St. Paul	3.25	16.25	11.5
New York	2	22	19.75
Philadelphia	8	16.75	17
Phoenix	15.25	3.5	6.5
Portland	9.75	9.25	6.75
Riverside	18.75	2.25	5.5
Sacramento	15	9.75	12
San Diego	16.75	6.25	8.75
San Francisco	9.75	11.75	10.5
Seattle	6.75	11	6
St. Louis	16	16.5	19.25
Tampa	19	3	5.5
Washington, DC	12.75	10.75	9.75

[a] Data source: Tables 4.3, 4.4, 4.5, 4.13, 4.14, and 4.15.
[b] Lowest outward migration assigned rank 1, second-lowest assigned 2 rank, . . .

rates would get a better picture of the overall flow; however, I am more interested in how a metropolitan area ranks. The average out-migration ranking of Minneapolis-St. Paul is 3.25. The only metro with a lower average rank is New York. Minneapolis-St. Paul shows net in-migration at each interval; whereas, New York shows net out-migration at each interval. The average net-migration rank for Minneapolis-St. Paul is 11.5—just below the median. The average in-migration rank is 16.25. Detroit also has a low average ranking of outward migration—tied with Minneapolis-St. Paul. Detroit though also has a lower in-migration rank, with the region showing net outward migration in the last time period.[2]

To aid presentation of the stability in migration patterns for the different metropolitan areas, I present Figure 4.9. As with the Talent Migration Map, the vertical axis in Figure 4.9 presents net-migration and the horizontal axis presents outward migration. I divide each axis into three cells, which represent the highest tercile in ranking (ranks 1–7), the mid-tercile in ranking (ranks 8–15), and the lowest tercile in ranking (ranks 16–22). For a metropolitan area to be presented in a cell, it must fall into that cell for at least three of the four time periods for which I presented the migration data. For example, in three of the four data periods, Tampa's ranking is in the highest

	Lowest Tercile Out-Migration (Rank 1–7)	Mid Tercile Out-Migration (Rank 8–15)	Highest Tercile Out-Migration (Rank 16–22)
Highest Tercile Net-Migration (Rank 16–22)			Tampa[b]
Mid Tercile Net-Migration (Rank 8–15)	*Minneapolis-St. Paul*	*Washington DC* *San Francisco*	
Lowest Tercile Net-Migration (Rank 1–7)	*New York* *Chicago* Detroit Los Angeles		St. Louis

Figure 4.9 Stability of migration pattern of the highly educated, employed, and high-earning population[a]

[a] Data from Tables 4.3, 4.4, 4.5, 4.13, 4.14, and 4.15.
[b] Metropolitan areas in table fall in the corresponding position in the Talent Migration Map in 3 of the 4 time periods (1975–80, 1985–90, 1995–2000, 2007–11). *Italics indicate that metro areas fall into the corresponding position in all four time periods.*
    Not presented (i.e., less stability in migration pattern): Atlanta, Baltimore, Boston, Charlotte, Dallas, Houston, Philadelphia, Phoenix, Portland, Riverside, Sacramento, San Diego, and Seattle.

tercile of net-migration and in the highest tercile of outward migration. The four metropolitan area that are italicized are in the quadrant for all four the data periods.

Figure 4.9 shows that Minneapolis-St. Paul is consistently in the lowest tercile of out-migration and in the mid-tercile of net-migration. The other two metropolitan areas that have similar characteristics are San Francisco and Washington, DC. These metropolitan areas are consistently in the mid-tercile of net-migration and out-migration. Four metropolitan areas are in the lowest tercile of out-migration and net-migration. These are New York City, Chicago, Detroit, and Los Angeles. Finally, St. Louis is in the cell representing the lowest tercile of net-migration and the highest tercile of out-migration. The one time period where it does not fall in that cell is the most recent time period depicted in Figure 4.2. All metropolitan areas not on the table demonstrate less stability in migration pattern over the four periods of data that I present.

Table 4.18 repeats the analysis of the data for the educated, employed, high-earning population with the additional restriction that they have a school-aged child in the household. Again, the data are very consistent with the previous table—if anything they are more pronounced with respect to Minneapolis-St. Paul. In these data, the average out-migration rank is 2.25, which is the lowest among all of the metropolitan areas. The average

Table 4.18 Migration rank for highly educated, employed, high-earning population, with school-aged child[a]

Metropolitan Area	Average Outward Migration Rank[b]	Average Inward Migration Rank	Average Net-Migration Rank
Atlanta	17	2.75	3.75
Baltimore	9.75	12.5	10.25
Boston	10	19.5	19
Charlotte	18.5	4.75	6.25
Chicago	9.25	19.5	19
Dallas	14.25	7.5	7.25
Detroit	4.75	19.25	18
Houston	13.75	8.5	9.75
Los Angeles	5.5	19.5	18
Minneapolis-St. Paul	2.25	16	11.75
New York	2.5	22	21
Philadelphia	6.25	16.25	14.25
Phoenix	14.75	3.5	2.75
Portland	13	10.75	9.75
Riverside	20.25	3.25	7.75
Sacramento	10.5	7.5	7.25
San Diego	13.5	7	6.25
San Francisco	10	15	15.25
Seattle	7.5	10	6.25
St. Louis	18.5	14.75	18.75
Tampa	15.75	3	7
Washington, DC	15.5	10.25	13.75

[a] Data source: IPUMS-USA, University of Minnesota, www.ipums.org Author's analysis.
[b] Lowest outward migration assigned rank 1, second-lowest assigned 2 rank, . . .

	Lowest Tercile Out-Migration (Rank 1–7)	Mid Tercile Out-Migration (Rank 8–15)	Highest Tercile Out-Migration (Rank 16–22)
Highest Tercile Net-Migration (Rank 16–22)		Sacramento[b]	Charlotte Riverside
Mid Tercile Net-Migration (Rank 8–15)	*Minneapolis-St. Paul* Philadelphia	Baltimore San Francisco Portland	
Lowest Tercile Net-Migration (Rank 1–7)	*New York* Detroit Los Angeles		St. Louis

Figure 4.10 Stability of migration pattern of the highly educated, employed, high-earning population, with school-aged child[a]

[a] Data from Tables 4.6, 4.7, 4.8. IPUMS-USA, University of Minnesota, www.ipums.org. 2000 5% Sample, 1990 5% Sample, 1980 5% State Sample, author's analysis.
[b] Metropolitan areas in table fall in the corresponding position in the Talent Migration Map in 3 of the 4 time periods (1975–80, 1985–90, 1995–2000, 2007–11). *Italics indicate that metro areas fall into the corresponding position in all four time periods.*
 Not presented (i.e., less stability in migration pattern): Atlanta, Boston, Chicago, Dallas, Houston, Phoenix, San Diego, Seattle, Tampa, and Washington.

net-migration is 11.75, and again just below the median. Moreover, in each period the net-migration shows an inflow in each period. Finally, the average in-migration rank is 16.

Figure 4.10 shows a more stability by metropolitan areas in the migration pattern of high-earning, highly educated individuals with school-aged children in their household, with twelve metro areas being presented in the figure compared to nine in Figure 4.10. Once again, Minneapolis-St. Paul is in the lowest tercile of out-migration and the mid-tercile of net-migration for all four data periods. Philadelphia joins Minneapolis-St. Paul in that cell. New York, Detroit, and Los Angeles fall into the cell with the lowest tercile of out-migration and the lowest tercile of net-migration, as they did in Figure 4.6. Portland and Baltimore join San Francisco in the mid-tercile of out-migration and mid-tercile of net-migration. Sacramento lies in a position of consistently being in the highest tercile of net-migration and mid-tercile of out-migration. Charlotte and Riverside show high out-migration and high net-migration. Finally, as in Figure 4.6, St. Louis has a high level of out-migration and low level of net-migration.

Summary

Chapter 3 introduces my explanation that managers, mobility, and migration are key to understanding a headquarters economy. Central to my explanation is that the pattern of migration of a talented workforce for Minneapolis-St. Paul looks different than the other major metropolitan areas in the country.

In this chapter, I examine migration data of twenty-two of the largest metropolitan areas in the United States to assess if these data are consistent with my explanation from Chapter 3. Because my explanation focuses on a talent pool that is employed, educated, and well-compensated, I focus my analysis on this subset of the population.

The data support the inferences from my explanation. The Minneapolis-St. Paul region has a very small outflow of this talent base. Over the last thirty-five years it exhibits among the lowest out-migration rates across metropolitan areas. As I argue, low outflow promotes mobility between companies in a region.

Although the out-migration rate is low, the in-migration rate is also relatively low. It ranks in the lower tercile among these twenty-two metropolitan areas. Nevertheless, because the out-migration rate is so low, the net-migration rate is positive. Over the time period, the Minneapolis-St. Paul region tends to be around the median in terms of net-migration of this talent pool—always experiencing net inward migration to the region.

Further supporting my explanation is that the migration pattern that is key to my argument does not hold for the overall population of the Minneapolis-

St. Paul region. Rather, it holds for the subset of the population where I expect it to be applicable. In addition, the pattern is pronounced when I further restrict the focal demographic to those who have school-aged children in their household. I argue that many quality of life factors that hold people to the Minneapolis-St. Paul region revolve around raising families. This appears to be the case—although I cannot directly assess what determines this migration pattern. I should note that although the differences overall are small, it appears that talent retention (i.e., lower relative outflows of those with school-aged children) rather than talent attraction (i.e., greater relative inflows of those with school-aged children). This is consistent with my contention that many quality of life factors primarily affect talent retention and not talent attraction.

The metrics and Talent Migration Map I present can be useful tool to analyze migration patterns across many different segments of the population. The tool is useful because it acknowledges that focusing on net-migration can mask very different dynamics in talent movement. By visualizing net-migration and outward migration one can better assess different underlying dynamics and what that potentially means for the talent base of a region.

Notes

1. This requires that I use the ACS weighting of each observation.
2. In addition, with respect to the headquarters economy dynamic, Detroit has fewer and a less diverse set of headquarters compared to Minneapolis-St. Paul (see Table 2.7).

5

What Creates a Vibrant Headquarters Economy?

Survey Evidence

In Chapter 4, I highlight how the migration pattern of employed, highly educated, high-earning individuals is consistent with my argument that managers, mobility, and migration are the key building blocks of a headquarters economy. The migration pattern of this talent base into and out of Minneapolis-St. Paul differs in comparison to the other major metropolitan areas in the United States. Although these data provide supportive evidence for my explanation of what drives a headquarters economy, they leave open two important questions. First, what precisely drives this migration pattern? And second, can I find more direct evidence of managerial mobility across industries in the Minneapolis-St. Paul region?

The analyses in Chapter 4 provide some insight into the former question. I show that the pattern of migration for Minneapolis-St. Paul is especially pronounced for employed, highly educated, high-earning individuals in households with school-aged children. This combined with the data on the nature of the household income and proportion of the high-earning population with school-aged children in their household suggest that quality of life issues with respect to child-rearing are important. Nevertheless, this cannot be on the only factor because a significant proportion of the population do not have school-aged children at any point in time. Moreover, the data in Chapter 4 rely on demographic characteristics of education, employment, and earnings to isolate the professional managerial and administrative talent pool from the overall population. Although the managerial and administrative talent pool will exhibit these characteristics, so will other professional talent pools—such as engineers.

To further the research and address these issues, I collect data that more directly tackles these questions. The most direct way to do this is to survey managerial and administrative employees. The benefit of a survey is that I can ask those who make up the talent base specific questions about their background, work experiences, mobility across employers, and migration to or from the region. A difficulty of a survey is getting access to these employees in meaningful numbers. To do this, I focus my efforts in surveying professional managerial and administrative employees within the Minneapolis-St. Paul metropolitan area.

Survey Procedure

I approached several companies in the Minneapolis-St. Paul metropolitan area to survey their managerial and professional headquarters employees. Twenty-three companies agreed to participate. These companies include large publicly-held headquartered firms (i.e., Fortune 500 companies), large privately held headquartered firms, hidden headquarters, mid-sized headquartered firms, and, in two cases, large local offices of professional service firms headquartered elsewhere.

The survey process was the following. Participating companies identified "managerial and professional administrative employees" that I would survey. I chose to have each company make this assessment because job titles and pay grades vary across industries. Therefore, having each company identify its professional and managerial workforce provides the most meaningful sampling across a large number of diverse companies.

Having identified the pool managerial and administrative employees, each company emailed their employees an introduction and a link to a web-based survey. In many cases the chief executive officer or another senior executive introduced the survey. The introduction stated that the company supported research about the local economy conducted by a professor at the University of Minnesota and encouraged participation. Upon entering the survey, participants confirmed that they consented to the research. The consent request was based on University of Minnesota Institutional Review Board procedures for human subjects. Those who consented to participate continued the survey. Those who did not were terminated from the survey. The participating companies sent an email a reminder about survey participation approximately ten days after the initial invitation. A professional market research company handedly survey programming and data collection.

All surveys were anonymous in that I did not collect any personal identifier. Participating companies sent all invitations so that the company controlled all employee contact. The processes of getting corporate approval and timing the launch so that it did not conflict with other survey efforts within these companies resulted in the surveys being fielded over a year time frame: from April of 2014 to April of 2015.

The survey contained 104 questions. However, respondents did not necessarily see all questions based on how they answered previous questions. The majority of the questions had scaled responses. However, of the 104 questions, ten required open-ended responses and an additional eleven required typing textual answers. My research assistants coded the open-ended questions. The textual answers were coded to map equivalent answers to common codes. For example, coding LA and Los Angeles as the same response.

I received 2,872 responses to the survey. The overall response rate of those who received an email invitation to participate is 40 percent. Across the twenty-three companies that participated in the survey, response rates range from a high of 95 percent to a low of 25 percent. I am very pleased with this response rate. Although sanctioned by the participating companies, this is not a company survey. In addition, those who participated in the survey appeared to be actively engaged. Ninety-three percent of survey participants who entered the survey ran it to completion. Many spent a lot of time on the open-ended questions and provided very detailed answers. The University of Minnesota disclosure requirements place my contact information and disclose the motivation for the research on the consent form. A few participants contacted me to say they were happy to complete the survey and found it engaging.

Survey Results

The remainder of the chapter presents the survey data. I present three sets of results. First, I report demographic information about the sample. In Chapters 3 and 4, I rely on demographic generalizations about the managerial and administrative talent pool. With the survey data, I empirically verify the validity of those generalizations. The demographic data also allow me to gather information about the managerial and administrative workforce within the Minneapolis-St. Paul headquarters economy.

The second set of results assesses the mobility of this talent base across companies—and especially across companies in different industries. As I mentioned in Chapter 4, such data are difficult to obtain for a comprehensive sample. The survey allows me to gather this information for professional managerial and administrative employees. I am able to analyze mobility patterns across different demographic subsets within the survey data.

The third set of results allows me to better isolate what underlies the migration patterns that I presented in Chapter 4. The American Community Survey provides comprehensive information about migration patterns. Although the way in which the pattern of migration varies across different demographic subsets provides insight into what underlies the migration patterns, those data do not directly assess the issue. Because I formulate the survey to focus on identifying what underlies migration, these data provide direct evidence of whether my description of the underlying dynamic of what drives a headquarters economy holds.

Demographic Makeup

EARNINGS AND EDUCATION

I expect a professional managerial and administrative workforce to be highly compensated. Table 5.1 presents response data on household income. I asked respondents to place their household income into one of six categories—or respond that they would rather not disclose this information. For calibration, recall that the Minneapolis-St. Paul region's median household income in 2012 is US$66,282, which is fifth among the largest twenty-five metropolitan areas in the United States. The category with the highest household income (more than US$200,000) had the largest frequency of responses (35 percent). It is clear that these are high-earning individuals.

Because I wish to focus on professional and high-earning individuals, for the following analysis I drop the respondents who reported household incomes of less than US$75,000. This is only 5 percent of the survey respondents. The overall results do not materially change if I include these respondents. I do, however, retain individuals who state they did not want to disclose their income because many of their other responses parallel those with the highest earnings. As a result, the following analysis draws upon 2,728 survey responses.

The second demographic characteristic that I wish to verify is educational attainment. Table 5.2 presents these data. As expected, this is a well-educated workforce. Just over 90 percent of this workforce possess a college degree. Over 41 percent possess a graduate degree. Recall, I do not select survey participants based on educational attainment, per se. Rather, I selected them because of the nature of their work (i.e., their employer identifies them as professional managerial and administrative workers). This confirms that well-educated

Table 5.1 Household income

Household Income Range US$	Respondents %
Less than 50,000[1]	1.29
50,000 to 75,000[2]	3.73
75,000 to 100,000	6.84
100,000 to 150,000	24.14
150,000 to 200,000	24.00
More than 200,000	34.91
Would rather not answer	5.09

Notes: n = 2872. [1]Dropped from subsequent analyses. [2]Dropped from subsequent analyses.

Table 5.2 Education attainment

Highest Level of Education	Respondents %
High school degree	2.35
Two-year technical degree or some undergraduate	7.41
Undergraduate degree	48.81
Graduate degree	41.44

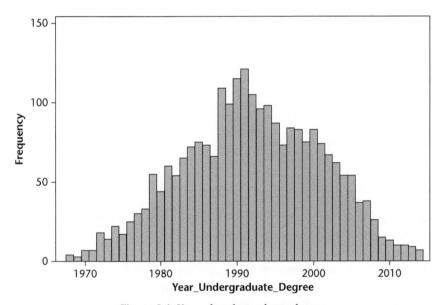

Figure 5.1 Year of undergraduate degree

high-earning individuals populate the workforce of interest with respect to headquarters talent.

Figure 5.1 presents the histogram of when those with a college degree completed their undergraduate degree. This demonstrates that the data are comprehensive in covering employees who are in the workforce for relatively long periods of time and those who are relatively new to the workforce. Although I do not ask respondents their age, one can estimate their age based on the date of their undergraduate degree. The sample, therefore, includes workforce participants across the recent generational cohorts in the United States including baby boomers, generation-X (gen-X), and millennials.

GENDER, MARITAL STATUS, AND CHILDREN

Table 5.3 presents other demographic descriptions. Panel A reports the gender of the respondents: 56 percent of the respondents are male and 44 percent female. Although not equal, it is a somewhat balanced gender representation.

Table 5.3 Gender, marital status, and children

Panel A: Gender

Gender	Respondents %
Male	55.75
Female	44.25

Panel B: Marital Status

Marital Status	Respondents %
Married	84.84
Single	8.11
Divorced	5.76
Widowed	0.73
Separated	0.55

Panel C: Children

Have Child/Children	Respondents %
Yes	81.06
No	18.94

Panel B reports marital status: 85 percent of respondents are married. Of those who are married, I ask if they are a dual career household. The question defines dual career as both spouses "having career responsibilities and aspirations." I do not define dual career as both spouses working. Sixty-nine percent respond yes. Once again, this is consistent with my expectation that individuals in this workforce have spouses with career aspirations because of the likelihood that they are also well-educated.

Panel C of Table 5.3 presents data with respect to children: 81 percent respond that they have children; 47 percent say that they have school-aged children living at home. This latter number—those with school-aged children in their household—is consistent with many considerations. First, in combination with the histogram of when people completed college, this confirms my expectation that a large portion of this workforce is in the child-rearing stage of their lives. Second, with such a large number of respondents with school-aged children at home, this reinforces why education-related issues would play a highly salient role for this talent pool.

For those with school-aged children, I gather additional information about their school choices. I ask them to identify the types of schools that their children attend or attended—distinguishing between public schools, private schools, and home schooling. The responses are public schools (85 percent), private schools (23 percent), and home school (1 percent). Because children can attend different schools over time and different children within the same household can attend different schools, these percentages sum to more than

Table 5.4 School choices by respondents with school-aged children[1]

	Entire Sample	Household Income (US$)				
		75,000-100,000	100,000-150,000	150,000-200,000	200,000+	Would rather not disclose
% Public Schools	85	89	90	87	82	80
% Private Schools	23	16	18	18	29	27
% Home School	1	1	3	1	1	0

Note: [1]Can sum to greater than 100 percent because respondents can send different children to different types of schools or send the same child to a different type of school over time.

100 percent. These data show a very strong prevalence of public school education. A simple calculation shows that 76 percent of respondents exclusively use public schools for their child's or children's education (i.e., subtract from 100 percent the percentages that ever send children to private school or home school).

I investigate the sensitivity to the use of public schooling across income levels. The data show that the use of public schools and private schools is invariant across all but the highest income segment I measure (i.e., household income of more than US$200,000 per year). The differences in schooling choices are not statistically different across the income groups up to US$200,000 in income. The group above US$200,000 has a higher use of private schools. Nevertheless, 82 percent sent their children to public schools, with 70 percent exclusively using public schools. Table 5.4 presents the breakdown of schooling across the income levels.

WHERE THEY WERE RAISED AND WHERE THEY WERE EDUCATED

I also inquire where survey respondents were raised—if they were raised in multiple locations the location in which they most identify—and where they went to college. Table 5.5 presents the data of where respondents were raised. Approximately one-third are raised in the Minneapolis-St. Paul metropolitan area (35 percent). Approximately one-quarter are raised in Minnesota outside of the Minneapolis-St. Paul metropolitan area (24 percent). Interestingly, the proportion of this workforce that come from the Minneapolis-St. Paul metropolitan area compared to the rest of the state mirrors the proportion of the overall population in Minneapolis-St. Paul metropolitan area compared to the rest of the state. For the remainder of the workforce, 36 percent are raised in the United States outside of Minnesota. Almost half of these respondents come from the four bordering states to Minnesota: Wisconsin, Iowa, South Dakota, and North Dakota. Only 5 percent of this headquarters workforce is raised outside of the United States.

Table 5.5 Location raised as a child

Location	Respondents %
Minneapolis-St. Paul	34.98
Minnesota, outside of Minneapolis-St. Paul	23.91
Within the United States, outside of Minnesota	36.19
Outside of the United States	4.91

Table 5.6 Location of undergraduate college

Location	Respondents %
Minneapolis-St. Paul	29.70
Minnesota, outside of Minneapolis-St. Paul	24.08
Within the United States, outside of Minnesota	42.76
Outside of the United States	3.46

Table 5.7 Location of graduate school

Location	Respondents %
Minneapolis-St. Paul	59.75
Minnesota, outside of Minneapolis-St. Paul	2.48
Within the United States, outside of Minnesota	34.75
Outside of the United States	3.01

Table 5.6 presents data on where the respondents went to college. These data show less representation from the Minneapolis-St. Paul area. Thirty percent graduated college in the Minneapolis-St. Paul metropolitan area, 24 percent graduated college in Minnesota outside of the Minneapolis-St. Paul metropolitan area, and 43 percent graduated college outside of Minnesota but in the United States. Only 3 percent graduated college outside of the United States.

Table 5.7 presents data on where those with graduate degrees attended graduate school. This sample is much more weighted to the Minneapolis-St. Paul metropolitan area. The data show that 60 percent of respondents attended graduate school in the Minneapolis-St. Paul metropolitan area; only 2 percent attended graduate school in Minnesota outside of the Minneapolis-St. Paul metropolitan area. Thirty-five percent attended graduate school in the United States outside of Minnesota and 3 percent attended graduate school outside of the United States.

These data show that the Minneapolis-St. Paul headquarters talent pool relies on regional talent. Nevertheless, it is misleading to say that is the only source of this talent. In addition, those who were raised or went to college in the region might have spent parts of their professional career elsewhere. I directly address this with survey questions that inquire about individual's migration.

SUMMARY OF THE DEMOGRAPHIC DATA

The demographic characteristics of the headquarters employees that I survey are very consistent with my expectations. They are high-earning. They are highly educated. The vast majority is married; most are in dual career situations; and almost half have school-aged children in their household. Although the talent base draws heavily from Minnesota and bordering states, approximately one-quarter come from the other places in the United States and internationally. Finally, the geographic imprint of where they went to college is less regionally concentrated than where they were raised. Nevertheless, the population that went to graduate school is heavily represented by those who attended graduate school in the Minneapolis-St. Paul metropolitan area.

Job Mobility

CURRENT EMPLOYMENT CHARACTERISTICS

One of the advantages of the survey data is that I am able directly assess the mobility of managerial and administrative talent across many different companies. Although I do not have similar data for other metropolitan areas, the advantage of these data is that they provide information on the nature and degree of job mobility for these individuals. Before discussing their work history, let me describe aspects of their current employment.

I ask each respondent to identify their role in the organization using the following classifications. Individual contributor, which I define as "you do not have anybody reporting to you." Manager, which I define as "you have individual contributors reporting to you." Senior leadership, which I define as "you have some level of management reporting to you." Table 5.8 presents these results. Fourteen percent of respondents report being an individual contributor. These constitute professional employees who do not have direct reports. This includes finance professionals, legal professions, and human resource professionals, among others. Fifty percent indicate that they manage others and 36 percent indicate that they are senior management. These data highlight that a large majority of the headquarters professionals have managerial responsibilities, although some jobs do not.

Table 5.9 lists the range of functional roles of the survey participants. These data verify the wide array of functional expertise held by the professional

Table 5.8 Current role in their company

Role	Respondents %
Senior leadership	36.25
Manager	50.11
Individual contributor	13.64

Table 5.9 Current functional role in their company

Role	Respondents %
General management	12.13
Human resources	6.74
Finance	18.33
Legal	4.77
IT	18.95
Marketing	7.95
Sales	5.06
Manufacturing	1.65
R&D/Product development	6.56
Logistics	0.99
Quality/Reliability	1.72
Other	15.14

managerial and administrative employees within headquarters. It also highlights the wide array of roles that the companies consider within their professional managerial and administrative workforce. The functions with the greatest level of response are information technology (IT), finance, general management, marketing, and research and development (R&D)/product development. The high rate of IT responses is likely—in part—a reflection of the nature of the companies that agreed to participate in the survey.

I ask respondents how long they have been in their current job. The average is 4.6 years. I also inquire how long they had been with their current company. The average is 11.7 years. These data suggest longevity within their current jobs. I highlight this because it is not necessarily inconsistent with mobility across companies or migration within the workforce. What this suggests is that this workforce—overall—does not rapidly churn between jobs and companies.

RECENT JOB HISTORY

I ask survey participants to describe their previous position relative to their current position along six dimensions. Was it at a different level (i.e., they were an individual contributor and are now a manager), in a different geographic location, with a different company, in a different industry, non-corporate, or they did not have a previous position. As one would expect, many indicate that their current position is at a different level than their previous position (46 percent). That is, they were previously a manager and are now senior leadership or they were an individual contributor and are now a manager. Only a small fraction indicate that this is their first position (2 percent) or that their previous position is non-corporate (5 percent).

The remaining dimensions provide information on the mobility of the workforce. Thirty-two percent state that their previous position is with a different company. More interesting with respect to mobility is that 18 percent report that their previous position is in a different industry. I find this meaningful because it indicates that about one out of five previous positions involve a switch of industry. Nevertheless, it is difficult to calibrate if this is pronounced compared to other regions because I only survey professional and managerial employees in the Minneapolis-St. Paul region. However, to aid in calibration I also inquire whether or not their previous position is in a different metropolitan area. Twelve percent of survey participants indicate this. Therefore, among these respondents I see that industry switches occur at a 50 percent greater frequency than geographic relocations (eighteen is 150 percent of twelve).

When I ask about their previous two positions, 47 percent report working in a different company, 26 percent in a different industry, and 18 percent in a different metropolitan area. These data reinforce the mobility among the managerial and administrative professionals in the region.

I examine the functional area in which respondents work to further assess the importance of mobility within this workforce. Having information on the function in which a person works, I am able to compare those who work in R&D/product development to all other respondents. I make this comparison for two reasons. First, many R&D/product development jobs draw on specific technologies or skills to an industry. For example, many employees in R&D positions at a company like General Mills have food science backgrounds; whereas, many employees in R&D positions at a company like Medtronic are biomechanical engineers. The technical backgrounds have notable industry focus and would often not be interchangeable. As a result, I expect to see less movement of R&D/product development employees across industries. Second, existing research draws upon patent data to examine the mobility of scientists and research engineers across companies (e.g., Almeida and Kogut, 1999; Marx et al., 2009; Marx, 2011). Examining the mobility of the R&D/product development respondents allows me to calibrate my findings with this research.

Table 5.10 presents the results. Overall, the R&D/product development workers' previous positions compared with other respondents are similar

Table 5.10 Previous position: R&D/product development compared to all others

Compared to Current Position	R&D/Product Development (% Responding Yes)	All Others (% Responding Yes)
Different Company*	22	33
Different Industry*	13	18
Different Metro Area	13	12
Different Level	46	46
Was non-corporate	4	5
Did not have one	4	2

Notes: * Percentages for R&D/product development and all others test different (p < 0.05: two-tailed test).

in all but two dimensions. The data show that R&D/product development workers' previous positions are less likely to be in a different company and less likely to be in a different industry compared to the other workers in the sample. R&D/product development worker's previous positions are equally likely to be in a different metropolitan area, at a different level, non-corporate, or non-existent.

These differences support my expectation that R&D/product development positions have more industry-specific components compared to other professional administrative and managerial positions, which are more general in their applicability. Moreover, these results suggest that the discussion of job mobility in research that focuses on scientists and engineers likely underestimates the prevalence of this phenomena in the broader professional workforce.

Looking across the different functional roles of the employees that I survey, those with the highest mobility across industries are in human resources (32 percent report their previous position was in a different industry), marketing (22 percent report their previous position was in a different industry), and manufacturing (22 percent report their previous position was in a different industry). The functional roles with the least mobility across industries are sales (10 percent report their previous position was in a different industry), legal (12 percent report their previous position was in a different industry), and R&D/product development (13 percent report their previous position was in a different industry).

HYPOTHETICAL EMPLOYMENT SCENARIOS

Another benefit of collecting survey data is that I can have respondents reveal potential choices that they would make if confronted with different job opportunities. Therefore, I construct six scenarios of possible job moves and assess respondents' willingness to consider these alternatives. These data allow me to assess to what extent this workforce sees its human capital specific to its industry and specific to large headquartered firms. They also allow me to assess respondents' willingness to consider opportunities that require relocating to another metropolitan area.

The first scenario that I present is whether a respondent would consider a career-advancing opportunity with their current employer that requires relocating to a different metropolitan area. In this scenario I inform respondents that a similar position might arise locally in the future, but one does not currently exist. I measure their willingness to consider this job opportunity on a five-point scale that ranges from (1) I would not be likely to consider this opportunity, to (5) I would be extremely likely to consider this opportunity. Thirty-one percent of survey participants report that they are likely or extremely likely to consider this move (i.e., respond with a 4 or a 5 on this scale). I also ask respondents to explain why they made this assessment in an open-ended question.

Assessing this effect is not straightforward. Some people might not be looking to move under any circumstance, some might be looking to move under any circumstance, or some might have recently visited a location where they would consider moving. Documenting that 31 percent are willing to consider this opportunity does not provide insight into whether this is a lot or little compared to other regions. Rather than focusing on this number in isolation, I use it as a benchmark for other scenarios I present. Therefore, I wish to focus on how the willingness to consider other employment opportunities changes across scenarios using this percentage as a baseline.

The second scenario is the same as the first one—it involves a career-advancing transfer with their current employer—but with one exception. Unlike the first scenario, I indicate that in the foreseeable future there will not be a similar opportunity locally. My expectation is that this increases the likelihood that survey participants consider relocating. The data support my expectation. The percentage of respondents who are likely or extremely likely to consider this opportunity increases by 4 percent to 35 percent. These data provide some assurance that participants are reading, thinking through, and assessing the differences in the scenarios that I present them.

Having set a baseline and verified the sensitivity to considering this baseline, I then present scenarios that allow me to assess to what extent respondents consider opportunities that involve switching industries or locations. The third scenario is one that leverages their current skills in the same industry; however, it requires relocating to another metropolitan area. Specifically, I tell them an executive search firm looking to fill a position that draws directly on their skills and experiences approaches them. It is in the same industry as their current employer; however, this position requires that they relocate to another major metropolitan area in the United States. They are told that this is a career-advancing move and although such an opportunity would be possible with their current employer, one does not currently exist. In other words, this is most similar to the first scenario that they were given with respect to future opportunities if they remain in their current position. Twenty-two percent respond that they are likely or extremely likely to consider this opportunity compared to 31 percent who respond that they are likely or extremely likely to consider the first scenario. These results show that the respondents are 40 percent more likely to consider an internal transfer in the company to an external opportunity that requires relocating (thirty-one is 41 percent greater than twenty-two). These data appear reasonable in that employees are more willing to stay with their current employer as a motivation for a move compared to relocating and switching employers.

The fourth scenario assesses respondents' willingness to change industries but remain in the Minneapolis-St. Paul metropolitan area. The scenario is that an executive search firm approaches them with an opportunity in a different industry that *would not* require relocating. I tell them that the position draws on their skills and experiences yet requires that their skills be adapted or that they learn additional skills for the position. As in the previous scenarios, I tell them that this is a career-advancing move and although such an opportunity is possible with their current employer, one does not currently exist. Fifty-three percent respond that they are likely or extremely likely to consider this opportunity.

These data support my arguments about career mobility within the Minneapolis-St. Paul region. I see that survey participants are much more inclined to consider taking a position in a new industry and adapting or enhancing their skills, compared to considering a geographic transfer with their current employer (53 compared to 31 percent). They are also much more inclined to consider taking a position in a new industry and adapting or enhancing their skills compared to relocating and working in the same industry (53 compared to 22 percent).

The final two scenarios assess another part of the mobility dynamic that I argued is key for Minneapolis-St. Paul; the movement of talent from large headquartered companies to smaller and start-up companies. In the fifth scenario, I present respondents with an opportunity to move to a small company in the Minneapolis-St. Paul region. I tell them that a former co-worker who is working at a small company with twenty employees approaches them about a job opportunity at that company. I tell them that the small company is poised for growth and that the position would draw directly on their experiences. In this scenario, 32 percent respond that they are likely or extremely likely to consider this opportunity.

I find these results illuminating. This is almost exactly the same percentage of survey participants who are willing to consider a within-company transfer (32 percent in this scenario compared to 31 percent in the initial scenario). Likewise, respondents are much more likely to consider this option than they are to consider relocating within the same industry for an opportunity brought to their attention by an executive search firm (32 percent in this scenario compared to 22 percent in the relocation scenario).

The final scenario is very similar to scenario that I just described. The difference is that the opportunity in the small company requires relocating to another major metropolitan area in the United States. Respondents demonstrate little appetite to consider this option. Only 9 percent state that they are likely or extremely likely to consider it.

Table 5.11 summarizes the proportion of respondents who are likely or extremely likely to consider the various employment opportunities.

Having demonstrated this pattern in Table 5.11, I wish to assess if the pattern holds across various subsets of respondents. In particular, I am curious if respondents without school-aged children in their household exhibit this

Table 5.11 Employment scenarios

Scenario	Likely and Extremely Likely to Consider (% Respondents)
Company transfer out of metropolitan area—possibility of local opportunity in the future	31
Company transfer out of metropolitan area—no local opportunity in the future	35
Opportunity in same industry but different firm and different metropolitan area	22
Opportunity in different industry but same metropolitan area	53
Opportunity at a start-up in the same metropolitan area	32
Opportunity at a start-up in different metropolitan area	9

Table 5.12 Employment scenarios: by school-aged child in household

Scenario	Likely and Extremely Likely to Consider (% Respondents)	
	School-aged Child in Household	No School-aged Child in Household
Company transfer out of metropolitan area—possibility of local opportunity in the future	27	34
Company transfer out of metropolitan area—no local opportunity in the future	31	39
Opportunity in same industry but different firm and different metropolitan area	19	25
Opportunity in different industry but same metropolitan area	55	51
Opportunity at a start-up in the same metropolitan area	33	31
Opportunity at a start-up in different metropolitan area	8	10

pattern or if this pattern only reflects that respondents with school-aged children are less willing to move. Likewise, respondents in dual career situations might drive the pattern of results. Or respondents who were raised in Minnesota and wish to stay geographically close to where there were raised might drive the pattern of results. If the former two scenarios are true, it does not invalidate my arguments because these demographic characteristics are central to the underlying drivers that I discussed in Chapter 3. If native Minnesotans not wanting to leave entirely drive the results, then that would not be entirely consistent with my arguments. However, if I can show that the general pattern of willingness to consider these opportunities is manifest across these different demographics, then it highlights the persistence of these preferences in the data and provides stronger support for the mobility and migration dynamics that are central to my arguments.

Table 5.12 splits the data by respondents who have school-aged children in their household and those who do not. Consistent with my expectations, for any scenario that involves geographically relocating, the percentage of respondents likely to consider the option is higher for those without school-aged children in their household. For instance, 34 percent of respondents without school-age children in their household are likely to consider an intra-firm transfer that requires relocation. In contrast, only 27 percent of respondents with school-aged children are likely to consider such an opportunity. Likewise, 25 percent for respondents without school-age children in their household are likely to consider an opportunity in the same industry in a different metropolitan area compared to 19 percent of respondents with school-aged children. Unlike relocating, the proportion of respondents willing to consider an opportunity in the same metropolitan area but in a different industry holds across sub-samples. Moreover, the rate at which they would do so is very similar across groups: 55 percent for respondents with school-age children compared to 51 percent for respondents without school-aged children. The data also reveal that the proportion that would consider moving to a local entrepreneurial venture is also very similar whether or not they have school-aged children in their household. Thirty-three percent of respondents with school-age children would consider a local venture compared to 31 percent of respondents without school-aged children. These last three comparisons suggest that the data do not simply reflect that those with school-aged children are risk averse and do not wish to change jobs. Overall, the data in Table 5.12 show that the general pattern of results holds whether or not respondents have school aged children in their household.

Table 5.13 presents the data separated by those who are in dual career situations and those who are not. These results parallel the previous split of the data. Consistent with my expectation, those who are not in dual career situations are more likely to consider relocating. Thirty-six percent of respondents not in dual careers situations would consider an intra-firm transfer that

Table 5.13 Employment scenarios: by dual career

Scenario	Likely and Extremely Likely to Consider (% Respondents)	
	Dual Career	Not Dual Career
Company transfer out of metropolitan area—possibility of local opportunity in the future	26	36
Company transfer out of metropolitan area—no local opportunity in the future	32	40
Opportunity in same industry but different firm and different metropolitan area	19	23
Opportunity in different industry but same metropolitan area	53	48
Opportunity at a start-up in the same metropolitan area	33	30
Opportunity at a start-up in different metropolitan area	9	9

Table 5.14 Employment scenarios: by raised in Minnesota

Scenario	Likely and Extremely Likely to Consider (% Respondents)	
	Raised in Minnesota	Not Raised in Minnesota
Company transfer out of metropolitan area—possibility of local opportunity in the future	26	37
Company transfer out of metropolitan area—no local opportunity in the future	29	45
Opportunity in same industry but different firm and different metropolitan area	18	27
Opportunity in different industry but same metropolitan area	53	53
Opportunity at a start-up in the same metropolitan area	33	30
Opportunity at a start-up in different metropolitan area	8	11

required relocation, whereas 26 percent with dual careers would consider the transfer. Likewise, 23 percent of respondents not in dual careers situations would consider an opportunity in the same industry but in a different metropolitan area; compared to 19 percent for respondents in dual career situations. Fifty-three percent of those in dual careers would consider an opportunity where they would change industry but not have relocate; whereas 48 percent of those without dual careers would consider this option. In parallel, the percentage that would consider a move to a small venture in the region was very similar: 33 percent of those with dual career situations and 30 percent of those not with dual career situations would consider the opportunity. The data in Table 5.13 continue to show that the general pattern of results holds whether or not respondents are in dual career situations.

Finally, Table 5.14 splits the data by those who were raised in Minnesota and compares it to those who were not raised in Minnesota. These data show that respondents who were not raised in Minnesota are more likely to consider opportunities that would require relocation. Again, this is consistent with my expectations. For instance, 37 percent of respondents raised outside of Minnesota would consider an intra-firm transfer that required relocation, whereas 27 percent of respondents raised in Minnesota would consider the transfer. Likewise, respondents who would consider an opportunity in the same industry but in a different metropolitan area is 27 percent for those raised outside of Minnesota compared to18 percent for respondents raised in Minnesota. However, the proclivity to consider an opportunity requiring switching industries in the same metropolitan area is equal between the groups at 53 percent. In parallel, the percentage of respondents who would consider a move to a small venture in the region was very similar: 33 percent of those raised in Minnesota and 30 percent of those raised outside of Minnesota

131

responded that they would consider the opportunity. Once again, the general pattern of results holds across these subsamples. This is important to show that the affinity to considering jobs in the region is not solely a reflection of preferences by those who were raised in Minnesota.

SUMMARY OF THE JOB MOBILITY DATA

Overall, the survey data lend support to the dynamic I present in Chapter 3. I show there is notable movement of managerial and administrative talent in the Minneapolis-St. Paul region. This level of movement is more pronounced than job moves into the region.

The data also capture differences in individuals' willingness to consider various job opportunities. Overall, I find that respondents are much more likely to consider leveraging their skills in a new industry—provided that they do not have to relocate—than they are to consider a within-company transfer or an opportunity in the same industry that requires relocating. In addition, their likelihood to consider moving to a start-up venture in their current location is approximately the same as their likelihood to consider a within-company transfer to a new metropolitan area.

These preferences among job opportunities are robust across many demographic characteristics. Although the pattern is pronounced for respondents with school-aged children in their household, those in dual career situations, and individuals raised in Minnesota, the overall pattern holds for respondents without these characteristics. This variation helps identify some important elements that make the mobility effect stronger. Moreover, the results also highlight the pervasiveness of the underlying effect.

Talent Migration

The data in the preceding section demonstrate greater employee mobility across companies in the region than migration into the region for the respondents' previous two jobs. Although mobility plays a pronounced role, the data also suggest that migration is important. Many data elements from the survey support this.

I return to the data in Table 5.5 that show where respondents were raised as a child. Recall that a minority of survey participants (35 percent) is raised in the Minneapolis-St. Paul region. Of the respondents who were raised in Minneapolis-St. Paul, 59 percent attended college and graduate school—if they went to graduate school—in the Minneapolis-St. Paul metropolitan area. As a result, only 20 percent of the respondents were raised in Minneapolis-St. Paul and obtained all of their post-secondary schooling in the region. This means that 80 percent of the surveyed workforce decided to migrate to Minneapolis-St. Paul at some point in time. Moreover, of this 20 percent of respondents who were raised in Minneapolis-St. Paul and obtained all of their post-secondary schooling in the region, 25 percent spent part of their professional career outside of the metropolitan area.

Therefore, migration plays a very important role in building the regional talent base and can be under appreciated by focusing only on respondents' recent job history. Although a large proportion of respondents who are not raised in Minneapolis-St. Paul are raised elsewhere in the state or in neighboring states, it is a strong assumption to believe that they would necessarily migrate to the Minneapolis-St. Paul metropolitan area. Even though Minneapolis-St. Paul is the proximate urban center for a vast area of the north-central United States, individuals from this area could continue to live where they were raised or where they went to school. Alternatively they could choose to move to other metropolitan centers, whether within or beyond the area. For this reason, it is important to assess migration in order to understand the talent base of the Minneapolis-St. Paul region.

WHAT ATTRACTED WORKING PROFESSIONALS TO THE REGION?
Because the region's workforce is not merely a reflection of inertia, conscious choice to live in region impacts the regional workforce. To assess what attracts managerial and administrative talent to the region, I choose to focus on the experiences of individuals who worked in another location and chose to relocate to the Minneapolis-St. Paul region. To do this, I ask respondents to identify if they had worked and lived in another metropolitan area over the course of their career. By asking if they worked and lived in a different location I wish to isolate survey participants whose professional lives have been in areas beyond the Minneapolis-St. Paul region. Forty-two percent of survey participants indicate that they have lived and worked elsewhere.

If respondents answer that they worked and lived elsewhere, I then ask them to identify up to two different locations where they worked and lived—focusing on the two where the spent the most time if they worked and lived in more than two places. These data show great variety in the workforce's previous geographic locations. Eighteen percent respond that they worked and lived outside of the United States—identifying forty-five different countries. For those with work experience in the United States but outside of the Minneapolis-St. Paul region, their experience is in forty-five states (including Minnesota outside of the Minneapolis-St. Paul region), Puerto Rico, and the District of Columbia.

To assess these respondents' motivation to move to the Minneapolis-St. Paul region, I ask the open-ended question, "What motivated your move?" I choose to provide opportunity for an open-ended response because I do not want to seed responses or restrict responses to a set of motivations that

Table 5.15 Motivations for relocating to Minneapolis-St. Paul

Motivation for Relocating	Respondents %[1]
Job-related (self or spouse)	65
Family/Friends/Relationships	36
Other quality of life factors	20
School (self or children)	8

Notes: [1]Data from an open-ended question where respondents could list as many reasons as they wanted. Therefore, percentages add up to over 100%.

I predetermined. Therefore, survey participants are open to provide any answer to this question. An advantage of asking this question directly is that this is not a hypothetical question. Each respondent relocated to the Minneapolis-St. Paul region. Because relocating is a meaningful life event and it can be emotionally and monetarily costly, I expect that all respondents were cognizant of their motivations to move.

I summarize the motivations in Table 5.15. Although there are more nuanced responses, I classify responses into the following broad categories. First, the motivation was job-related—whether the employment opportunity was theirs or their spouse's. Second, the move was for family, friends, or other relationships. I consider this a quality of life factor because it is a factor outside of employment. Moreover, in seeing the data, when respondents mention that they moved for family reasons that often encapsulates motivations like moving for schools or other factors that will keep their family happy. Third, the move was for quality of life factors that do not revolve around family, friends, or other relationships. This includes stated motivations such as "quality of life," "culture," and "amenities." Finally, I identify if the motivation was explicitly education-related—either for the respondent or the respondent's children.

Because this is an open-ended response, participants can provide several motivations. For this reason, the sum of the percentages in Table 5.15 is greater than 100 percent. The motivation with the highest frequency of responses reflects job-related motivations. Approximately two-thirds (65 percent) of respondents list a motivation that centers on the respondent's employment or their spouse's employment. This is consistent with my argument that for this talent base, job-related issues are the primary determinant of talent attraction.

Approximately one-third of respondents (36 percent) identify quality of life factors attributable to family, friends, or other relationships as their motivation to move to Minneapolis-St. Paul. One-fifth (20 percent) of respondents identify other quality of life factors; and 8 percent of respondents identify education. If I combine all of these non-employment-related factors, they are present in 52 percent of all responses. Recall individuals can report multiple responses so this is not the simple sum of the underlying three categories. Fifty-two percent is notably less than the percentage of respondents who identify employment-related motivations and further reinforces my conclusion that employment plays the central role in attracting this talent base.

WHAT AFFECTS ATTRACTION TO OTHER REGIONS?

I use the experiences of those who decided to move from another region to assess what affects talent attraction to the Minneapolis-St. Paul region. The benefit of these data is that I rely on the actual experiences of survey participants to assess what motivated their move. To corroborate these findings, I ask all survey participants to rate the importance of nineteen different quality of life factors *if they were considering whether or not to move to a different location*. These questions appear after the open-ended questions about relocation so as not to seed the open-ended questions with quality of life dimensions that I assess here.

The quality of life factors I ask respondents to consider include elements such as family nearby, low taxes, good climate, and availability of good jobs. The first column of Table 5.16 lists all of the factors that I include. As reflected in the wording of the question, my intent is not to ask if respondents valued these factors overall—but to assess their value under the specific circumstance of considering relocating.

Table 5.16 Quality of life factors if considering to relocate

Quality of Life Factor	Very or Extremely Important (% Respondents)
Availability of good jobs for me	90
Strong local economy	76
Good place to raise children	72
Good quality public schools	69
Availability of high quality healthcare (e.g., high quality medical facilities nearby)	67
Outdoor activities (e.g., parks, water sports, wilderness areas)	67
Availability of good jobs for my spouse/significant other	65
Favorable cost of living	62
Family located nearby	55
Amenities such as restaurants and shopping	55
Community that shares my values	54
Good transportation/easy to get around	53
Ease of travel to other US or international cities	45
Good climate	45
Friends located nearby	44
Availability of cultural events (e.g., music and theater)	43
Low taxes	36
Availability of professional and college sports events	26
Strong religious community with which I am affiliated	20

I code the importance of these quality of life factors on a five-point scale with the following options: (1) Not at all important, (2) Somewhat important, (3) Important, (4) Very important, and (5) Extremely important. I randomize the order that the respondents see these factors in order to mitigate the chance that the order of presentation biases response. To most effectively display the results, I present the percentage of survey participants who indicate that a factor is very important or extremely important (i.e., 4 or 5 on the five-point scale). The interpretation of the results does not materially change if I examine mean values of these scales. Column 2 of Table 5.16 presents these data.

Before delving into the results, I wish to highlight the significant variation in the scores across factors. This is noteworthy because each factor is a positive quality of life indicator. They are all "good" things. For example, "good" climate, "good" public schools, and "low" taxes. If survey participants are not thoughtful in answering this question, then they would rate all factors as important and there would be little variance in the data. With the wide range of values across these quality of life factors, it appears that survey participants engaged and carefully in evaluated what dimensions they considered important and what dimension they did not consider important.

Turning to the results, the five most important quality of life factors that this workforce identifies (with the percent that rate them very or extremely important in parentheses) include availability of good jobs for me (90), strong local economy (76), good place to raise children (72), good quality public schools (69), and availability of high quality healthcare tied with outdoor activities (67).

The first two are especially noteworthy because they represent economic factors as key to affecting the desire to relocate—as I have consistently highlighted. These responses parallel the data regarding participants' stated motivations to relocate to the Minneapolis-St. Paul metropolitan area. The seventh highest ranked factor (with 65 percent of indicating that it is very or extremely important) is the "availability of good jobs for my spouse/significant other." To calibrate the importance of this factor, recall that 85 percent of the sample is married and 69 percent of them indicate they are in dual career situations. If all of these respondents responded that jobs for their spouse was very or extremely important and only these respondents thought that this factor was very or extremely important, then the response rate for very and extremely important on this factor would be approximately 59 percent (69 percent of 85 percent). However, 65 percent of the sample rates this as very or extremely important. This indicates that many of the non-married respondents or married respondents not currently in dual career situations express the importance of dual career opportunities where they live.

The next two elements—good place to raise children and good public schools—focus on issues related to raising children. Again, this is consistent with the data showing that those with school-aged children in their household are especially hesitant to leave the Minneapolis-St. Paul metropolitan area. It is also interesting to note that this effect appears to be much more pronounced than to only reflect the immediate concerns of households with school-aged children. To see this, note that 70 percent of respondents find this very or extremely important. The demographic summary show that that 47 percent of respondents have school-aged children at home. This suggests that many respondents who currently do not have school-aged children consider this important. It is an open question of whether this is something that they want in the future or something indicative of other quality of life factors that they value in the community.

The final two factors in the top five are also quality of life factors that that reflect regional amenities. One is the availability of healthcare. The other is access to outdoors recreation.

The lowest five responses are (with the percent that rate them very or extremely important in parentheses): strong religious community with which I am affiliated (20), availability of professional and college sports events (26), low taxes (36), availability of cultural events (43), and friends located nearby (44).

This is an interesting list with some surprises. Low taxes, availability of sporting events, and availability of cultural events are all on this list. Keeping in mind that respondents are high-income individuals, I would expect that they be more sensitive to tax burden compared to lower income individuals in the region. Also, because of the costs of attending professional sporting events, these individuals have the financial means to do so and having attended college they have collegiate ties and likely have greater motivation to attend these events. However, this does not appear important. Likewise, one might expect that the availability of cultural events should play a more important role because this population is highly educated and high-earning. However, this too does not appear in the data.

An interesting pattern begins to emerge when one considers the elements at the top of the list and those at the bottom of the list. For many individuals, the lower ranked items are issues that they tend not to experience on a day-to-day basis. For example, interactions with their religious community, sporting events, cultural events, and interactions with friends are often not daily interactions. The elements that appear most important have a more consistent influence. For instance economic condition and family situation would appear to have more day-to-day impact on an individual.

Having identified the overall results, I want to assess the stability of the quality of life ratings across subsets of the survey respondents. I choose two splits that can potentially produce different findings. First, I split among those with school-age children in their household and those without school-age children in their household. Second, among those with college degrees

137

Table 5.17 Quality of life factors if considering to relocate: by school-aged child in household

Quality of Life Factor	Very or Extremely Important (% respondents)	
	School-aged Child in Household	No School-aged Child in Household
Good place to raise children	93	53
Availability of good jobs for me	92	87
Good quality public schools	86	53
Strong local economy	76	77
Outdoor activities (e.g., parks, water sports, wilderness areas)	69	65
Availability of high quality healthcare (e.g., high quality medical facilities nearby)	67	68
Availability of good jobs for my spouse/ significant other	65	64
Favorable cost of living	61	63
Community that shares my values	56	52
Family located nearby	54	55
Amenities such as restaurants and shopping	50	59
Good transportation/easy to get around	50	56
Good climate	44	46
Friends located nearby	42	45
Ease of travel to other US or international cities	40	50
Availability of cultural events (e.g., music and theater)	37	48
Low taxes	35	37
Availability of professional and college sports events	27	25
Strong religious community with which I am affiliated	22	18

I split by those who obtained their undergraduate degree in 1997 or later from those who obtained their undergraduate degree in 1996 or prior. This will tend to map to those who are 40 and under, and those who are over 40—respectively.

Table 5.17 presents the rankings split by those with school-age children and those without school age children. Although this is an important difference among survey respondents, the pattern of results is not markedly different. Expectedly, the importance of good schools and the environment to raise children are more important for the group with school-aged children. However, the other rankings are very similar. Moreover, over half of the respondents in the group without school-aged children consider good public schools and a good environment to raise children as very or extremely important. The ratings across those with and without school-aged children are so similar that the correlation of the importance of quality of life factors across the two groups is 0.78.

Table 5.18 presents the ranking split by when the respondent graduated from college. Here the overall rankings of quality of life dimensions show even less variation than in the previous table. The correlation of ratings between

Table 5.18 Quality of life factors if considering to relocate: by year of undergraduate degree

Quality of Life Factor	Very or Extremely Important (% Respondents)	
	Undergraduate Degree Prior to 1997	Undergraduate Degree 1997 or Later
Availability of good jobs for me	89	91
Strong local economy	78	73
Availability of high quality healthcare (e.g., high quality medical facilities nearby)	69	64
Outdoor activities (e.g., parks, water sports, wilderness areas)	69	64
Good place to raise children	69	77
Good quality public schools	66	72
Favorable cost of living	62	62
Availability of good jobs for my spouse/significant other	60	73
Community that shares my values	57	50
Amenities such as restaurants and shopping	56	53
Good transportation/easy to get around	55	50
Family located nearby	54	56
Availability of cultural events (e.g., music and theater)	48	34
Ease of travel to other US or international cities	48	41
Good climate	48	40
Friends located nearby	44	44
Low taxes	37	34
Availability of professional and college sports events	27	24
Strong religious community with which I am affiliated	22	17

those who graduated prior to 1997 and those who graduated in 1997 or later is 0.94, which is exceedingly high. Therefore, in these data I see little divergence in the factors that respondents consider important when relocating based on this age split.

WHAT KEEPS EXISTING TALENT FROM RELOCATING?

In order to assess what affects retention, I use two different approaches. First, I follow on from the quality of life factors that respondents deem important when considering moving to a different region with questions on their beliefs of how the Minneapolis-St. Paul region fares on each of these quality of life factors. From here I assess how the region's performance on these dimensions match what respondents consider import. Second, I ask if survey participants would prefer to live elsewhere. If they respond affirmatively, I inquire what prevents them from moving. I describe the results from each set of analysis, in turn.

I ask for respondents' perceptions of how the Minneapolis-St. Paul metropolitan area performs relative to other regions on the nineteen quality of life

Table 5.19 Quality of life factors: performance of Minneapolis-St. Paul relative to other regions

Quality of Life Factor	Minneapolis-St. Paul Performs Very or Extremely Well (% Respondents)
Good place to raise children	93
Availability of high quality healthcare (e.g., high quality medical facilities nearby)	93
Outdoor activities (e.g., parks, water sports, wilderness areas)	92
Amenities such as restaurants and shopping	88
Availability of cultural events (e.g., music and theater)	88
Availability of professional and college sports events	85
Availability of good jobs for me	83
Good quality public schools	81
Ease of travel to other US or international cities	81
Strong local economy	78
Friends located nearby	78
Availability of good jobs for my spouse/significant other	76
Family located nearby	72
Community that shares my values	70
Strong religious community with which I am affiliated	67
Favorable cost of living	42
Good transportation/easy to get around	42
Good climate	17
Low taxes	7

factors that I previously introduced. I use a five-point scale ranging from (1) Does not perform well at all to (5) Performs extremely well. Again, I randomize the presentation order of these questions to insulate against the possibility that question ordering affects responses. Table 5.19 presents the percentage of survey participants who indicate that the Minneapolis-St. Paul region performs very well or extremely well on each dimension.

Once again, I see significant variation in responses across these dimensions. Some factors—such as availability of quality healthcare—have almost unanimous response that the Minneapolis-St. Paul region performs very or extremely well. Others—such as low taxes—have only a small fraction of the survey participants indicating that the Minneapolis-St. Paul region performs well.

The five highest responses include (with the percentage that rate Minneapolis-St. Paul performs very or extremely well in parentheses): good place to raise children (93), availability of high quality healthcare (93), outdoor activities (92), amenities such as restaurants and shopping (88), and availability of cultural events (88). Not only are these ratings very high, for all five factors 1 percent or less of respondents rate these as 1 or 2 on the scale.

Only four of the nineteen quality of life factors have less than majority support that the Minneapolis-St. Paul region performs very or extremely well compared to other locations. These factors are (with the percentage that rate Minneapolis-St. Paul performs very or extremely well in parentheses): low taxes (7), good climate (17), good transportation/easy to get around (42), and favorable cost of living (42). Although the rating of cost of living and good transportation are relatively low compared to the other ratings, only a minority of respondents reports that the metropolitan area does not fare well. Sixteen percent of respondents report that cost of living does not fare well (scores it 1 or 2 on the five-point scale), and 20 percent of respondents report that transportation does not fare well.

In comparison, a minority of respondents—17 percent—report that the climate is good relative to other areas; yet 50 percent report that the metropolitan area does not fare well. Finally, only 7 percent report that taxes are favorable compared to other regions. Almost two-thirds (65 percent) report that the metropolitan area does not fare well.

Three patterns in the data warrant comment and likely contribute to the high retention rate of managerial and professional talent within the Minneapolis-St. Paul region. First, all but four factors show that over half of the survey participants believe that the region performs very well. Second, of the factors that the survey participants report Minneapolis-St. Paul performs poorly, these coincide with the factors that the survey participants do not consider important when assessing relocating. Third, among the most highly ranked factors are the factors that the survey participants indicate are the most important if considering relocating.

I investigate if the assessment of how the Minneapolis-St. Paul region fares compared to other regions varies across the subsets of the sample that I examined previously. I assess how the responses compare between those with school-age children in their household in contrast to those without; and those who graduated college prior to 1997 in contrast to those who graduated in 1997 or later. The results show very little difference in either comparison. The nineteen quality of life factors scores for those with and without school-aged children in their household correlates at 0.99. The correlation among the nineteen quality of life factors for those who graduated college prior to 1997 and for those who graduated in 1997 or later is also 0.99. Because the rankings are so similar across these groups, I do not to present them separately.

PREFERENCE TO LIVE ELSEWHERE
Another question that I ask all survey participants is whether there is another place that they would prefer to live. Directly asking this question, aids my assessment of what factors play an important role for retaining talent. This also allows me to assess if quality of life factors play different roles in attracting and retaining talent.

Twenty-eight percent of the survey participants respond that there is another place where they would prefer to live. That, of course, translates to over 70 percent of the survey participants indicating that there is not a place that they would rather live. Although I cannot calibrate the response of this question across metropolitan areas, the magnitude is large and is consistent with the migration data showing high retention rates in the Minneapolis-St. Paul metropolitan area. The percentage of respondents who answer affirmatively does not vary much across different demographic segments. For example, for those with school-aged children at home 27 percent report that there is another place where they would rather live; for those without school-aged children at home 29 percent report that there is another place where they would rather live. This difference is not statically significant. Among those who are married, those in dual career situations 25 percent report that there is another place where they would rather live; for those not in dual career situations 31 percent report that there is another place where they would rather live. This difference is statistically significant but arguably the difference in magnitude is not exceedingly large. Finally, those with college degrees granted in 1997 or later (likely under 40 years of age) report the same likelihood that there is another place where they would rather live to those whose college degrees are prior to 1997—at 28 percent.

For the survey participants who indicate that they would rather live elsewhere, I ask them to identify the location. Ninety-four percent of list locations are in the United States. The five most prevalent states are California (19 percent), Colorado (13 percent), Florida (8 percent), Texas (8 percent) and Arizona (7 percent). Only one other country—Canada—had more than five mentions (i.e., greater than 1 percent of responses).

After identifying survey participants who would prefer to live elsewhere, I ask what prevents them from moving there. Once again, this leverages the advantages of collecting primary data on a focal population. Although I can infer what quality of life factors relate to whether someone would prefer to live elsewhere, directly asking this question is possible. Many people may have actively considered moves and ruled them out or have not actively considered moves because of the situation in which they find themselves. For example, not wanting to move children or being caregivers to parents. In either situation, respondents should have little problem detailing their choices.

Table 5.20 compiles the reasons presented. As in the question that assesses why respondents move to the Minneapolis-St. Paul metropolitan area, this is an open-ended question. I ask this question before the questions that present the quality of life dimensions, in order not to seed potential responses. I collapse the responses into five categories: job-related (self or spouse), family/friends/relationships, cost/hassle of relocating, other quality of life factors, and retirement/timing. The last category reflects desires to move to other (often warmer) locations upon retirement.

These data show that employment opportunities and quality of life factors play a similar role in retaining talent. Fifty-two percent of respondents state

Table 5.20 Motivations for not relocating from Minneapolis-St. Paul

Motivation for Not Relocating[1]	Respondents %[2]
Job	52
Family/Friends/Relationships	51
Cost/Hassle of Relocating	17
Other Quality of Life Factors	7
Retirement/Timing	5

Notes: [1] Sample restricted to respondents who indicate they would prefer to live elsewhere. [2] Data from an open-ended question where respondents could list as many reasons as they wanted. Therefore, percentages add up to over 100%.

that family/friends/relationship keep them from moving and 52 percent of respondents state that job-related issues keep them from moving. When I combine the quality of life-related categories "family/friends/relationships" and "other quality of life factors" into one category, 56 percent of respondents identify this general overall quality of life affect. This is greater than those who highlight job-related factors, although the difference is not statistically significant.

SUMMARY OF THE JOB MOBILITY DATA

The survey data provide broad-based support for several insights with respect to migration that I introduce in Chapter 3. First, the data support the claim that job factors are of primary importance when it comes to attracting professional managerial and administrative talent to a region. By having respondents describe what motivated their move to the region, I see that quality of life factors—including family/friends/relationships—play a less important role.

Second, both quality of life factors and job factors play an important role in retaining talent. When I ask why people do not move to a place where they would prefer to live, job and quality of life factors play an equally important role. The magnitude to which job factors affect retention in this situation is less than its impact on attraction. The magnitude to which non-job-related quality of life factors affect retention is greater for retention than it is for attraction.

Finally, the data show that the region fares very well on a number of quality of life factors. Nevertheless, there is variance on a factor-by-factor basis. However, the factors in which the region fares worse are fewer than in which it fares very well. The specific factors where it fares worse are also the factors that respondents note are relatively less important when considering to relocate. The match between what respondents desire in a new location and their perceptions of how the Minneapolis-St. Paul area fares along these dimensions, explains why over 70 percent of those surveyed indicate that there was not another metropolitan area in which they would prefer to live.

Advantages and Disadvantages of Living the Region

In addition to questions about migration to and from the Minneapolis-St. Paul region, I survey individuals' perceptions of the advantages and disadvantages of living in the region. To assess this, I ask two opened-end questions, "What are some of the biggest advantages" of living the Minneapolis-St. Paul area and "What are some of the biggest disadvantages" of living in the area. I ask these open-ended questions prior to the nineteen quality of life dimensions to avoid priming or prompting certain responses.

ADVANTAGES

Respondents are very engaged with this question. Many list several different advantages of living in the Minneapolis-St. Paul region—in part, because there is no character limit to the response. Very few respondents (5 percent) leave this question blank. Of the 95 percent who answer, they list between one and sixteen advantages, with the average response consisting of 4.7 advantages. Table 5.21 summarizes the ten most frequent responses. Because respondents can list multiple advantages, the total sums to greater than 100 percent. In trying to stay as specific as possible to the respondents' statements, I am not aggressive in combining similar answers. For example, I leave separate "attitude of the people who live in the region," which is an advantage 13 percent of respondents identify, from "mid-western values," which is an advantage 2 percent of respondents identify.

Table 5.21 Advantages of living in Minneapolis-St. Paul

Advantage[1]	Respondents %[2]
Schools	35
Family	30
Recreation	27
Music/Art Scene	22
Culture	21
Weather	17
Job opportunities	17
Sports teams	16
Lakes/Rivers	14
People	13

Notes: [1]Ten most frequent responses presented. [2]Data from an open-ended question where respondents could list as many reasons as they wanted. Therefore, percentages add up to over 100%.

The most frequent response, with over a third mentioning it, is the existence of good schools and quality education. This is followed by family (30 percent). Next comes recreation, which includes the possibility of indoor and outdoor hobbies (27 percent). The following two responses are the music/art scene (22 percent) and culture more generally (19 percent). Interestingly, weather is listed as an advantage by 17 percent of respondents. Many of these responses explicitly note the existence of four seasons. Rounding out the list are job opportunities (17 percent), various local sports teams (16 percent), lakes and rivers (14 percent), and attitude of the people who live in the region (13 percent).

DISADVANTAGES

As with the advantages, the vast majority of respondents provide an answer to this question—only 8 percent leave it blank. However, the disadvantages are more focused than the advantages. Those who answer listed between one and eight disadvantages, with an average of two.

Table 5.22 presents the six most frequent answers. I report only six because all other responses are mentioned in less than 5 percent of cases. The most frequently listed disadvantage is the weather, especially winter, with 76 percent of respondents highlighting this. I should note that many companies launched the survey in April of 2014, which was a month with an abnormal number of late-season snowfalls. Although this might have amplified the sentiment, the overall results are not misleading because this is a frequent response in other time periods when I fielded the survey. The second most prevalent response is taxes with 21 percent of respondents noting this. The only other response noted by more than 10 percent of respondents is traffic and commute (20 percent). The next three responses are public transit—the lack of options (8 percent), cost of living (5 percent), and road system/infrastructure (5 percent).

Table 5.22 Disadvantages of living in Minneapolis-St. Paul

Disadvantage[1]	Respondents %[2]
Weather	76
Taxes	21
Traffic/Commute	20
Public Transportation	8
Cost of living	6
Road systems/infrastructure	5

Notes: [1]All responses with 5 percent or greater. [2]Data from an open-ended question where respondents could list as many reasons as they wanted. Therefore, percentages add up to over 100%.

SUMMARY OF ADVANTAGES AND DISADVANTAGES OF LIVING IN THE REGION

These data map very closely with other data I capture about how respondents rate Minneapolis on nineteen quality of life factors. This highlights the validity of the data because different types of questions produce very consistent findings. In addition, the similarity between the open-ended questions and the nineteen quality of life factors assure me that the nineteen dimensions do not miss important elements of respondents' perceptions about the advantages and disadvantages of living in the region.

These data also reinforce that respondents tend to find many more advantages than disadvantages to living in the region. Moreover, the advantages tend to map closely to the quality of life factors that they consider important when relocating. The disadvantages do not map closely to the quality of life factors that they consider important when relocating. These observations further suggest that the low out-migration rate from the region stems from a match between the demands of this talent pool and the amenities that the region provides.

These data also highlight that what people consider the greatest advantages of a region are not necessarily the factors they find most important when considering whether or not to move to a region. Because there might be overwhelming agreement in what disadvantages exist, those too might not drive migration decisions. This suggests that sorting out preferences—as I designed many parts of the survey to do—is more important than showing how a region performs in quality of life dimensions when assessing the determinants of migration to and from a region.

Summary

I develop a proprietary survey and gather data from approximately 3,000 professional managerial and administrative employees in twenty-three headquarters within the Minneapolis-St. Paul region. The motivation of the survey is to collect primary data and allow me to confirm or disconfirm elements of the dynamic that I argue underlies a headquarters economy. The data are consistent with my arguments. The survey data also allow me to better highlight the factors that drive mobility and migration.

Managers

The survey data confirm many of the observations and generalizations about this talent pool; which in turn, are central to predicting important factors that affect this talent pools' mobility across companies and migration into the region. I confirm that this group is well-educated. Ninety-three percent have a college degree and 41 percent have a graduate degree. They come from households with relatively high income. Thirty-seven percent of survey participants were in households earning over US$200,000 per year. A majority is in a dual career situation. Of the 85 percent who are married, 69 percent report that they are balancing dual careers. Forty-seven percent of the respondents report having school aged children. In addition, a very high proportion sends their children to public schools.

Mobility

The survey data also provide evidence of job mobility that supports my explanation of what drives a headquarters economy. Many note that their previous position (or the one before that) was in a different industry than their current position. Moreover, the percentage that reports this is higher than reports that their previous position was in a different metro area.

To better assess the proclivity of the professional managerial and administrative talent to apply their skills across industries rather than to look for opportunities in the same industry in a different location, I present survey participants with hypothetical job opportunities. Using a career advancing relocation outside of the Minneapolis-St. Paul metropolitan area within their current employer as a benchmark, I find the following. They are much more inclined to consider a career advancing opportunity in a different industry within the Minneapolis-St. Paul region compared to a relocation with their current employer. They are just as likely to consider a move to a small start-up company within the Minneapolis-St. Paul region as they are to consider a relocation with their current employer. They are less likely to consider an opportunity outside of the region in the same industry with a different company than they are to consider a relocation with their current employer. Overall, these data point to the potential for managerial and administrative talent to consider opportunities in the regional that leverage their skills across companies than to consider opportunities that require relocation.

Migration

The data also provide insights into the migration of this talent base to and from the region. Because a small minority of the workforce is raised, educated, and spend their entire career in the Minneapolis-St. Paul metropolitan area (15 percent), migration plays an important role in building this talent base. Although the majority who migrate to the metropolitan area are raised in Minnesota or from neighboring states, a sizable portion of the talent pool come from beyond the region. Moreover, a significant portion of the workforce has work experience in other geographic areas.

To gauge what affects mitigation into Minneapolis-St. Paul, I ask those who have work experience in other locations why they moved to the region. The primary determinant is economic opportunity—jobs for them or their spouse. Quality of life factors are also mentioned; however, much less frequently than job-related factors. I also ask survey participants if there was another place that they would prefer to live; and if so, what prevents them from moving there. A minority of those surveyed—just over a quarter of respondents—reply that they would rather live elsewhere. When I ask why they do not move, economic opportunity and quality of life factors play much more equal roles. Overall, the data support my expectation that job opportunities primarily drive attraction to the region; whereas, job opportunities and quality of life factors affect retention.

Finally, I report how survey respondents assess the importance of nineteen quality of life factors if considering moving to a different location. These data show great variation in the importance that respondents place on different quality of life factors. Of greatest importance are factors related to economic opportunity and raising families. Of least importance are factors related to religious communities, sports teams, low taxes, and cultural events. When I ask respondents to assess how the Minneapolis-St. Paul metropolitan area performs on these same dimensions compared to other regions, the majority of respondents state that Minneapolis-Paul performs very or extremely well in all but four factors. The factors where respondents rate the region poorly are the factors that respondents consider of least importance.

Combined, the data suggest that one of the reasons for low outward mobility in the Minneapolis-St. Paul metropolitan area is a strong mapping between the regional factors that this talent base values and the benefits that the region provides.

6

Headquarters Economy Attributes and Strategy/Policy Foundations

The previous chapters provide evidence that managers, mobility, and migration are key building blocks to a headquarters economy. Having identified these building blocks, I highlight the implications that this has for interested parties wishing to build or sustain a headquarters economy. This includes policy makers, who want to foster this approach to economic development. It also includes corporate managers, who want to find ways in which to foster competitive advantage by tapping regional benefits of where they locate their headquarters operations.

Why Focus on a Headquarters Economy?

A headquarters economy is an engine for regional economic and social vitality. Nevertheless, this is not the only path to regional prosperity. Economic and social vitality in many regions revolve around other drivers of success. For example, many highlight how industry clusters drive a region's economic and social vitality (e.g., Porter, 1990; Saxenian, 1994). Others highlight how the creative economy and its requisite talent base contribute to economic and social prosperity (Florida, 2002).

The possibility that there are different paths to prosperity is important to acknowledge when drawing implications from my research. For this reason, I do not suggest that all regions should strive to create a headquarters economy. Some regions will be better served by pursing other paths. Nevertheless, there are benefits that stem from a headquarters economy that are not necessarily prevalent in other paths to prosperity. I highlight several.

First, in most instances professional management skills (i.e., skill of the talent pool that form the basis of a headquarters economy) are not industry bound. This means that temporal market forces that favor or disfavor certain companies or industries can be accommodated by the adaptability and transferability of this talent base's skills. These individuals' skills are redeployable in many companies and industries. This is especially important because headquarters jobs can be transitory due to the inherent turbulence in companies and industries. Companies merge, are acquired, transition into and out of product lines, and sometimes fail. Industries are born, mature, and often decline. Having a pool of workers whose economic future is not tied to one employer—or even to one industry—affords a region greater adaptability when confronted with economic forces beyond its control.

Of course, this is not to say that the talent base that forms the other paths to regional prosperity is inadaptable or is stuck with a focused skill set. However, as I discuss and demonstrate in Chapter 3, there are many examples where managerial talent can easily move into seemingly unrelated businesses and find ways in which to deploy their skills effectively.

Second, a headquarters economy—as I define it—is a diverse economy. Diversification has the benefit to limit the amplitude of swings in the economy for a community. Regions where there are concentrations of industries are often not afforded this. The potential benefits of avoiding amplified contractions in the economy are obvious. In fact, a place like the Minneapolis-St. Paul metro area weathered the great recession with lower unemployment than all but one other major metropolitan area in the United States, Washington, DC, over that period.[1]

The benefits of less amplified up-swings in the economy might not be as readily apparent. However, when economies are over-heated several factors can limit growth and lead to social problems that offset economic advantages. For example, increased demand on a region's infrastructure can have an adverse effect on quality of life. Home prices might rise, schools might be stretched to capacity, and transportation systems become extremely congested. This is less likely to occur under the condition of more tempered or consistent growth.

A diversified economy will also accelerate the movement of individuals and ideas between companies compared to industry-focused economies, because a diversified economy mitigates the effectiveness of worker non-compete agreements. As Marx (2011) notes, nearly half of technological employees in the United States sign non-compete agreements and such agreements decrease employee mobility (Marx et al., 2009). However, in a region with diversified companies, where employees are likely to move across industries, non-compete agreements are unlikely to decrease mobility because the employee would not be moving between competitors.[2]

Third, in addition to the diversification benefits that regions experience from housing companies from different industries, corporate headquarters provide more stable employment during industry and regional economic downturns compared to other types of establishments (Kolko and Neumark, 2010). This makes a region with a high concentration of headquarters less prone to experience large employment swings compared to a region with fewer headquarters—even if the business distribution across industries is identical (with the non-headquartered jobs being establishments such as manufacturing or research). Moreover, it suggests that a regional-specific downturn affects employment less when the region is home to headquarters and not to other types of establishments such as manufacturing plants.

Fourth, professional managerial and administrative jobs tend to be high paying jobs. There are many benefits to this. This includes the effect on the local tax base and the ability to finance quality of life amenities that this talent base demands. Higher earning individuals are also more likely to invest in philanthropic organizations that in turn affect the quality of life in the region where they live (e.g., Card et al., 2010). Like-educated and like-employed individuals tend to invest in and demand similar amenities. Therefore, concentration increases the likelihood of this talent base receiving the amenities that they desire (e.g., Waldfogel, 2007). Although this would hold true for a concentration of any type of workforce, it reinforces the other benefits I describe.

Fifth, a headquarters economy employs professional managers at all stages of their career. There are jobs better suited for novice employees and jobs that require substantial experience. As a result, employers within a headquarters economy value talent across the span of their career path. Therefore, the talent pool will comprise of those just out of college and of those with substantial experience. Employers do not necessarily rely on labor of whom a small fraction can progress in their organization. This means that headquarters economies are places where talent can make longer term investments.

Sixth, although managerial talent tends to be well-educated, it comes from a broad array of academic backgrounds and possesses many types of college degrees. As a business school professor, I firmly believe that many important managerial and technical administrative skills come from business school education. However, not all managers pick up these skills from degree programs or even formal business training. Professional managerial and administrative employees have degrees in a myriad backgrounds including liberal arts, sciences, law, healthcare, education, and engineering.

Contrast this with the technical skills that are often associated with industry clusters. For example, biotechnology research and development (R&D), or electrical engineering. These technical professionals possess much more focused academic backgrounds and training. They come from a narrower set of colleges or degree programs than the talent base that forms a headquarters economy. This means that a headquarters economy will have a much broader and more eclectic pull of talent compared to many industry clusters.

With such an array of benefits that flow from a headquarters economy, one might conclude that all regions should focus their efforts on building a headquarters economy versus other alternatives. However, I do not believe that this should be the case. An important impediment is that the underlying dynamic of a headquarters economy, creative economy, or industry cluster is one where strengths are compounded and amplified.

Therefore, the current talent base and corporate base in a region profoundly influences viable paths forward. In particular, many regions are better building from their existing strengths versus trying to start a new path forward. Regions with existing headquarters activities—including hidden headquarters—or pools of managerial and administrative talent would be in relatively better positions to build a headquarters economy.

Managerial and Administrative Talent as the Underlying Foundation

For regions or companies within regions that wish to engage in actions that enhance the formation of or sustain a headquarters economy, the research and data I present provide the structure from which to build meaningful implications. In particular, I highlight the three building blocks of a headquarters economy: managers, mobility, and migration. The logical point from which to start when drawing implications is the foundational building block—managers.

In order to draw meaningful implications, it is important to focus on individuals within the managerial and administrative talent pool and consider them as decision-makers. These individuals make many different choices that subsequently impact the creation and continuation of a headquarters economy. Among these choices are the types of investments they wish to make in their skills. They decide where to attend school, where to live, and where to work. They choose the jobs that they apply for, the jobs they accept, and the jobs they decline. They also make choices in their personal lives on whether and whom they partner with and whether and when to start families. The choices that they make are shaped by how the various alternatives affect their well-being. That includes their well-being as individuals and, depending on their life situation, the well-being of their spouse, partner, children, or extended family. As a result, the foundation for what creates and sustains a headquarters economy is the choices made by thousands, if not millions, of individuals.

The underlying demographics of the managerial and administrative talent pool shape the choices that they make. I wish to reiterate and summarize many of these demographic characteristics. I should note that many of these characteristics are found in other pools of talent. However, the entire set of characteristics make this talent pool different from many others.

Educated

The vast majority within this talent pool will possess college degrees. Many will have graduate degrees. As a result, this is a highly educated workforce. A point of differentiation compared many other talent pools is that the educational backgrounds of these individuals are heterogeneous. Not all in professional managerial and administrative roles have business school educations. Part of this reflects that some skills can be learned on the job and that analytical and interpersonal skills from other backgrounds are readily applied to business. For example, it is quite common to have individuals with liberal arts degrees working in professional managerial and administrative functions. It is unusual to have these same individuals working in technical R&D functions. Moreover, some technical administrative skills draw on a wide array of backgrounds. For example, companies often hire math or economics graduates when seeking to staff entry finance-related jobs.

High-earning

Professional managerial and administrative positions tend to be well-compensated. A high-earning population will demand certain types of amenities. For example, they are likely have greater demands for restaurants, cultural events, and sporting events compared to individuals who earn less. Because of their earning power, they are able to afford to participate in these activities. In addition, higher earning individuals are better able to make investments in regional quality of live factors because of their earning power and how that translates into increased philanthropic giving. Finally, greater earning power provides regional governments with a greater tax base and heightened ability to make public good investments.

Educated Spouses or Partners

Because this talent pool is educated, there is a very high likelihood that if they have a spouse or partner, that person will have a similar level of educational attainment. As a result, dual career concerns for professional occupations are often very salient within this talent base. Although it is likely that educational attainment might be similar, this does not mean that they share similar educational background. Therefore, regions with a variety of career opportunities might be especially valuable for this talent pool when seeking to satisfy dual career aspirations.

Child-rearing

Many in this talent pool will be in the child-rearing stages of their life when they are actively advancing in their careers. Therefore, they will often value amenities or quality of life features that revolve around raising children. This includes a safe place to live, good schools, good recreation, and other types of child-rearing amenities.

Decision-making within a Set of Interconnected Actors

Although I focus on the choices that managers make with respect to where they work and where they live, other actors and institutions influence their choices. Some influences are very direct. For example, although someone might prefer to live in a specific region, there is no guarantee that they can find suitable employment there. Or if there is a suitable employer in the region, there is no guarantee that the employer would want to hire this individual. Other influences are can be more indirect. For example, a group of neighbors start a youth sports association, which in turn is an amenity that affects the happiness of someone's children.

As I developed the arguments in Chapter 3, I noticed that four sets of actors—four constituents—repeatedly impacted individuals' decisions. These are companies, governments, non-governmental institutions, and the pool of similar talent. I discuss each in turn. In the following discussion, my focus is on the relationship between these constituents and individuals in the managerial talent pool. I do not present a broader discussion or analyses of the multitude factors that affect these constituents.

Companies

The first constituent is companies because without companies there can be no corporate headquarters. Therefore, companies are an important and indispensable actor. Companies make many decisions that affect individuals' well-being, and, turn, the decisions that these individual will make. Companies choose where they locate their operations. If they locate in more than one region, they choose how to allocate various activities across the regions in which they operate. Ultimately, they choose whom to offer jobs, whom to continue to employ, and what types of benefits and compensation to offer. These corporate decisions have a direct impact on individuals' decision calculus.

One corporate decision that I wish to highlight is the willingness to hire and onboard managers from outside of their industry. In the examples that I present in Chapter 3, each of these companies demonstrated a willingness to look outside of their industry to fill roles. In doing so, they expected some onboarding as their hire became familiar with the new industry. I have also seen instances where companies are unwilling to make such hires. To the extent that such preferences are pervasive within a region, the benefits of cross-industry managerial movement will not be realized.

Although companies' decisions directly impact the choices of individual managers, individual managers' choices also affect companies. In other words, the relationship between companies and the managerial talent tool is recip-rocal. For example, should a company wish to set up a headquarters operation in a region, there is no guarantee that the requisite talent resides there or will relocate there. Likewise, if a company offers a job to an individual, the recipi-ent of the offer has the freedom to accept or decline the offer. By highlighting the influence that companies can have on individuals' decisions, I wish to establish that they are an important and interconnected constituent. I do not suggest that they play a more important or dominant role.

Although companies affect the managerial talent pool in a region directly through employment, this is not their only influence. Most companies are active players in their communities in other ways. Many engage in philan-thropy or provide resources to the regions in which they reside. Such resources can be in the form of support to local businesses, governments, or other institutions. These company actions likely impact the decisions of individuals in the managerial talent pool—albeit in more indirect ways.

Governments

The second constituent is government. A key role that the government plays is setting the rules or the laws within the regions where this talent base works and lives. Many of these government decisions directly impact the choices that individuals make. For example, governments can affect the nature of employment contracts. Likewise, they affect employees' take-home compen-sation through taxation policies.

Governments also determine the extent and nature of public goods that they provide to residents. For example, they are often important providers of education. They provide infrastructure that facilitates transportation and recreation (e.g., parks). They make decisions with respect to public health and public safety. All of these factors influence the quality of life within a region and, in turn, can affect managerial talent's decision calculus.

Another direct role that governments play is as the employer of managerial and administrative talent. Many governmental agencies require manage-rial and administrative skills similar to what for-profit companies employ. It is for this reason that managerial and administrative talent can move between jobs in the public and private sectors. Nevertheless, government jobs alone will not create a headquarters economy. Therefore, professional managerial and administrative jobs in the public sector can complement the dynamics of a headquarters economy. However, the direct employment effect is much less pronounced than the employment provided by the private sector.

As with companies, it is important to note that although governments are important actors, their choices are reciprocally influenced by talent in a region. The most direct influence from individual managers to government is through voting in democratic regions. If government enacts policies that are not consistent with the preferences of individuals, individuals often exercise their vote to enact changes in government and policy. If not successful, individuals have the ability to move from a region when their preferences are not fulfilled by government policy.

Non-governmental Institutions

The third set of constituents are non-governmental institutions. Many regional quality of life factors rely on non-governmental institutions to manage and maintain their output. In turn, quality of life factors affect individuals' decisions. Non-governmental institutions play an important role because many activities are beyond the purview of the government and individuals. Non-governmental institutions can play especially important roles in coordinating government, business, and non-governmental actors.

For example, even if schools are funded and run by governmental agencies, non-governmental organizations impact their effectiveness. This includes parent organizations, educational foundations, and teacher-centric organizations like certification boards and unions. Private schools are important non-governmental institutions that affect the choices of the administrative and managerial talent base. Other examples of non-governmental organizations that coordinate quality of life factors include arts councils, museums, recreational providers, and religious organizations.

Once again, although non-governmental institutions influence the choices of individual actors, choices of individual actors also influence these institutions. Many non-government institutions are volunteer-driven organizations that rely on the time and talents of individuals from the professional and managerial talent pool. Likewise, many of these organizations are non-profits and rely on the funding from individuals in this talent pool. This includes art councils, religious organizations, and community leagues.

Some non-governmental organizations are large and have wide scope; they require professional managerial and administrative talent to guide their organization. When one thinks of many important foundations that are professionally managed, this description rings true. Therefore, non-governmental organizations can directly influence the talent base through job opportunities.

However, like equivalent government jobs, a headquarters economy cannot rely on non-governmental organizations as the main source of professional administrative and managerial employment. However, it can be an important complementary source, where professionally managerial and administrative talent moves between these jobs and equivalent jobs in the business sector.

Others in the Managerial and Administrative Talent Pool

The final set of constituents that can have an important impact on the decisions made by individuals within the managerial and administrative talent pool is the group of other individuals that form the talent pool. There are many ways in which the pool of talent influences individual decision-makers. For instance, professional norms can affect individuals' decisions. For example, different regions have distinct business cultures. In part, this can reflect differences in the types of companies in the region and the businesses in which they participate. For example, regions with a strong presence in investment banking will have a different corporate cultures compared to regions with a strong emphasis on start-up companies.

Other ways in which the pool of similar talent affects individual decision-makers is indirectly through the provision of valued amenities. The more similar individuals in a region, the greater the demand for similar amenities. Greater demand for amenities increases the likelihood that such amenities will be funded. This can be through focusing public monies. It can also be through the contributions of these individuals. For example, there are many fixed costs involved in funding a children's theater. Therefore, the contribution required to fund this activity is less per individual when there are 100,000 interested individuals compared to when there are 10,000 interested individuals.

The reciprocal nature of this relationship is straightforward. Any one person is part of the collective of similar talent for other decision-makers in the talent pool.

Interconnectedness of the Constituents

The interconnectedness of these parties is manifest by these four constituents influencing the individual decision-makers within the professional administrative and managerial talent pool and the individuals in this talent pool, likewise, can affect these different constituencies. Yet the degree of interconnectedness goes further than this. These various constituents influence each other.

For example, just because government wishes to offer corporate incentives in order to spur economic development through a headquarters economy, this does not mean that companies will consider or accept such offers. Companies consider a broader range of issues and are not myopically focused on government incentives when making these types of decisions. Likewise, competing regions might offer incentives that trump the offers for other regions that offer incentives. Companies can lobby or exert other influence to shape government policy. Therefore, company actions and corporate policies can be connected.

In the same way there are relationships between companies and non-governmental institutions. Companies can be important sources of funding and resources for these various institutions and thus affect the decisions and actions that these institutions take. These institutions through the services that they provide and the community involvement that they engender can affect the decisions of companies.

A parallel set of arrangements occur between these non-governmental institutions and the regional governments. They potentially affect each other's decisions through the services each provides. They might have incentives not to offer duplicate services. In other cases they might wish to in order to enhance the effectiveness services within a region.

Finally, because of the interrelationship between individual decision-makers and corporations, regional government, and non-governmental institutions, there will be interrelationships between the pool of talent and these constituencies. This logically follows from the pool of talent being the collection of the individuals.

Figure 6.1 highlights the relationships that I just described. At the center is the individual—the professional manager or administrator—central to my discussion. They make decisions of how and where to apply their skills. Around them are the four constituents. Although these constituents do not make the decision of how and where the individual manager employs their skills, their actions affect the decision-making of the individual. Moreover, the individuals' decision reciprocally can influence these constituencies.

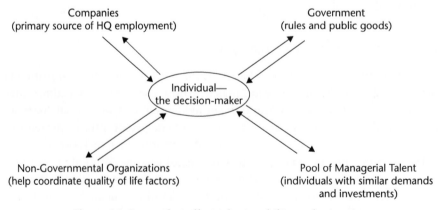

Figure 6.1 Forces that affect talent mobility and migration

Emergent versus Managed System

In light of the interrelated decisions-makers, it might appear incongruent—or even misguided—to suggest that one can draw implications for action because there is no one entity that manages or oversees the process. For example, in the Minneapolis-St. Paul context, the positive dynamic unfolded without an entity overseeing its creation. Rather, it emerged.

I, however, hold the view that understanding this dynamic has important implications to guide action for the following reasons. First, although one entity does not guide or manage the set of constituents, constituents' choices ultimately influence the overall system. Therefore, while not deterministic, some actions support a dynamic that facilitates a headquarters economy and others do not. If we wish to promote outcomes that build and sustain a headquarters economy, then it is important to know what actions by which actors can influence this dynamic.

Second, although no actor coordinates the overall process, it is possible to coordinate actions across the various constituents. In fact, the existence of these interconnections among decision-makers exemplifies why there are benefits for actors to try and work across boundaries and coordinate their efforts. Admittedly, such collaboration is difficult and often times will not be possible. This can reflect different objectives of the various actors. Even when constituents share the same objectives, coordination might be too difficult. Nevertheless, understanding the underlying dynamic and the various mechanisms that lead to this dynamic has the potential to bring together and better coordinate these different constituents.

Third, although the actions of an individual actor in isolation might not do a lot to build this dynamic, the actions of an individual actor can have a disproportionately large effect in harming the dynamic. It is difficult envisioning why any one of the constituents might want to purposely short-circuit the positive dynamic that underlies a headquarters economy. Therefore, to the extent that such actions are undertaken they are likely unintentional. For this reason it is important to derive implications from understanding what not to do.

Fourth, although no one actor can control the entire system, actors often choose if and how to tap the benefits of the system. For example, although one company might not be able to affect the system, the company can make choices to locate in a region that possesses this dynamic. By this action, they are able to access managerial practices that they would not be able to access had they located elsewhere. Likewise, companies can make choices of where to locate regional or divisional headquarters; they also make choices of where to house certain skills, and how they seek to attract employees to their companies. Tapping into the dynamics that underlie a headquarters economy can affect their success in these activities.

Finally, another reason why trying to shape the actions of constituents can be important is that this dynamic can switch from a virtuous to a vicious cycle. Any actions that can mitigate this possibility can have an important impact on a region. Many cities have seen concentration of headquarters activities wane over time. Once on a sustained trend in this direction it is often difficult to turn things around.

Summary

A headquarters economy is a source of economic and social vitality. Because other paths to economic or social prosperity by industry clusters or creative economies dominate discourse, there is relatively little discussion about vitality stemming from a headquarters economy. In addition to drawing attention to this type of economy, I highlight that there are unique and beneficial elements of a headquarters economy compared to the other sources of economic and social prosperity that dominate attention.

The key implication for guiding policy to build and sustain a headquarters economy and corporate strategies to tap a headquarters economy is the insight that the professional managerial and administrative workforce is the foundation from which to assess any action. Many other actors—such as companies, governments, and non-governmental agencies—influence the building of a strong headquarters economy. However, managerial and administrative talent considerations are central because the actions of other constituents ultimately flow through these individuals' decisions.

Because managerial and administrative talent is a different foundation than economies focused around industry clusters and creative talent, implications drawn from these other perspectives do not necessarily parallel with building, sustaining, and tapping into a headquarters economy. For this reason, refined prescriptions for regions, companies, or individuals requires an understanding of how these actions impact the managerial and administrative talent pool.

The framework that I introduce in this chapter reveals that a set of interconnected actors affect the decisions of the managerial and administrative workforce, whether or not these actors are cognizant of this. Therefore, choices made by these actors affect the talent base whether or not they are deliberate or purposeful. It means that ignorance of an influence does not prevent it from affecting the important parties and the overall economy. However, it also suggests that moving from ignorance to understanding can have a positive impact on building, sustaining, and leveraging a headquarters economy.

Notes

1. Data source is the Bureau of Labor unemployment statistics compiled by metropolitan area. I assess unemployment rates of the twenty-five metropolitan areas, which are my focus in Chapter 4.
2. Minnesota is generally considered a low-enforcement non-compete state (e.g., Stuart and Sorenson, 2003).

7

Five Novel Insights for Regional Economies and Company Strategies

In this chapter, I synthesize the arguments and evidence from the previous chapters and present five elements to consider when formulating meaningful implications for building, sustaining, and tapping into a headquarters economy. These five elements accentuate aspects of a headquarters economy that differ compared to other paths to economic and social prosperity. In doing this, I highlight the novel insights from my research.

These elements, which I discuss in detail, include: focusing on talent that is specialized by role not industry; understanding that talent attraction and retention are different phenomena; recognizing that talent is often more geographically bound than business headquarters; acknowledging that many headquarters jobs are hidden headquarters jobs; and discerning that a region's quality of life strengths can differ from quality of life factors that attract and retain talent.

Talent Specialized by Role and Not by Industry

Many discussions of economic development focus on the role of industry clusters (e.g., Porter, 1990). The observation is that competitive and successful firms within an industry are often geographically collocated. Proponents of this perspective argue that collocation is advantageous because of technology spillovers among companies, specialized supporting industries that companies tap into, and a high quality specialized labor force from which companies can hire (Marshall, 1890). The last element on this list—drawing on a specialized labor force—suggests similarities between the discussion of what facilitates industry clusters and my discussion of what facilitates a headquarters economy.

Despite the similarity that talent or human capital is central to economic and social vitality, there are important differences between my perspective and discussions about industry clusters. The industry cluster perspective centers on industry-specialized talent. However, talent that is critical to a headquarters economy possess skills that are applicable beyond a particular industry or set of industries that form a cluster. In a headquarters economy, it is important to appreciate that skill specialization reflects the functional role that an individual plays in a business organization. It is professional managerial and administrative talent.

As I demonstrate in the previous chapters, professional managerial and administrative skills are not industry-bound. All successful businesses require managerial and administrative oversight. This applies to high-tech businesses as much as it applies to firms that are not technology-focused. It applies to nascent or entrepreneurial businesses and it applies to established industrial giants. Managerial talent is important for companies when economic conditions are favorable because managerial talent is important to guide a growing business. Managerial talent is also important for companies when economic conditions are unfavorable because managerial talent is important to seek for new opportunities or to effectively rationalize a shrinking business.

Focusing on skills that are specialized by function and not industry can lead to different prescriptions compared to focusing on skills that are specialized by industry. I discuss several points of distinction.

Role specialization allows for broader talent search than industry specialization

When companies look to hire employees to fill managerial and administrative roles, they need not restrict their search to candidates within their own industry. Although the implications from discussions of industry clusters focus on the benefits of industry expertise, I discuss how companies benefit from looking beyond their immediate industry—especially when looking for professional managerial and administrative skills. This is because many skills are not industry specific.

In addition, the examples that I present in Chapter 3 show that when industry-focused managerial practices exist, bringing in managerial and administrative skills from other industries imports new skills or serves as a force to overcome inertia within the organization or industry. Therefore, there are advantages to injecting skills and experiences from outside of an industry rather than continually specializing and drawing upon skills and experiences from within an industry.

Role Specialization, Compared to Industry Specialization, Can Mitigate Negative Effects from Talent Mobility

There are also implications when one considers the broader impact that talent mobility has on companies. To see this, it is important to recognize that when discussing employee mobility, focusing on talent arriving at a new employer is only part of the impact. When a company hires a new employee, most often, this employee leaves another employer. Therefore, a company attracting talent is generally paired with a company that is losing talent; and the latter being made worse off. The exception being when the company losing talent is actively trying to reducing its workforce. Because talent mobility leads to the movement of talent into some companies and the movement of talent out of others, it has positive and negative impacts on companies within a region.

It follows, then, that when a company locates in a region where it can more easily access talent from its competitors, it also becomes more susceptible to have competitors access its talent. This downside of industry clustering has typically not attracted a lot of attention. For an exception, see Shaver and Flyer (2000). Nevertheless, it is an inherent element of any economy where employee movement between companies is pronounced.

A headquarters economy mitigates this negative aspect of talent mobility compared to in an economy characterized as an industry cluster. The reason is that talent tends to move across industries in the case of a headquarters economy compared to moving within industries in the case of an industry cluster. To see why this mitigates the negative effects of talent mobility, consider the following. When talent moves between companies in the same industry, it means that it moves between competitors. If an employee leaves their current employer, not only does that firm lose an employee, their competitor gains the employee. Therefore, the company's loss is simultaneously accompanied by a competitor's gain.

In contrast, when an employee leaves their current employer and leverages their skills in another industry, the overall effect to the company that the employee departs is dampened. Although the company from which this employee departs still loses an employee, this employee does not go to their competitor. It is not accompanied by a competitor's gain. Therefore, while the loss of an employee can be detrimental, it is less damaging compared to the situation where the employee moves to a competitor.

The same effect that mitigates the negative effect of talent mobility can also change the calculus of companies' willingness to support regional talent investments. When the losses associated with talent mobility are muted, companies are more likely to see greater benefits to promoting a labor pool from which many companies can draw. In turn, this provides increased net benefits for such communal investments and increases companies' incentives to make these investments.

But this is not the only way in which a headquarters economy—with its talent base possessing skills that are applicable across industries—creates differing incentives for making communal investments compared to an industry cluster—with its talent base possessing skills are more industry-focused. I draw attention to two aspects of how a headquarters economy can incentivize companies, governments, and non-governmental agencies to make investments in promoting a headquarters economy compared to other means to economic and social vitality.

HEADQUARTERS ECONOMY CAN BE MORE ADAPTABLE TO ECONOMIC TURBULENCE

A talent pool that possesses skills applicable in many different industries is more adaptive to changing business conditions compared to a talent pool with industry-focused skills. For example, talent with industry-specific skills likely face heightened pressures to relocate if a key employer leaves the region—whether by relocating or shuttering their operations. A talent pool with industry-specific skills might have little option other than to relocate if they want to effectively apply their skills. Such an outcome is less likely for employees whose skills are broadly applicable. Even if opportunities in their current industry of employment vanish locally, they can often apply their skills in other industries within the region—provided that such opportunities exist. This latter situation better describes the plight of managerial and administrative talent.

For example, when Pfizer closed its research and development (R&D) facilities in Ann Arbor Michigan, it dealt an economic blow to the region. The majority of these highly educated and high-earning individuals had to relocate because there were few other pharmaceutical research options locally.[1]

Contrast this with the outcome when Delta Airlines moved the former Northwest Airline's headquarters operations out of Minneapolis-St. Paul, post-acquisition. Although some of the headquarters talent relocated to Atlanta, many did not. In parallel with Pfizer leaving Ann Arbor, there were no other major airlines headquartered in Minneapolis-St. Paul when Delta closed the former Northwest Airlines headquarters. However the headquarters talent from Northwest Airlines that did not relocate applied their skills in other industries in the region. I know of many who disseminated to companies like United Healthcare and Ecolab. As a result, a much greater proportion of the former Northwest Airlines headquarters talent remained in the Minneapolis-St. Paul compared to the situation of when Pfizer left Ann Arbor.

The propensity for talent to remain in the region affects the incentive for various constituencies to make investments in this type of talent base compared to a talent base focused on one industry. For instance, making investments in talent that is more likely to remain in the region should be more attractive to regional governments and regional non-governmental agencies compared to investments in talent that is more likely to leave the region.

Companies, by their nature, focus on their workforce needs. As a result, they are equally disincentivized to invest in talent that will leave their company and move out of the region, as they are to invest in talent that will leave their company yet stay in the region. Nevertheless, they might be willing to make investments in talent that is likely to stay in the region—if other companies are willing to do the same. In other words, companies are less likely to view this as subsidizing other companies when other companies also make this type of investment. Therefore, a key issue becomes finding ways to mobilize collective action among companies in a region rather than there being little incentive to make the investment.

The other way in which a talent pool with broadly applicable skills affects the incentives to build this talent pool is that a more flexible talent pool dampens the risk of the investment. For instance, if regional entities focus their efforts on building talent for a particular industry, they make a bet on that industry. If the industry thrives, it is a good bet because the region captures the resulting spillovers. However, if the industry does not thrive in the region, then the talent base—with their industry-focused skills—is likely to disperse and leave the region. In this situation, actors in one region contribute resources while those in another region capture the benefits.

The above outcome is less likely to occur for investments in skills that are applicable across many industries. Here, investments are in widely applicable skills compared to industry-specific skills. For the region to benefit from an investment in more general skills, it is not necessary for a particular industry to fare well. When skills that are applicable across many industries are the focus of investments, market forces can guide the allocation of talent to the industries in which it is best utilized. This differs from betting on a specific industry.

TALENT BASE OF A HEADQUARTERS ECONOMY HAS DIVERSE EDUCATIONAL BACKGROUNDS

Entry-level talent in the managerial and administrative talent pool come not only from business schools but from a wide array of educational backgrounds. This breadth in background—especially for those entering this workforce—provides a much broader and diverse source of talent compared to economies that focus on industry-specific skills. In turn, such breadth of background has two direct implications.

First, it provides employers with more options from where to find talent compared to if they are looking for industry-specific skills. This has the potential to mitigate competitive pressure that employers face in assembling talent—especially when supply and demand conditions favor those looking for employment.

Second, this observation suggests that headquarters economies will tend to have more employment opportunity—for the broad set of people entering the workforce—compared to regions where the skills are more industry-focused. Because a large number of college graduates fill entry-level managerial and administrative positions, headquarters economies become "landing spots" for job-seekers from a variety of backgrounds. This has the advantage of seeding the local economy with young talent—many of whom might permanently stay. It also has the advantage of providing opportunities for couples looking to satisfy dual-career demands. Moreover, regions that attract significant numbers of college graduates tend to create an atmosphere and provide amenities that just-out-of-college employees value. This has the potential to make the region more attractive compared to regions that do not have the similar talent base and reinforces its attractiveness for such talent.

Talent Attraction and Talent Retention Are Different Phenomena

I present substantial evidence that talent attraction and talent retention are not simply mirror images of each other. Therefore, talent strategies of companies, governments, and non-governmental agencies need to align the outcomes that they wish to stimulate with the levers best enabled to enact changes.

Multiple sources of data I present in the previous chapters demonstrate the distinction between talent attraction and retention. The broadest representation of this conclusion comes from examining the migration data from the major metropolitan areas in the United States. Figure 7.1 presents data I initially presented in Chapter 4 in a different manner. In this figure I plot in-migration rate on the vertical axis against out-migration rate on the horizontal axis. The data reflect the subset of the population that is over 23, employed, college educated, and in a high-earning household. This figure exhibits a positive relationship between in-migration and out-migration rates. Namely, lower in-migration rates tend to be associated with lower out-migration rates. One would not expect to see this relationship if the determinants of in-migration and out-migration were similar. If the determinants were similar, then regions with high inflows would have low outflows and regions with low inflows would have high outflows. In other words, the relationship between in-migration and out-migration would be negative. This figure also demonstrates that focusing on net-migration can be misleading because it suppresses differences of in-migration and out-migration flows.

The survey data in Chapter 5 provide direct evidence that decision-makers differentially weigh factors with respect to moving to or remaining in a region. When I ask those who relocate to Minneapolis-St. Paul what motivates their move to the region, the predominant motivation centers on job opportunities. When I ask those who report that they would prefer to live in another location what prevents them from moving there; the predominant answer is quality of life factors.

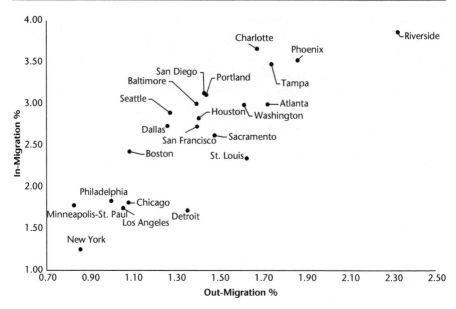

Figure 7.1 Inward and outward migration: highly educated, employed, and high-earning

Quality of Life Factors Play a More Prominent Role in Retention versus Attraction

The data support the conclusion that quality of life factors are especially important for talent retention. They play a less important role for talent attraction. This conclusion is at odds with the "if you build it, they will come" rationale that companies, governments, and non-governmental agencies should invest in quality of life amenities in order to foster economic vitality. The data I show indicate that economic opportunities—for individuals and their partners—are especially important for attracting managerial and administrative talent.

I want to be clear that these are not absolutes with respect to talent attraction and retention. I do not expect a region with quality of life amenities to have exceptional rates of talent retention if economic opportunities do not exist or disappear. Likewise, even highly valued economic opportunities can be insufficient to attract talent to regions devoid of quality of life amenities. The survey data that I present in Chapter 5 reinforce this. Although career opportunities are of paramount importance for talent attraction, quality of life factors play an important role for many respondents. Although quality of life factors play a more important role with respect to talent retention, career opportunities still play an important role.

Regional Quality of Life Factors Are Often Experience Goods

I believe that quality of life factors play a more important role for talent retention because many quality of life features are experience goods. By this I mean that many people cannot evaluate the day-to-day quality of life implications of living in a region until they actually experience living in that region. This allows them to tangibly assess the following types of questions. What is the commute like? Am I able to adjust to utilize the regional amenities? How available are amenities that I especially value given my lifestyle? Once these factors are tangible, they can play a more definitive role in decision-making compared to when they are abstract.

Nevertheless, some quality of life factors are more tangible or appear more tangible. Quality of life factors where data are readily available, interpretable, and comparable fall into this category. Two examples of such data that appear to play prominent roles in the discussion of regional attractiveness are the weather—especially average temperatures—and the tax rate. These data are available for all locations and are easily comparable. It is relatively easy to generate a list of regions and rank based upon these data. Although tangible and often used in decision-making, the ways in which even these quality of life features affect living in a region are often more experiential in nature. For example, average temperature is not the only factor that determines how weather affects quality of life. For example, a better assessment revolves around how well-adapted a region is to dealing with the weather it receives. Different weather factors might be more or less important for a specific person. For example, someone with asthma might find the same weather conditions unattractive compared to an individual without the same medical condition.

If one of the reasons why quality of life factors play a less important role in talent attraction is because they are experience goods, then it suggests strategies to leverage quality of life factors to attract talent. When quality of life factors are experiential, they are most effective when attracting individuals who previously lived in the region or who have had experiences in the region. For example, individuals who were raised in the region but moved elsewhere for college or graduate school might be attracted back to the region by focusing on quality of life aspects. Likewise, quality of life factors might disproportionately influence individuals who went to college or graduate school in the region.

The previous discussion further highlights why the "if you build it, they will come" mantra for economic development is challenged to work. However, to the extent that regions or companies wish to focus on quality of life amenities to attract talent, it suggests that promoting regional quality of life factors should go beyond simple descriptions and better document how these factors tangibly affect the day-to-day experiences of the target audience. Likewise, regions with such quality of life benefits will often experience greater success attracting talent to the region if they have had previous experiences in the region. These regions and companies might also benefit from actions that broaden the scope of potential talent who experience the region.

Talent Attraction and Retention Forces Might Vary by Talent Base

Although the data I present demonstrate that talent attraction and talent retention forces differ, the data from which I draw this conclusion reflect the focal talent base of my investigation. The professional managerial and administrative talent that comprises a headquarters economy likely focus on job-related issues because of their investments in education and the nature of their career trajectories. Individuals with other skills might focus on different attributes. Moreover, the demographics of the professional managerial and administrative talent base lead to quality of life factors related to dual-careers and child-rearing being especially important. For a different groups of individuals, other factors might be more important.

In light of this, the data I present in the previous chapters will not necessarily generalize to other pools of talent. Relatedly, this cautions regions and companies from simply mimicking talent attraction and retention strategies from other regions and companies without calibrating the target of these talent attraction and retention efforts. Differences in the talent that regions and companies hope to attract can make such strategies ineffective or even counterproductive.

Talent Can Be More Geographically Bound than Corporate Headquarters

My research suggests a view of mobility with respect to individuals and corporations that challenges intuition and received wisdom with respect to the geographic stickiness of talent compared to the companies for which they work. We tend to consider individuals as mobile. They can choose where they live and can—relatively easily—move. And we tend to picture companies as more permanent. Unlike individuals, companies do not have a finite life expectancies. Many iconic businesses, which have existed for a long period of time, are fixtures in their local communities.

However, the data I present highlight—as have others—that the roster of the largest companies in the United States is very fluid. Moreover, this fluidity is manifest across metropolitan areas in the country. Part of this fluidity is that small companies grow and large established companies decline and die. However, an important determinant of this fluidity reflects other factors. Among these are that companies relocate, merge, expand, retrench, and divest.

This means that the loss of a headquarters from a region is not necessary the result of a company failing and looking to shed jobs. Headquarters can disappear when companies are performing well and become the acquisition target of another company. Likewise, well-performing companies can choose to change the location of their operations. As a result, the fluidity of corporate headquarters need not reflect the underlying vitality of the businesses or the economic conditions of the region.

Turning to the geographic mobility of employees, many individuals stay with an employer for extended portions of their career. And of those who actively move from employer to employer over the course of their career, many do so while staying within the same geographic region. They need not relocate to find new opportunities. This reflects that relocation is accompanied by transition costs—for by the individual and others members of their family. Therefore, if individuals looking to move from their current employer can do so without relocating, many will prefer to do so. In addition, individuals who relocate rarely do so with every job switch. Many will relocate and subsequently look for options in their new location due to the costs of relocating.

Acknowledging that individuals are potentially more geographically stable than companies has many implications for regional economic and social vitality policies and for companies within these regions. Foremost, it reinforces the need to look at talent as the foundation of economic prosperity, in general, and for a headquarters economy, in particular. The volatility of the geography of companies versus the geography of talent suggests that policies to build a headquarters economy that focus primarily on companies versus the underlying talent can be misguided.

Regional Policies toward Attracting and Retaining Talent versus Companies

When one combines the insight that individuals might be more location-bound than companies with the previous insight that talent attraction and talent retention are different forces, a more comprehensive view on policies to foster economic and social vitality arises. To see this, let me distinguish between regions that already have a talent base and company base from regions lacking a talent base and company base.

For regions with an existing talent base and company base, a primary focus would be to retain what they have and build upon their success. With retention a key element of this approach, investments in talent retention are likely more impactful than investments in company retention. This reflects that when talent is more location-bound, investments in quality of life for talent

171

will have a greater multiplier effect on the local economy compared to direct corporate incentives.

In addition, incentives to companies do not always ensure economic activity remains within a region. To see this, it is important to reflect on the reasons why headquarters leave a region. Many are not at the discretion of the management of the local company. For example, changes in technology or other external factors might be the source of a company's decline. No company chooses to perform poorly—these are not decisions of the company's management. Well-intentioned companies might not deliver on economic growth even when incentivized. Likewise, when a company is acquired, this reflects choices of the acquiring company and not the target. This is not to say that the target companies are uninvolved bystanders. However, when faced with a credible offer for their company at a premium over the current stock price, the target firm's managers have limited ability to outright decline the offer for fear of shareholder backlash. Such changes in ownership and control affect regional operations.

For regions without an existing talent and company base, focusing on retention would not be warranted. Instead, attraction becomes key. If the goal is to attract the talent pool central to my arguments, the data I present show that economic opportunities attract this talent pool—not quality of life investments. This means that policy investment in talent attraction for these regions will have lower multiplier effects compared to incentives to bring economic opportunities for this talent base the region. I stress the phrase "for this talent base" because bringing any type of economic activity will not necessarily have the desired effect.

Headquarter Stability and Hidden Headquarters

One might question if some of the data I present call into question if individuals are more geographically stable compared to companies. Most notably, I present considerable evidence that hidden headquarters play an important role in a headquarters economy. In addition, many of the hidden headquarters that I identify were corporate headquarters of a previously independent company that was acquired.

Rather than invalidate my observation that individuals are more geographically stable than companies, the existence of hidden headquarters support it. The main reason is that it is not a foregone conclusion that a hidden headquarters emerges once a company is acquired. To be a foregone conclusion, hidden headquarters would exist simply because of inertia or some sense of obligation of the acquiring company to the target company's region. Although these influences can play a role, the main reason why a hidden headquarters exists is because the acquiring company assesses that it would be costly, disruptive, or infeasible to try and move the operations.

An important reason why this occurs—especially with headquarters operations—is that the acquiring company assesses it cannot readily replace the managerial and administrative talent of the previous headquarters. This is often true if the assessment is that the talent from the acquired operation would not relocate if the headquarters were consolidated. Likewise, the incentives that the acquiring company would have to provide to induce the talent to relocate would make relocation economically infeasible.

In summary, although individuals have considerable flexibility where they work, their preference to stay regionally bound can provide a substantial anchor to corporate locations. In some scenarios, this suggests that investments to retain talent might be more enduring than investments to retain companies.

Many Headquarters Jobs Are "Hidden"

The notion of what comprises a headquarters is well-accepted. It is the administrative center of a company. Although this might be conceptually clear, what it means in practice is often less clear.

Large companies operate multiple lines of business and many of these businesses have separate administrative centers. For example, many companies operate in multiple countries or regions of the world and house important administrative roles in these countries or regions. As a result, the managerial and administrative workforce of many companies does not concentrate in one location. Rather, it is spread across many different regions.

When we consider the variety in the scope and organization of companies, the term "headquarters" can mean different things in practice. However, by focusing on what constitutes a headquarters, rather than the moniker of "headquarters" per se, resolves this issue. In particular, focusing on the location of managerial and administrative talent helps resolve this issue. This brings to light that pools of managerial and administrative talent outside of the corporate headquarters (i.e., the hidden headquarters) should be of great interest for those who wish to build or sustain a headquarters economy.

For example, existing research shows that among the largest companies in the world corporate headquarters span a wide array of sizes (Collis et al., 2007). In these very large companies, leaner corporate headquarters tend to be associated with other headquarters activity within the company. When there are fewer managerial and administrative positions at the corporate headquarters, these activities are often decentralized in business unit headquarters, geographic headquarters, or both. Other things equal, smaller corporate headquarters have larger hidden headquarters presence. Moreover, having headquarters activities spread across disperse geographic regions tends to be pronounced for the largest companies. For this reason, many Fortune 500 firms have substantial hidden headquarters operations.

Because of their importance, regional development discussions that do not take into account the role that hidden headquarters play are under informed. Regional development efforts that fail to focus or capitalize on the role that hidden headquarters play in economic and social vitality miss worthwhile opportunities. The ability to entice or engage with location strategies of hidden headquarters might be easier to facilitate than with corporate head-quarters. Likewise, regional efforts might be better able to engage with local companies that are acquired and seek to assess if they will remain in the region and provide a hidden headquarters presence.

In summary, many of the contributions that headquarters make to a regional economy go underappreciated without taking a broad view of head-quarters activities that include hidden headquarters. This broader view of headquarters activities also opens consideration to a greater range of oppor-tunities and tools for regions that wish to build and foster a headquarters economy compared to focusing only on corporate headquarters.

A Region's Advantages are not Necessarily Drivers of Talent Attraction or Retention

The survey data that I present in Chapter 5 demonstrate that the quality of life factors respondents describe as having the greatest impact on retention and attraction are not necessarily the same factors that they list as the quality of life strengths of their region. This reflects that respondents distinguish a region's strengths from the factors that most directly affect their motivation to migrate to or remain in a region.

I highlight this point because it cautions regional development and corpor-ate recruiting efforts from focusing on what a region does well—or what its inhabitants highlight as the greatest benefits—as the focus for talent attrac-tion and retention efforts. Discussions of a region's quality of life strengths or testimonials from its residents on the virtues of living in the region can be an important input for regional development efforts and corporate recruiters. These efforts can be effective if the region's strengths map to the quality of life factors central to the decision calculus of those that the region wishes to attract or retain. However, these efforts are not necessarily effective when the region's strengths do not map well to the quality of life factors demanded by the talent base that they wish to attract.

The insight that residents can easily distinguish between the quality of life strengths of a region and the quality of life dimensions that attract or retain talent reinforce the importance of explicitly understanding regional attributes that map most directly to the focal talent base's quality of life demands. Focusing on a region's strengths or assessing the demand of those outside of the focal talent base will often not produce the desired results.

Summary

In the previous chapters, I show that managers, their mobility across companies, and their migration affect why some regions develop and sustain a headquarters economy. In making this case, I uncover five novel considerations for regional economic and social vitality and corporate talent attraction that have not been part of the common discourse.

Most important among these considerations is focusing on an underlying talent base whose skills and expertise are applicable across industries rather than a talent base whose skills are industry-focused. Current discussions of economic and social vitality based on the development of industry clusters highlight the benefits of talent with industry-specific expertise. However, I show there are advantages to developing a talent pool that is specialized by function—or what they do. Moreover, there are advantages when this talent base can deploy their skills across industries—rather than in a particular industry. Professional managerial and administrative talent has this characteristic.

Focusing on the talent base that underlies a headquarters economy reveals the factors affecting talent attraction and retention can differ. In particular, I demonstrate that among professional managerial and administrative professionals job-related factors play a primary role in talent attraction. However, quality of life factors play a primary role of talent retention. This nuanced effect of talent attraction and retention is important to guide policies and collective action for regional talent development.

The data I present also show that talent can be more geographically bound than the companies for which they work. This view challenges conventional wisdom that individuals can easily move and that companies tend to be stable with regional historic roots. This suggests that in many situations, regional development efforts that focus on attracting and retaining key talent can be more beneficial than regional development efforts that focus on attracting and retaining companies.

This focus on the talent that underlies headquarters activities and the fluidity in the largest companies underscores the importance that hidden headquarters can play in regional economic and social vitality. Large complex organizations house pools of managerial and administrative talent in many regions. This reflects that many companies have business unit headquarters distinct from corporate headquarters and that companies disperse managerial oversight to the geographic areas in which they operate around the world. As a result, hidden headquarters can play as large or an even larger role than corporate headquarters with respect to a region's economic and social vitality.

Finally, the managerial and administrative talent base from which I gather data distinguish between quality of life factors that they value and quality of life strengths of their region. The former are factors that affect whether or not they migrate to or remain in a region. The latter are the quality of life characteristic in which their region is relatively strong. That professional managerial and administrative talent makes this distinction is understandable. An educated, well-earning talent base will possess nuanced assessments of where they live and why they live there. Nevertheless, this distinction suggests that understanding regional strengths should not necessarily be the focus when developing regional development or corporate recruiting policies. Rather, it suggests the importance of developing policies based upon understanding the demands of the talent base central to a region's economic and social vitality.

Note

1. http://blog.mlive.com/annarbornews/2008/01/one_year_later_pfizer_labs_emp.html

8

Prevalence of Headquarters Economies

Applying these Insights

Understanding managerial and administrative talent is key to understanding a headquarters economy. Headquarters economies typically achieve economic and social prosperity because of type of jobs they provide and the nature of the talent that fills these jobs. Nevertheless, a headquarters economy is a type of regional economy that has not garnered significant attention compared to other regional economies such as industry clusters or creative economies.

In order to draw attention and insight into headquarters economies, a goal of my research is to demonstrate the mechanisms that lead to a headquarters economy and not just to describe prosperous regions with concentrations of headquarters activity. I argue that cross-pollinating and sharing managerial practices across companies in a region is what aids corporate competitiveness within a headquarters economy. This, in turn, benefits regional companies and initiates a virtuous cycle that strengthens a region's companies and builds its pool of managerial talent. Therefore, understanding managers, their mobility across companies in a region, and their movement to and from a region are key to understanding a headquarters economy.

In order to identify and document these forces, the previous chapters focus on an exemplar headquarters economy—Minneapolis-St. Paul. Focusing on the region yields research design advantages that allow me to isolate these underlying mechanisms. Nevertheless, focusing on a specific region can raise questions about the wider applicability of my findings.

To demonstrate the breadth of ways in which the insights that I advance are applicable across many different regions, I first highlight metropolitan areas around the world that house concentrations of headquarters from the world's largest companies. This provides initial guidance as to other regions where my research is most applicable. However, as I discuss in this section, this is only initial guidance because the key element of my research is documenting the mechanisms that advanced the headquarters economy in Minneapolis-St. Paul. Focusing on the underlying mechanisms suggests that the results have a much wider scope of applicability than might initially be perceived.

After I present regions with concentrations of headquarters and discuss the applicability of my research findings, I draw attention to an empirical regularity that I uncover in this exercise. Many "secondary" cities (i.e., not the largest global cities) have very high concentrations of corporate headquarters activities.

In the second section of the chapter, I return to the observation with which I open the book. Examining headquarters requires that one understand the pool of professional managerial and administrative talent that resides within corporate headquarters. Over the course of researching the book, several ways in which these talent pools influence the regions in which they reside appeared repeatedly. I discuss four key influences.

I conclude the chapter and book by highlighting ways in which future study can advance the research that I present. I highlight areas that are fruitful paths to extend the work. I also document limitations of my work and discuss how addressing these limitations can guide further investigation.

Regional Headquarters Concentrations of the World's Largest Companies

As a starting point for considering regions where the implications from my research are applicable, I highlight metropolitan areas around the globe that have concentrations of headquarters of the world's largest companies. To make this assessment, I follow a similar analysis to the one I present in Chapter 2 where I present the metropolitan regions in the United States with the largest number of corporate headquarters. For the global assessment, I draw upon the 2016 Fortune Global 500. Like the Fortune 500, which focuses on US companies, the Global 500 ranks the largest companies in the world by revenues.

To ascertain which metropolitan areas have concentrations of headquarters, I undertake the following steps. First, I note each company's headquarters city. I then assign headquarters cities into metropolitan regions. In Chapter 2, I use the United States Office of Management and Budget's definitions of Metropolitan Statistical Areas to define metropolitan regions. However, such a standardized measure is not readily available across countries. Therefore, the following process guides my assignment of companies to metropolitan areas. Many headquarters formally reside within well-known metropolitan areas (e.g., Beijing or Paris). In these cases, the assignment of headquarters to metropolitan region is straightforward. When this is not the case, I search the Internet for evidence of whether or not the corporate headquarters city resides within a metropolitan area for a specific country—as defined by that

Table 8.1 Fortune Global 500 companies by metropolitan area, 2016

Rank	Metropolitan Area	Number of Companies
1	Beijing	57
2	Tokyo	39
3	Paris	27
4	New York	25
5	London	23
6	Seoul	12
7	Chicago	11
7	Zurich	11
9	San Francisco	10
10	Guangzhou	9
10	Shanghai	9
12	Rhine Rhur	8
13	Hong Kong	7
13	Washington	7
13	Osaka	7
13	Houston	7
13	Toronto	7
18	Minneapolis-St. Paul	6
18	Taipei	6

Source: 2016 Fortune Global 500 list.

country. I use these country-specific definitions to define metropolitan areas even though they are not standardized across countries. I then use these definitions to collect population data in order to assure alignment in population and headquarters classification.

As a result of this process, I document 138 metropolitan areas with at least one Global 500 headquarters. Table 8.1 lists the nineteen metropolitan areas that have six or more Global 500 companies. The metropolitan areas with the largest number of headquarters are major global metropolitan areas: Beijing, Tokyo, Paris, New York, London, and Seoul. Of the top six, five are the most populous metropolitan area in their country and five are national capitals.

To provide an indicator of the concentration of large global headquarters relative to metropolitan area size, I scale headquarter counts by population. I restrict this analysis to metropolitan areas with at least four Global 500 companies to assure that there is a notable concentration of large headquarters in the region. Thirty-two metropolitan areas have four or more Global 500 headquarters. Table 8.2 ranks metropolitan areas by headquarters per capita. The metropolitan areas with the highest concentration of headquarters per capita are Zurich, Beijing, Paris, Amsterdam, and Rotterdam. Apart from Rotterdam, most of these are cities I hear referenced when I discuss metropolitan areas with concentrations of large headquarters.

The analysis in Table 8.2 reaffirms the conclusions that I present in Chapter 2 about the concentration of headquarters activity in the Minneapolis-St. Paul

Table 8.2 Fortune Global 500 headquarters per capita by metropolitan area, 2016

Metropolitan Area	HQs per Million	HQs
Zurich	2.89	11
Beijing	2.29	57
Paris	2.20	27
Amsterdam	2.17	5
Rotterdam	1.82	4
London	1.68	23
Minneapolis-St. Paul	1.67	6
Munich	1.54	4
Toronto	1.19	7
Chicago	1.16	11
Washington	1.15	7
Houston	1.15	7
San Francisco	1.14	10
Boston	1.06	5
New York	1.05	25
Tokyo	1.03	39
Hanover	1.03	4
Hong Kong	0.96	7
Melbourne	0.87	4
Guangzhou	0.87	9

Sources: 2016 Fortune Global 500 list, population sources described in text.

region when I focus only on US data. Minneapolis-St. Paul is home to six of the Global 500 companies, which ranks the region tied for eighteenth worldwide. The region ranks seventh for Global 500 headquarters per capita, at almost the same level as London. It has the highest Global 500 headquarters per capita of any US city. One other US metropolitan area, Chicago, factors into the top ten and other US cities rank eleventh through fifteenth.

Seeing the list of metropolitan regions in Tables 8.1 and 8.2 raises the question of whether or not the mechanisms and implications that I draw out over the course of this book would be applicable across all of these regions with high counts or high per capita levels of headquarters. Many other sources of economic and social vitality will come to mind when one initially thinks about the history of these different metropolitan areas and the nature of their economies.

Although initial impressions that other historical or economic factors influence the economies of these metropolitan areas, it requires a logical leap to conclude that the mechanisms of managerial mobility and migration that I identify do not exist in these regions. To see this, it is important that I highlight two issues. First, the mechanisms that are central to my arguments can coexist with other sources of regional vitality. Second, the mechanisms that are central to my arguments are not the only determinants of headquarters locations and regional vitality; therefore, other factors—in isolation of my arguments—could drive the concentration of corporate headquarters. Although the latter point calls into question using simple headquarters rankings as indicators of headquarters economies, it also suggests that the inverse might be true. That is, locations that do not factor high on these simple comparisons might exhibit the mechanisms related to a headquarters economy. The following sections discuss these issues.

A Headquarters Economy Need Not Be an Exclusive Source of Regional Vitality

Many of the metropolitan areas that I list in Tables 8.1 and 8.2 are economies with attributes that extend beyond concentrations of publicly held corporate headquarters. For example, many of the metropolitan areas are national capitals, national and international financial centers, or national and regional population centers. One could argue that if these other factors play important roles, then my arguments have limited application. Continuing this line of logic, if my arguments have limited application in metropolitan areas with the highest concentrations of large corporate headquarters, then they must have limited application overall.

Such reasoning, I believe, is erroneous. The arguments that I advance do not preclude that other factors determine regional economic and social vitality. In other words, they do not constitute a necessary condition for regional economic and social vitality. For example, within a region with diverse companies can be pockets of industry concentration. Industry clusters can coexist within a headquarters economy. My arguments are that an industry cluster, per se, does not reflect a headquarters economy. Likewise, companies might choose to locate in major financial centers or in national capitals where they are close to political power. Even if focused on these motivations, headquarters in these regions can still benefit from the cross-pollinating and sharing of management practices.

To the extent that regional economic and social vitality assessments discuss these alternative determinants, they become the focus of what drives regional vitality for these metropolitan areas with concentrations of corporate headquarters. Focusing on these issues can mask the existence and importance of the mechanisms that I advance. I believe this is an important reason why discussions of a headquarters economy and the mechanisms that I advance do not receive the same attention as other forces for regional vitality. Nevertheless, to the extent that the mechanisms of managerial movement and sharing of managerial practices across diverse businesses exist, then they play the role I highlight. The mechanisms that I identify can be an important source of regional vitality—whether tapped or untapped—even though it coexists with other determinants of regional vitality.

One of the research design advantages of building my arguments from the case of Minneapolis-St. Paul is that other factors play a less prevalent role in that region. It is not a national capital, it is not a global or national finance hub; it is an exemplar headquarters economy. This allows me to identify, isolate, and verify the importance of the movement of managers and managerial practices across diverse companies. Focusing on this underlying mechanism, rather than simply describing the concentration of headquarters in the region, allows me to look to regions where other forces might eclipse the mechanisms central to my arguments and highlight the potential importance of the mechanisms that I identify.

For example, after the Brexit decision (when Britain voted to leave the European Union), many question if London will retain its role as a major international financial center. Arguably, the agglomeration of financial services in the city is a key element of London's economy. However, there is also a large concentration of diverse corporate headquarters outside of the financial services sector. To the extent that there is movement of managerial and administrative employees among the headquartered companies that share and advance managerial practices, the headquarters economy dynamic would mitigate the anticipated effect on the city compared to considering the financial sector as the sole driver of the region. Therefore, the mechanisms that are central to my arguments might have an impact on the region's vitality. Recognizing this can lead to different policy implications and corporate strategies compared to considerations that focus on agglomerations of finance functions as the only important driver of London's economy.

For this reason, the implications of my findings and the extent of their applicability is likely more pronounced and wide ranging than might be considered at first glance. If a requirement to draw implications for other regions is that these other regions must look exactly like Minneapolis-St. Paul, then my findings have limited applicability. However, if one understands that Minneapolis-St. Paul provides insight into underlying mechanisms that exist in many regions—even regions where other factors exist—then the implications are wide ranging. Moreover, they provide the opportunity to broaden the discussion and offer novel insights because they go beyond the more-often-discussed drivers of regional vitality, which can act as blinders to understanding and action.

Regional Concentration of Headquarters is a Useful but Imprecise Indicator of a Headquarters Economy

As I just discussed, many of the metropolitan regions listed in Tables 8.1 and 8.2 can exhibit the headquarters economy mechanisms that I document in the book; even though one might not reach this conclusion at first glance.

However, I also caution drawing the conclusion that all of these regions exhibit the mechanisms that underlie a headquarters economy. This is because having a large concentration of large corporate headquarters in a ranking like the Global 500 is not a necessary condition for a headquarters economy, nor is it a sufficient condition for a headquarters economy.

A concentration of large corporate headquarters in a ranking like the Global 500 is not a sufficient condition because a key element of my definition and the mechanisms that I discuss is the sharing of managerial practices across companies and industries. For this to occur, I highlight the importance that the concentration of headquarters reflect a diverse range of business and industries. A large proportion of headquarters might arise from a concentration of companies in one or a few industries. For example, the Global 500 lists seven headquarters in Houston. However, these companies tend to be concentrated in the energy sector.

The reason that a concentration of large corporate headquarters in a ranking like the Global 500 is not a necessary condition is that such rankings are limited in the scope of the headquarters activities that they classify. For instance, the Global 500 tracks corporate headquarters of extremely large, publicly traded companies. It omits other forms of headquarters activity. For instance, it does not include privately held companies or "mid-sized" publicly traded companies. Moreover, rankings of large companies might not include government-held companies. Likewise, most lists of headquarters fail to include hidden headquarters such as business unit or regional headquarters, which can have prominent headquarters activities. Some metropolitan areas are especially notable for their concentration of regional headquarters (e.g., Zhao, 2013). With this in mind, many other metropolitan areas that do not appear in Tables 8.1 and 8.2 are likely headquarters economies.

I would, however, caution concluding that all metropolitan areas with concentrations of regional headquarters are headquarters economies. The reason is that some of these metropolitan areas will not exhibit the underlying mechanism that I present. For example, if most of the key managerial and administrative talent in these regions are expatriots, who come to the region on temporary assignments and then leave the regions as their companies transfer them, then the dynamics of cross-pollinating management practices will not occur. Hubs of regional headquarters will more likely be headquarters economies if there is a pronounced local talent base that moves between companies (i.e., it is not predominantly an expatriot workforce on temporary assignment to the region), or that individuals arrive as expatriots but leave their employer to stay in the region. Not all metropolitan areas with concentrations of regional headquarters will exhibit this, but some will.

The definitional issues that I allude to might give the sense that more comprehensive lists of corporate headquarters would be meaningful in identifying headquarters economies. This would certainly be beneficial. However, it would still focus on the existence of headquarters operations and not on the mechanisms that I argue are key to sustaining the benefits of a headquarters economy. For this reason, the ideal metric would not only compile the extent of headquarters activity in a region, it would also reflect the breadth of the headquarters. In addition, it would assess the movement of talent across these companies to be able to assess the applicability of my findings.

"Secondary Cities" and Headquarters Concentrations

In terms of raw counts, Bejing, Tokyo, Paris, New York, and London house the largest number of Global 500 headquarters. These are among the largest cities of the world. They are also cities that many refer to as global cities. Nevertheless, many smaller cities play a prominent role in terms of headquarters concentrations—both in terms of counts and especially on a per capita basis. Although I use the term "smaller cities," these still tend to be major metropolitan areas (e.g., Beaverstock et al., 1999; Chen and Kanna, 2012; Goerzen et al., 2013).

To see this, examine the rankings of the cities with the highest per capital concentration of corporate headquarters for the Global 500 in Table 8.2 or per capital concentration of Fortune 500 headquarters in the US in Table 8.3 (which reproduces Table 2.8). Table 8.2 includes the metropolitan areas of Zurich, Amsterdam, Minneapolis-St. Paul, Rotterdam, and Munich in the top ten. Table 8.3 includes metropolitan areas of Minneapolis-St. Paul, Charlotte, Omaha, Richmond, Cincinnati, and Hartford.

This raises a question of whether the dynamics that scholars argue lead to global cities (e.g., Sassen, 2001) make these regions less compelling places for corporate headquarters. Alternatively, is it that the headquarters economy dynamics that I identify are muted in global cities? Although I cannot offer hard evidence, the following conjectures appear consistent with this.[1]

To the extent that global cities are international financial centers, they play a role that surpasses the role that these cities played when they were national financial centers. Therefore, the agglomeration effect of the global city attracts activities that were previously located in other regions. For example, as European financial services activities concentrated in London, many other European nation's financial centers declined in importance. The concentration of financial services in some regions has the potential to push out other business services such as headquarters.

For instance, the concentration of financial services in a region can increase the cost for businesses and individuals to locate in these regions. Concentrations of businesses and the demands for real estate and services to house these businesses can bid up the cost relative to other regions. In addition, many high earning individuals in a region can increase the cost of living for skilled

Table 8.3 Fortune 500 companies per capita, 2011

Metropolitan Statistical Area	HQs per Capita	Number of HQs
Minneapolis-St. Paul-Bloomington, MN-WI	5.79	19
Omaha-Council Bluffs, NE-IA	5.78	5
Charlotte-Gastonia-Concord, NC-SC	5.12	9
Bay Area	5.02	31
Richmond, VA	4.77	6
Cincinnati-Middletown, OH-KY-IN	4.69	10
Hartford-West Hartford-East Hartford, CT	4.12	5
Greater NY	3.99	79
Denver-Aurora, CO	3.93	10
Milwaukee-Waukesha-West Allis, WI	3.86	6
Houston-Sugar Land-Baytown, TX	3.70	22
Pittsburgh, PA	3.40	8
Cleveland-Elyria-Mentor, OH	3.37	7
Columbus, OH	3.27	6
Detroit-Warren-Livonia, MI	3.26	14
St. Louis, MO-IL	3.20	9
Dallas-Fort Worth-Arlington, TX	3.14	20
Washington-Arlington-Alexandria, DC-VA-MD-WV	3.05	17
Chicago-Naperville-Joliet, IL-IN-WI	2.96	28
Boston-Cambridge-Quincy, MA-NH	2.42	11
San Antonio, TX	2.33	5
Seattle-Tacoma-Bellevue, WA	2.33	8
Atlanta-Sandy Springs-Marietta, GA	2.28	12
Philadelphia-Camden-Wilmington, PA-NJ-DE-MD	2.18	13
Phoenix-Mesa-Scottsdale, AZ	1.67	7
Los Angeles-Long Beach-Santa Ana, CA	1.64	21
Miami-Fort Lauderdale-Pompano Beach, FL	0.90	5

Sources: 2011 Fortune 500 list, United States Census Bureau.

talent that works within headquarters. Anecdotally, many financial service companies have individuals that earn very high wages that out-strip the wages of other professional employees. Educated and skilled workers who hold more traditional managerial positions typically earn less, even though they are well-paid in comparison to the median wage. In these situations, one can envision equilibrating forces where jobs with the highest paid individuals cluster in global cities. Other skilled, high earning jobs might find it preferable to cluster in relatively smaller or secondary international cities. In other words, one can envision cities that "bankers" find more attractive than "managers."

Exacerbating these cost of living effects for potential headquarters employees in global cities can be the draw of these cities to wealthy individuals who might not directly participate in the local economy. For example, individuals who create their wealth elsewhere or draw upon other regions to create and sustain their wealth might look to tap the quality-of-live benefits of living in a global city. Many of the secondary cities that are home to concentrations of headquarters do not have the same allure of the global cities for wealthy individuals looking to live in global cities or speculate on real estate. With this dampened effect on cost of living forces, secondary cities can often provide less costly benefits for headquarters talent compared to global cities.

To the extent that financial services agglomerate in global cities, it suggests that headquarters need not co-locate with financial centers. If headquarters and the finance functions central to financial services needed to co-locate, we should observe one of the following. First, as financial services agglomerate into financial centers, corporate headquarters follow in order to be geographically proximate. Second, if financial centers and corporate headquarters need to co-locate, and corporate headquarters do not follow the financial service firms as they agglomerate, then financial service firms will de-agglomerate over time. Data do not appear to support either of these trends.

Rather, as financial services specialize and concentrate in global cities, corporate headquarters often remain in other regions and access these services through the service provider's satellite offices. For example, London is a financial center in Europe that Danish, Spanish, or Italian companies can access via financial services company networks. Therefore, while financial service providers benefit by agglomerating with other financial service providers, this does not preclude them from having a broad reach of clients in other regions. For example, in the case of Minneapolis-St. Paul, my acquaintances in the financial sector in New York know of the companies in Minnesota, have contacts in these companies, interact with these companies, and eagerly pursue business opportunities with them. Therefore, the fact that Minneapolis-St. Paul is not an international financial center does not preclude the local companies from tapping into the network of international financial services. Moreover, to the extent that local financial entities exist, they find ways to compete in light of the globalization of financial services. Often this comes from specializing their offering to benefit local companies.

These data raise the possibility that the specialization of global cities into hubs of financial services might create forces where secondary cities become larger headquarters economies. Although I require additional data to verify this conjecture, the possibility that it exists suggests that major metropolitan areas that are not considered global cities might be especially sensitive to the arguments that I advance.

Headquarters as Pools of Managerial Talent

I wish to reinforce a key insight from my research: that in order to understand headquarters and their impact on the regions in which they reside, one must focus on the essence of a headquarters—the pool of managerial and administrative talent. This focus allows me to gain traction in isolating the mechanisms that underlie a headquarters economy. Having discussed these mechanisms over the course of the book, I wish to return to the issue of managerial and administrative talent in order to highlight four aspects of managerial talent that have implications across many different regions.

Managers Matter

Many discussions of economic vitality and regional growth tend to focus on entrepreneurs or technically skilled individuals. We celebrate these individuals' insights and perseverance in pushing forward their ideas and advancing a region's economy. Although entrepreneurs and technically gifted individuals often warrant the attention and deserve the praise, this focus neglects the role that skilled management provides in creating the overall impact in these endeavors.

For instance, it takes more than an idea, technology, or patents to create a technology company. It takes more than individual determination to transform an idea into a company, and to transform a fledgling company into a going concern. Likewise, there are important skills required to scale-up a going concern and transform it into an organization that can realize the potential of the underlying idea. All of these transformations require management. Moreover, companies require a different and increasing set of managerial and administrative skills after each of each of these transformations. Many companies, such as Uber, make missteps when they grow and rely on their founders rather than handing over the reins to a team of managers with the skills to guide the growing business.

I would go further and claim that many high-profile entrepreneurial exits, where the founders sell their venture to a larger company, are indications that these ventures require professional managerial expertise from the larger company. One of the reasons that they receive high valuations is that the acquiring firm foresees a way to scale-up the venture's operations. This effort requires professional and managerial expertise that likely resides in the acquiring firm and not in the venture.

One might question why there are such great returns to entrepreneurs if the managerial and administrative skills that the acquirer provides are so important. Skilled managerial and administrative talent resides in many companies. To the extent that companies compete to purchase an entrepreneurial venture, many of the returns from the managerial and administrative talent will go to the successful entrepreneurs. Nevertheless, the entrepreneurs had to bear a lot of risk. Many entrepreneurs fail, are never approached by other companies to take their idea to scale, and do not see such returns. Moreover, the companies that offer such valuations would not rationally do so unless they envisioned ways in which they could take the nascent businesses to scale. Therefore, when one sees a successful and high-profile entrepreneurial exit, it not only reflects the importance of the underlying business concept, it also reflects the insight and expectation of how to manage it to scale.

In addition, to the extent that the media focuses on managers for their actions and insights, I find that much of this focuses on celebrity chief executive officers (CEOs). It does not focus on the set of managerial and administrative skills within the company. Although many CEOs have an indelible impact on the companies that they lead, it is not possible that they manage the company on their own. A large company requires hundreds or thousands of individuals working in unison in order to achieve superior results. Recognizing that certain individuals are especially skilled at orchestrating this, might at times leave the false impression that an individual is more important than the entire pool of management.

Skills, Education, and Demographics Shape Choices

Because I argue that managers play an important role in headquarters and headquarters profoundly affect the regions in which they reside, I focus on this talent pool. Within sizable metropolitan regions, this talent pool consists of thousands of individuals who are unique in many dimensions. However, in the process of my research I see certain commonalities that warrant focus.

A managerial and administrative talent pool consists of well-educated individuals who invest in the development of their human capital. Understanding this provides insight into where they come from, the skills that they possess, who they partner with in their personal lives, and what they value in the regions in which they live. In light of this, my research finds that issues such as economic opportunities for themselves and their spouses and a favorable environment in which to raise children are key locational factors that this talent base values. In some ways, these issues might seem pedestrian compared to discussions about the importance of quality of life factors associated with, for example, bohemian lifestyles (e.g., Florida, 2002; Wojan et al., 2007). Nevertheless, to the extent that these are the most important factors for this talent base, it is important that they become focal considerations for the policy makers and companies wishing to attract this talent base.[2]

Some people ask if, by focusing on a talent base that is highly educated, employed, and well-compensated, I am ignoring parts of the population. Likewise, am I discussing regional policies and company strategies that will leave behind those who are not in this talent base? I do not believe so for two reasons.

First, by documenting the nature of the talent that drives a headquarters economy, I highlight the skills that allow individuals to most directly participate in such an economy's success. Knowing who centrally participates and why is important for understanding existing outcomes and formulating policies and company strategies. For example, if history, demographics, or discrimination precludes individuals from participating centrally in a headquarters economy, then isolating these issues is an important step in formulating policy and highlighting potential solutions.

Second, the skilled headquarters jobs that I highlight are among the types of jobs that have pronounced spillovers to regions (Moretti, 2012). Therefore, understanding the nature of an economy allows policy makers to assess if other paths toward regional development will lead to superior outcomes. It is important to compare alternative engines of regional development rather than compare existing outcomes to an ideal outcome (Coase, 1960). Being able to understand what drives an economy, and an economy such as a headquarters economy, is key to having fruitful discussions on many policy issues related to economic and talent development.

Mobile Talent Leads to Immobile Companies

When I reflect on my research there is an irony that strikes me. The professional managerial and administrative talent that resides in headquarters are among the most mobile individuals. They have the economic ability to move. They possess skills sought in many regions. Most have lived in more than one geographic location when one considers where they were raised, attended college, attended graduate school, and worked throughout their careers.[3] Therefore, these individuals have the ability to relocate, possess skills valued in many regions, and have experiences of living in more than one region.

The irony stems from having a group that is arguably so movable deciding that they do not want to move. When they choose where to live, this has an impact on where companies locate because they require access to this talent pool. In this way, my work is consistent with of Florida's (2002) assertion that understanding where talent wishes to work is important for an economy. His focus is on the creative class; mine is on professional and managerial talent.

Departing Headquarters Have a Lasting Legacy if Their Talent Does Not Leave with Them

During my research, I encountered many managers who had chosen to stay in regions after headquarters operations where they had previously worked ceased to exist there. In some cases the headquarters moved. In other cases, the headquarters ceased to exist because the company shut down or because an elsewhere-headquartered acquirer purchased the company.

In these situations, when the headquarters talent remains in a region the headquarters can have an important legacy—especially if the company was well-managed and managerially innovative for a period of time. Some of the talent likely ends up in other prominent headquarters jobs, should those opportunities exist. However, it also can end up in an array of smaller companies where it might go unnoticed.

An example of the legacy of management from the Minneapolis-St. Paul region is Control Data Corporation (CDC). It was, at one point, a large player and pioneer in the computer industry. In fact, the Minneapolis-St. Paul region had a notable cluster of computer companies in the 1960s and 1970s, much like Silicon Valley and Route 128 (Misa, 2013).

In my discussions of CDC with a former CEO, Robert Price, I asked him why he left California to join the operations of CDC in Minneapolis. His response was that he was attracted by the company, especially by how innovative it was. This is consistent with my expectation that job opportunities drive talent attraction to a region. It was also understandable because the company was considered to be an innovative computer company and Price was coming from a technical background. However, as he continued he added elements that I had not considered.

He said that CDC was not only innovative in the products that it developed but it was also very innovative in its managerial approach and practices. He mentioned that CDC developed managerial practices that were very novel at the time, if more commonplace now. For example, the CDC was a pioneer in the corporate use of wellness programs for their employees. Another example is that CDC created a 'committee for corporate responsibility' in 1972.[4] CDC contributed to the headquarters economy of Minneapolis-St. Paul as talent moved into and out of this company and into and out of other companies in the region.[5]

When CDC began to decline and then ceased to exist in the entity that it had been previously, much of the talent from this company stayed in the region. Therefore, although the company is formally gone—and has been for over twenty-five years—its legacy is not just a memory of a once-mighty company. The talent that it formally housed continued to influence the region's companies. Although as time passes and many of these individuals retire, I continue to hear about the company, its management techniques, and its impact on the region in discussions about the Minneapolis-St. Paul economy.

Continuing the Investigation

This book reflects my focus on the phenomenon of a headquarters economy. Drawing on data from the exemplar headquarters economy of Minneapolis-St. Paul, I advance the explanation that the sharing and cross-pollination of managerial practices is key to understanding the region's economic vitality. In doing that I note how managers, their mobility across companies, and the pattern of their migration into and out of the region facilitates this outcome. I then turn to additional data sources and present analyses that are consistent with the explanation that I advance. Although I believe that this approach provides an empirically validated understanding of the phenomena, it is a first step in providing a complete understanding. In particular, there are three important ways to advance the research that I present.

First, like every theory of positive spillovers or virtuous cycles, the issue of what initiates the dynamic and what then leads to the positive spillovers is difficult to untangle. I focus my attention in Chapter 2 on the positive spillover and only briefly describe the initial seeding of industry in Minneapolis-St. Paul because the data show that the ability to reinvent and generate new headquarters is key to understanding the experience of the region. However, I could not directly address the factors that differentiated Minneapolis-St. Paul from other regions that had concentrations of headquarters fifty, a hundred, or 150 years ago yet did not develop this dynamic. Additional insight into this would be worthwhile.

Second, the data I use to show that migration patterns differ between Minneapolis-St. Paul and the other major metropolitan areas in the United States in Chapter 4 is comparative. However, the survey data in Chapter 5 that assesses the mechanisms that I advance are not. Although such primary data are difficult to gather, especially with meaningful sample sizes, gathering such data across many regions would provide powerful insights.

Third, although I seek empirical support for my arguments with different data than the data that guide my theory generation, this empirical support is not conclusive. In particular, many of the analyses do not meet our highest demands for causal inference. My hope is that advancing novel theory and providing consistent empirical evidence with that theory motivates further studies that carefully refine the theory and look for ways to advance better tests.

This latter point is important because it reinforces the message of this chapter. The key insights from this book center on understanding the underlying mechanisms that drive a headquarters economy. Only by understanding these underlying mechanisms can one draw implications to many other regions and offer better-informed prescriptions for managers and policy makers.

Notes

1. Sassen (2001) presents evidence that the number of very large corporate headquarters declined in many of the world's largest cities between 1984 and 1999. Comparing these data to the data in Table 8.1 demonstrates a continuing decline in many of the world's largest cities. Nevertheless, inconsistent with this general trend is the notable increase of large global headquarters in Beijing and Seoul.

2. Storper and Scott (2009) note the difficulty in isolating how creative talent amenities drive economic development.

3. For example, only 15 percent of the professional managerial and administrative workforce that I surveyed in the Minneapolis-St. Paul region were raised, obtained all of their post-secondary education, and spent all of their professional career in the Minneapolis-St. Paul region.

4. http://www.cbi.umn.edu/collections/cdc/histtimeline.html

5. See Jensen et al. (2013) for a discussion of the Human Resource Innovations at Control Data Corporation. For a discussion of Robert Price's career at Control Data Corporation, see Misa (2012).

Relatedness of the Investigation to Other Academic Literatures

As I discuss in Chapter 1, a headquarters economy is a type of economy that has received relatively little attention compared to other regional economies. While many lines of academic inquiry investigate related phenomena, they do not directly assess a headquarters economy. In the main text of the book, I reference and discuss many of these lines of inquiry. My focus in the body of the text is to reference literature directly related to my arguments to logically build and assess the determents of a headquarters economy.

In this Appendix, I further discuss related academic literature. I highlight the relatedness and detail the differences between this scholarship and my arguments. Because my goal is to document the differences between my work and this scholarship, I do not review or extensively survey these literatures.

Many different fields of inquiry relate to my investigation. I structure the Appendix to highlight and discuss these individual areas of inquiry in separate sections. However, my goal is not to present a narrative connecting these diverse literatures.

Flow of Talent and Knowledge across Companies

The central element of my argument is the benefits that accrue to companies within a headquarters economy due to the cross-pollinating of managerial practices stemming from managerial mobility across companies and industries. In other words, benefits accrue from the flow of talent and the knowledge that it possesses. The general notion that there exist benefits from talent and knowledge flow between localized companies is central to many other discussions of regional economic vitality. Although conceptually related, the mechanism central to my argument differs in one or both the following ways compared to existing approaches in the literature: (a) I focus on the benefits of cross-industry talent and knowledge flows instead of the benefits of within-industry talent and knowledge flows; and (b) I focus on the dissemination of management practices versus technologies.

Within-industry Spillovers

As I note in the body of the text, a headquarters economy is a concentration of headquarters from diverse industries. It is not an industry cluster. The study of the benefits associated with industry clustering is a very large body of scholarship across multiple academic disciplines. Building from Marshall (1890), the literature discusses externalities that arise from the geographic concentration of industry. Some scholarship refers to this literature by the acronym MAR (Marshall Arrow Romer), recognizing the additions to Marshall's work by Arrow (1962) and Romer (1986) (see, e.g., Glaeser et al., 1992). The source of externalities from concentrations of industry often reflect mechanisms advanced by Marshall. These mechanisms include knowledge spillovers among competitors, specialized pools of labor, and specialized input providers (e.g., Krugman, 1991).

In addition, much of the literature on spillovers focuses on the movement of technological skills or capabilities among firms—often through engineer mobility. Among the influential scholarship that focuses on these mechanisms is the work of Saxenian (1994) and Klepper (2010). Klepper (2010), in particular, notes the role of talent movement from existing companies to new companies that spawn from these existing companies (i.e., spinouts).

Across-industry Spillovers

There exists scholarship that is closer to my investigation because it focuses on the potential benefits of spillovers when there exists regional industry diversity. The literature often refers to these as Jacobian externalities, referencing the discussion in Jacobs (1969). In her book, Jacobs argues that diversity of outputs generates more outputs— whether they be goods or services. At a conceptual level, these arguments and my arguments are the same in that they highlight benefits of diversity for spillovers across companies. However, there are three notable differences.

First, my arguments center on a particular type of diversity: managerial talent and practices, and the benefits that accrue from sharing these skills across companies and industries. This is different from diversity of outputs or underlying technologies that are the focus of Jacobs' arguments. For example, Jacobs (1969) provides examples of companies launching new products or services when they access diverse capabilities. Likewise, many large-scale empirical tests of Jacobian externalities look to assess the impact of technical diversity within regions (e.g., Feldman and Audretsch, 1999; and van der Panne, 2004).

Second, and related to the first point, some consider Jacobian externalities a "black box" where the underlying mechanisms are not specified (e.g., Desrochers and Leppälä, 2011). My arguments explicitly identify a mechanism in managerial mobility. Moreover, I further identify factors that facilitate this mechanism.

Third, Jacobs discusses how large companies are less likely to take advantage of product or service diversity to generate new outputs. Central to my argument is that large companies are repositories of management practices. For this reason, the spillovers that are central to my arguments are pronounced in large companies.

Movement to Post-industrial Work in Cities

An established body of research demonstrates cities moving away from specialization by industry sector to specialization by function (e.g., Duranton and Puga, 2004). The crux of the argument is that over time headquarters needed not be co-located with production, and they benefit from being proximate to business service providers from which they outsource services. As a result, cities become concentrations of business service providers and headquarters. The notion of a headquarters economy is certainly consistent with this because it reflects the concentration of skilled managerial and administrative jobs within a region.

Nevertheless, there are important distinctions between this work and my work, despite the relatedness. First, there are many types of business services, many of which are not the managerial and administrative skills housed within corporate head-quarters. Therefore, this literature tends to focus on business services that reside outside of headquarters (i.e., outsourced business services) and are concentrated within cities. This includes concentrations of financial services, advertising services, and management consulting services, among others.

Notable in this area of scholarship is the literature on global cities. In this literature, the discussion focuses on how global cities become home to post-industrial work (e.g., Sassen, 2001). A key point is that global cities become centers for business activities that companies outsource. This research often focuses on a particular business service—finance. In essence, these studies are about industry agglomerations, albeit in business services rather than other goods. For this reason, these studies more closely align with studies of industry clustering compared to my arguments of the benefits of diversity in industries where managerial talent works. Sassen's (2001) work reinforces this difference. She notes the importance of identifying a global city by the concentration of outsourced business services like finance and states that identifying a global city the concentration of corporate headquarters can be misleading (Sassen, 2001: 108).

There is, however, scholarship about global or world cities that more directly focuses on the existence of headquarters operations. However, this work is largely descriptive in that it notes or documents that headquarters and business services often co-exist (e.g., Friedmann 1986). This differs from my analyses, which highlights the conditions that lead to and sustain headquarters activities across different regions.

This scholarship also tends to focus on the extent that cities evolve to concentrations of business services and headquarters—in general. It does not offer an explanation why some cities appear to have disproportional concentrations of business services or headquarters. As I mention above, the global cities literature discusses why some cities exhibit especially strong agglomerations of business services compared to other cities—particularly with respect to the global finance function. My work describes why some cities develop and sustain pronounced concentrations of headquarters activities compared to other cities (Friedmann 1986, notes that such specialization is possible).

Industry Switching and Job Matching

There exists a nascent literature that examines how labor market size and local population density affect the likelihood that individuals will switch industries in which they work (Moretti, 2010b). Wheeler (2008) and Bleakly and Lin (2012) undertake such investigations. These authors start from the assumption that workers possess industry-specific skills. From here, they interpret industry switches by employees to indicate poor matches between employees' skills and industry. Employees leave their current industry looking for better job-skill matches in another industry. They find that dense or larger labor markets provide better opportunities for employees to find good matches.

Central to my argument is that managerial skills are not industry-specific but deployable across many industries. Moreover, importing managerial practices to new industries and combining them with what is known there can be beneficial. Therefore, my work starts from a very different assumption about the applicability of skills across industries. The empirical analyses in Chapter 5 differs from Wheeler (2008) and Bleakly and Lin (2012) because I investigate managerial and administrative employees only. I do not consider the broader workforce whose skills are arguably more industry-specific.

Strategic Human Capital

A key element of my arguments center on how managerial human capital affects companies' competitiveness. There is a burgeoning literature—often referred to as strategic human capital—that examines the relationship between human capital and corporate competitiveness (e.g., Coff, 1997).

Although related, my investigation does not map directly to major themes in the strategic human capital literature. These themes include assessing when companies can capture economic returns from human capital (e.g., Campbell et al., 2012; Chadwick, 2017). Of particular focus in this line of inquiry is the importance of firm-specific versus non-firm-specific human capital investments (e.g., Hatch and Dyer 2004; Raffiee and Coff, 2016). Relatedly, the literature also investigates why some companies might be better at retaining employees—especially when other employers value their skills—and how this can lead to corporate advantage (e.g., Reilly et al., 2014).

The streams of research in this literature closest to my investigation discuss broad topics to which my investigation relates. One stream advances that managerial human capital can be a source of firm competitiveness (e.g., Castanias and Helfat, 1991). Although more limited—especially empirically, the literature also discusses the importance of mid-level managers (e.g., Wooldridge et al., 2008) and not just top management teams (e.g. Hambrick and Mason, 1984). Relatedly, there is some discussion that managers can create competitive advantage for companies by developing and advancing new practices (e.g., Chadwick and Dabu, 2009). However, the empirical literature that investigates how managers' human capital affect companies tends to focus on chief executive officer (CEO)'s human capital and how it affects CEO turnover or compensation (e.g., Harris and Helfat, 1997; Buchholtz et al., 2003; Combs and Skill, 2003).

Another stream of research argues that combinations of general skills an individual possesses (Lazear, 2009) or combinations of individuals with complementary skills within a company (e.g., Ployhart and Moliterno 2011; Ployhart et al., 2014) can be sources of corporate competiveness. My argument that managers create value by bringing practices from their experiences to new employers in different industries is consistent with such general descriptions.

In summary, my arguments relate to the strategic human capital literature. However, I do not focus on hiring skilled individuals or "stars" who might be able to appropriate the return on their human capital. The notion of cross-pollinating or combining existing skills in a new setting creates a situation where both the incoming talent and the hiring organization have to bring something to realize the benefits of the cross-pollination of management practices. Therefore, it is not a situation where a company hires talent and where the individual is able to extract the total contribution that they make. Rather, it is the case where both individuals and the company can capture value from the employment relationship (e.g., Castanias and Helfat, 1991; Coff, 1997; Chadwick, 2017).

Creative Class

The central theme of Florida's (2002) book is that creative work has become a more important part of the modern economy; therefore, those who do this type of work play an increasingly important role in the economy. The demands of how this talent wants to work and live affects where creativity-based economic activity takes place. A key implication of this work is regional quality of life factors that appeal to creative talent will attract this workforce and economy. My work is similar in noting the importance of where talent wants to live and work being a key element of regional economic success.

In relation to my work, Florida considers skilled management a small subset of the creative class. He distinguishes it from the "Super-Creative Core," which includes scientists, engineers, artists, entertainers, university professors, and cultural figures—among others (Florida, 2002: 69). Florida considers management professionals as "creative professionals" that are beyond the core group (Florida, 2002: 69). This leads to different insights and implications.

Most notably, my investigation reaches different conclusions of how quality of life factors affect talent retention and attraction. I demonstrate that quality of life factors primarily retain talent once it resides in a region. Their primary role is not in attracting talent as attributed to the creative class arguments. I show that economic opportunities (i.e., jobs) are what primarily attracts professional managerial talent. These individuals have made large investments in human capital training, such as graduate school; and they look to earn returns on the investments that they have made. Once they reside in a region with economic opportunities, however, quality of life factors mitigate the incentives to pursue opportunities elsewhere.

I also highlight the quality of life factors that professional managerial and administrative talent value in Chapter 5. These factors do not necessarily map to the quality of life factors often noted in Florida's work (e.g., Wojan et al., 2007). Although Florida argues that regions should invest in amenities that all citizens value (Florida, 2002: 294), he focuses on the desirability of quality of life factors ascribed to the super-core creatives.

The differences between my findings and Florida's can reflect the differences in the focal talent bases. The differences can also reflect observations that other factors might drive the relationships between quality of life factors that creative talent desires and economic development (e.g., Storper and Scott, 2009).

References

Almeida, Paul and Bruce Kogut. 1999. Localization of knowledge and the mobility of engineers in regional networks. *Management Science*, 45: 905–17.

Arrow, Kenneth J. 1962. The economic implications of learning by doing. *Review of Economic Studies*, 29(3): 155–73.

Beaverstock, J., R. Smith, and P. Taylor. 1999. A roster of world cities. *Cities*, 16(6): 445–58.

Bell, James B. 2007. *From Arcade Street to Main Street: A History of the Seeger Refrigerator Company, 1902–1984*. St. Paul, MN: Ramsey County Historical Society.

Bill Wooldridge, Torsten Schmid, and Steven W. Floyd. 2008. The middle management perspective on strategy process: contributions, synthesis, and future research. *Journal of Management*, 34(6): 1190–221.

Bleakley, Hoyt and Jeffrey Lin. 2012. Thick-market effects and churning in the labor market: evidence from US cities. *Journal of Urban Economics*, 72: 87–103.

Boeker, W. and R. Wiltbank. 2005. New venture evolution and managerial capabilities. *Organization Science*, 123: 33.

Brainerd, Mary, Jim Campbell, and Richard Davis. 2013. Doing well by doing good: a leader's guide. *McKinsey Quarterly*, 4: 100–11.

Buchholtz, A. K., B. A. Ribbens, and I. T. Houle. 2003. The role of human capital in post acquisition CEO departure. *Academy of Management Journal*, 46(4): 506.

Campbell, B. A., R. W. Coff, and D. Kryscynski. 2012. Re-thinking competitive advantage from human capital. *Academy of Management Review*, 37(3): 376–95.

Card, David, Kevin F. Hallock, and Enrico Moretti. 2010. The geography of giving: the effect of corporate headquarters on local charities. *Journal of Public Economics*, 94(3–4): 222–34.

Castanias, R. P. and C. E. Helfat. 1991. Managerial resources and rents. *Journal of Management*, 17(1): 155–71.

Castle, Henry Anson. 1912. *History of St. Paul and Vicinity: A Chronicle of Progress and a Narrative Account of the Industries, Institutions, and People of the City and its Tributary Territory*. Chicago: Lewis Pub. Co.

Chadwick, C. 2017. Towards a more comprehensive model of firms' human capital rents. *Academy of Management Review*, 42(3): 499–519.

Chadwick, C. and A. Dabu. 2009. Human resources, human resource management, and the competitive advantage of firms: toward a more comprehensive model of causal linkages. *Organization Science*, 20(1): 253–72.

Chan, Che-Po and Wai-Kit Poon. 2012. The Chinese local administrative measures for building up the "headquarter economy": a comparison between Pudong and Shenzhen, *Journal of Contemporary China*, 21(73): 149–67.

Chen, Xiangming and Ahmed Kanna. 2012. *Rethinking Global Urbanism: Comparative Insights from Secondary Cities*. Routledge Advances in Geography. New York: Routledge.

Chiodo, Abbigail J., Rubén Hernández-Murillo, and Michael T. Owyang. 2010. Non-linear effects of school quality on house prices. *Federal Reserve Bank of St. Louis Review*, May/June, 92(3): 185–204.

Coase, R. 1960. The problem of social cost. *Journal of Law and Economics*, 3: 1–44.

Coff, R. W. 1997. Human assets and management dilemmas: coping with hazards on the road to resource-based theory. *The Academy of Management Review*, 22(2): 374–402.

Collis, D., D. Young, and M. Gould. 2007. The size, structure, and performance of corporate headquarters. *Strategic Management Journal*, 28: 383–405.

Combs, J. G. and M. S. Skill. 2003. Managerialist and human capital explanation for key executive pay premiums: a contingency perspective. *Academy of Management Journal*, 46(1): 63.

Costa, Dora L. and Matthew E. Kahn. 2000. Power couples: changes in the locational choice of the college educated, 1940–1990. *The Quarterly Journal of Economics*, 115(4): 1287–315.

Davis, James and J. Vernon Henderson. 2008. The agglomeration of headquarters. *Regional Science and Urban Economics*, 38(5): 445–60.

Desrochers, Pierre, and Samuli Leppälä. 2011. Opening up the "Jacobs Spillovers" black box: local diversity, creativity and the processes underlying new combinations. *Journal of Economic Geography*, 11: 843–63.

Duranton, Gilles and Diego Puga. 2005. From sectoral to functional urban specialization. *Journal of Urban Economics*, 57: 343–70.

El-Hai, Jack. 2013. *Non-Stop: A Turbulent History of Northwest Airlines*. Minneapolis, MN: University Of Minnesota Press.

Fedor, Liz. 2008. *Star Tribune*, July 23.

Feldman, Maryann P. and David B. Audretsch. 1999. Innovation in cities: science-based diversity, specialization and localized competition. *European Economic Review*, 43: 409–29.

Flood, Sarah, Miriam King, Steven Ruggles, and J. Robert Warren. 2017. Integrated Public Use Microdata Series, Current Population Survey: Version 5.0. [dataset]. Minneapolis: University of Minnesota. https://doi.org/10.18128/D030.V5.0

Florida, R. 2002. *The Rise of the Creative Class*. New York: Basic Books.

Fortune. 1936. Twin cities. *Fortune*, April, XIII(4): 112.

Friedmann, John. 1986. The world city hypothesis. *Development and Change*, 17: 69–83.

Galaskiewicz, Jospeh. 1991. Making corporate actors accountable: institution building in Minneapolis-St. Paul, in Walter W. Powell and Paul J. DiMaggio (eds), *The New Institutionalism in Organizational Analysis*: 293–310. Chicago: University of Chicago Press.

Galaskiewicz, Joseph. 1997. An urban grants economy revisited: corporate charitable contributions in the twin cities, 1979–81, 1987–89. *Administrative Science Quarterly*, 42(3): 445–71.

George, Stephen. 2003. *Enterprising Minnesotans: 150 Years of Business Pioneers*. Minneapolis, MN: University of Minnesota Press.

Georzen, Anthony, Christian Geisler Asmussen, and Bo Bernhard Nielsen. 2013. Global cities and multinational enterprise strategy. *Journal of International Business Studies*, 44: 427–50.

Glaeser, E. L., H. D. Kallal, J. A. Scheinkman, and A. Shleifer. 1992. Growth of cities. *Journal of Political Economy*, 100: 1126–52.

Gray, James 1954. *Business without Boundary: The Story of General Mills*. Minneapolis, MN: University of Minnesota Press.

Hambrick, D. C., and P. A. Mason. 1984. Upper echelons: the organization as a reflection of its top managers. *Academy of Management Review*, 9: 193.

Harris, D. and C. Helfat. 1997. Specificity of CEO human capital and compensation. *Strategic Management Journal*, 18(11): 895.

Hartsough, Mildred Lucile. 1925. *The Twin Cities as a Metropolitan Market: A Regional Study of the Economic Development of Minneapolis and St. Paul*. Studies in the Social Sciences (Minneapolis, Minn.) 18. Minneapolis, MN: University of Minnesota.

Hatch, Nile W. and Jeffrey H. Dyer. 2004. Human capital and learning as a source of sustainable competitive advantage. *Strategic Management Journal*, 25(12): 1155–78.

Henderson, J. Vernon and Yukako Ono. 2008. Where do manufacturing firms locate their headquarters? *Journal of Urban Economics*, 63(2): 431–50.

Hidy, Ralph W., Muriel E. Hidy, Roy V. Scott, and Don L. Hofsommer. 2004. *The Great Northern Railway: A History*. Minneapolis, MN: University of Minnesota Press.

Hitz, Hansruedi, Christian Schmid, and Richard Wolf. 1994. Urbanization in Zurich: headquarter economy and city-belt. *Environment and Planning D: Society and Space*, 12: 167–85.

Hughlett, Mike and Brooks Suzukamo, Leslie. 2004. Northwest Airlines CEO leaves for lesser post at UnitedHealth. *St. Paul Pioneer Press*, October 2.

Jacobs, Jane. 1969. *The Economy of Cities*. New York: Random House.

Jefferey, Kirk. 1989. The major manufacturers: from food and forest products to high technology, in Clifford E Clark, Jr (ed.), *Minnesota in a Century of Change*. St Paul, MN: Minnesota Historical Society.

Jensen, Mark with Norb Berg, Frank Dawe, Jim Morris, and Gene Baker. 2013. *HR Pioneers: A History of Human Resource Innovations at Control Data Corporation*. St. Cloud, MN: North Star Press of St. Cloud.

Kaplan, Greg and Sam Schulhofer-Wohl. 2017. Understanding the long-run decline in interstate migration. *International Economic Review*, 58(1): 57–94.

Klepper, Steven. 2010. The origin and growth of industry clusters: the making of Silicon Valley and Detroit. *Journal of Urban Economics*, 67: 15–32.

Klier, Thomas H. 2006. Where the headquarters are: location patterns of large public companies, 1990–2000. *Economic Development Quarterly*, 20(2): 117–28.

Kolko, Jed and David Neumark. 2010. Does local business ownership insulate cities from economic shocks? *Journal of Urban Economics*, 67: 103–15.

Krugman, P. 1991. Increasing returns and economic geography. *Journal of Political Economy*, 99(3): 483–99.

Larson, Don W. 1979. *Land of the Giants*. Minneapolis, MN: Dorn Books.

Lazear E. 2009. Firm-specific human capital: a skill-weights approach. *Journal of Political Economy*, 117(5): 914–40.

References

Lazear, Edward P., and Rosen, Sherwin. 1981. Rank-order tournaments as optimum labor contracts. *Journal of Political Economy*, 89: 841–64.

Marquis, Christopher. 2003. The pressure of the past: network imprinting in intercorporate communities. *Administrative Science Quarterly*, 48(4): 655–89.

Marshall, A. 1890. *Principles of Economics*, 8th edition. London: MacMillan.

Marvin, William W. 1969. *West Publishing Co.: Origin Growth Leadership*. St. Paul, MN: West Publishing Company.

Marx, Matt. 2011. The firm strikes back: non-compete agreements and the mobility of technical professionals. *American Sociological Review*, 76(5): 695–712.

Marx, Matt., D. Strumsky, and L. Fleming. 2009. Mobility, skills, and the Michigan non-compete experiment. *Management Science*, 55(6): 875–89.

Michael, Joel. 2015. Single sales apportionment of corporate franchise tax. The Research Department of the Minnesota House of Representatives, Minnesota, updated June.

Minnesota Mining and Manufacturing Company. 1977. *Our Story so Far: Notes from the First 75 Years of 3M Company*. St Paul, MN: 3M Company.

Misa, Thomas J. (ed.) 2012. *Building the Control Data Legacy: The Career of Robert M. Price*. Minneapolis, MN: Charles Babbage Institute.

Misa, Thomas J. 2013. *Digital State: The Story of Minnesota's Computing Industry*. Minneapolis, MN: University of Minnesota Press.

Molloy, Raven, Christopher L. Smith, and Abigail K. Wozniak. 2014. Declining migration within the U.S.: the role of the labor market. NBER Working Paper No. 20065.

Moretti, E. 2010a. Local multipliers. *American Economic Review: Papers & Proceedings*, May, 100: 373–7.

Moretti, E. 2010b. Local labor markets. *Handbook of Labor Economics*, 4b: 1237–313.

Moretti, E. 2012. *The New Geography of Jobs*. New York: Mariner Books.

Ono, Yukako. 2006. What do census data tell us about headquarters location? *Economic Development Quarterly*, 20(2): 129–41.

Ouchi, William. 1984. *The M-form Society: How American Teamwork Can Recapture the Competitive Edge*. Reading, MA: Addison-Wesley Publishing Company.

Ployhart, R. and T. P. Moliterno. 2011. Emergence of the human capital resource: a multilevel model. *Academy of Management Review*, 36(1): 127–50.

Ployhart, R., A. Nyberg, G. Reilly, and M. Maltarich. 2014. Human capital is dead. Long live human capital resources! *Journal of Management*, 40(2): 371–98.

Porter, Michael. 1990. *The Competitive Advantage of Nations*. New York: Free Press.

Powell, William J. 1985. *Pillsbury's Best: A Company History from 1869*. Minneapolis, MN: The Pillsbury Company.

Raffiee, Joseph and Russell Coff. 2016. Micro-foundations of firm-specific human capital: when do employees perceive their skills to be firm-specific? *Academy of Management Journal*, 59(3): 766–90.

Reback, R. 2005. House prices and the provision of local public services: capitalization under school choice programs. *Journal of Urban Economics*, 57(2): 275–301.

Reilly, G., A. J. Nyberg, M. Malrarich, and I. Weller. 2014. Human capital flows: using context-emergent turnover (CET) theory to explore the process by which turnover, hiring, and job demands affect patient satisfaction. *Academy of Management Journal*, 57(3): 766–90.

Rodengen, Jeffrey L. 1995. *The Legend of Honeywell*. Fort Lauderdale, FL: Write Stuff Syndicate.

Romer, Paul M. 1986. Increasing returns and long-run growth. *Journal of Political Economy*, 94: 1002–37.

Sassen, Saskia. 2001. *The Global City: New York, London, Tokyo*, 2nd edition. Princeton, NJ: Princeton University Press.

Saxenian, AnnaLee. 1994. *Regional Advantage: Culture and Competition in Silicon Valley and Route 128*. Cambridge, MA: Harvard University Press.

Schafer, Lee and Mark Brunswick. 2014. *Star Tribune*, June 16: A.1.

Schmid, Calvin F. 1937. *Social Saga of Two Cities: an Ecological and Statistical Study of Social Trends in Minneapolis and St. Paul*. Minneapolis, MN: Bureau of Social Research, The Minneapolis Council of Social Agencies.

Semple, R. Keith. 1973. Recent trends in the spatial concentration of corporate headquarters. *Economic Geography*, 49(4): 309–18.

Shaver, J. Myles and Fredrick Flyer. 2000. Agglomeration economies, firm heterogeneity, and foreign direct investment in the United States. *Strategic Management Journal*, 21(12): 1175–93.

Smith, K., T. Mitchell, and C. Summer. 1985. Top level management priorities in different stages of the organizational life cycle. *Academy of Management Journal*, 28(4): 799–820.

Stangler, Dane and Sam Arbesman. 2012. *What Does Fortune 500 Turnover Mean?* New York: Ewing Marion Kauffman Foundation.

Storper, Michael and Allen J. Scott. 2009. Rethinking human capital, creativity and urban growth. *Journal of Economic Geography*, 9: 147–67.

Storper, Michael, Thomas Kemeny, Naji Makarem, and Taner Osman. 2015. *The Rise and Fall of Urban Economies: Lessons from San Francisco and Los Angeles*. Stanford, CA: Stanford University Press.

Straus-Kahn, Vanessa and Xavier Vives. 2009. Why and where do headquarters move? *Regional Science and Urban Economics*, 39(2): 168–86.

Stuart, Toby E. and Olav Sorenson. 2003. Liquidity events and the geographic distribution of entrepreneurial activity. *Administrative Science Quarterly*, 48(2): 175–201.

van der Panne, Gerben. 2004. Agglomeration externalities: Marshall versus Jacobs. *Journal of Evolutionary Economics*, 14: 593–604.

Waldfogel, Joel. 2007. *The Tyranny of the Market: Why You Can't Always Get What You Want*. Cambridge, MA: Harvard University Press.

Walshok, Mary Lindenstein and Abraham J. Shragge. 2014. *Invention & Reinvention: The Evolution of San Diego's Innovation Economy*. Stanford, CA: Stanford University Press.

Wheeler, Christopher H. 2008. Local market scale and the pattern of job changes among young men. *Regional Science and Urban Economics*, 38: 101–18.

Wills, Jocelyn. 2005. *Boosters, Hustlers, and Speculators: Entrepreneurial Culture and the Rise of Minneapolis and St. Paul 1849–1883*. St Paul, MN: Minnesota Historical Society Press.

Wojan, T. R., D. Lambert, and D. A. McGranahan. 2007. Emoting with their feet: Bohemian attraction to creative milieu. *Journal of Economic Geography*, 7: 711–36.

Zhao, Simon X. B. 2013. Information exchange, headquarters economy and financial centers development: Shanghai, Beijing and Hong Kong. *Journal of Contemporary China*, 22: 1006–27.

Index

Index